Young People, Crime and Justice

Young People, Crime and Justice

Roger Hopkins Burke

WILLAN
PUBLISHING

Published by

Willan Publishing
Culmcott House
Mill Street, Uffculme
Cullompton, Devon
EX15 3AT, UK
Tel: +44(0)1884 840337
Fax: +44(0)1884 840251
e-mail: info@willanpublishing.co.uk
website: www.willanpublishing.co.uk

Published simultaneously in the USA and Canada by

Willan Publishing
c/o ISBS, 920 NE 58th Ave, Suite 300,
Portland, Oregon 97213-3786, USA
Tel: +001(0)503 287 3093
Fax: +001(0)503 280 8832
e-mail: info@isbs.com
website: www.isbs.com

First published 2008

Reprinted 2010

ISBN   978-1-84392-367-1 paperback
       978-1-84392-368-8 hardback

British Library Cataloguing-in-Publication Data

A catalogue record for this book is available from the British Library

FSC
Mixed Sources
Product group from well-managed
forests and other controlled sources

Cert no. SGS-COC-2482
www.fsc.org
© 1996 Forest Stewardship Council

Project managed by Deer Park Productions, Tavistock, Devon
Typeset by GCS, Leighton Buzzard, Bedfordshire
Printed and bound by T.J. International Ltd, Padstow, Cornwall

Contents

Part II: Explaining Youth Criminal Behaviour

Part III: The Contemporary Youth Justice System and its Critics

List of tables

Acknowledgements

I would like to offer my sincerest thanks to all those who have offered help, advice and support during the researching and writing of this book. It has all been most appreciated. In particular, thanks to Chris Crowther-Dowey, Natasha Chubbock and Paul Sparrow at Nottingham Trent University for their continued help and support and without whom the day job would be virtually impossible. A special thanks to my wife Kristan and our two wonderful and very talented boys, Thomas (now 10) and Oliver (now 7) who both love seeing their names in print and I am sure will continue to do so.

For
Kristan, Thomas and Oliver

Chapter 1

Introduction: the problem of youth crime

Young people and criminal behaviour have always been linked in the minds of the general public. Moreover, there are widely held common-sense notions that such activities are a recent phenomenon and invariably an outcome of the 'permissive 1960s' and the breakdown of the traditional nuclear family that has occurred in intervening years. It is also widely believed that in the past young people were orderly, disciplined, well behaved and law-abiding (Pearson 1983). This is a commonly held and extremely influential viewpoint which has had a considerable impact on political thinking and policy agendas.

The criminal behaviour of children and young people has become a significant political issue in both the USA and UK in recent years, with demands that if young people are prepared to break the law they should also be prepared to take responsibility for their actions and that this might well mean incarceration in the same institutions as adults. This is of course contrary to the dominant orthodoxy in both societies – and increasingly in the world beyond – throughout the twentieth century, that young people should be dealt with differently than their elders (Pitts 2003).[1]

These concerns about young people and their offending behaviour are, nevertheless, nothing new and they have reoccurred throughout history with a parallel erroneous assumption on the part of the public that things were always better in the past (Pearson 1983). Thus, for some, youth offending is little more than a recurring 'moral panic' – a notion which implies that the social reaction to a certain phenomenon is out of proportion to the scale of the problem (Young 1971; Cohen 1973) – and is thus a relatively minor social problem where many if not most children and young people commit criminal offences or acts of deviancy as part of a normal transition to adulthood and, left to their own devices, in the main simply grow out of this behaviour and become responsible, law-abiding citizens. For others, young people who offend are at risk of becoming persistent and serious offenders starting out on criminal careers which without an appropriate and timely intervention in their lives is likely to lead them to become the next generation of adult offenders readily equipped to inhabit the increasingly expanding prison estate.

The extent and distribution of youth offending

Statistical data about the prevalence of crime committed by children and young people are obtained from two main sources: first, the official crime statistics which consist of statistical data compiled by the police and the courts and are routinely published by the Home Office as indices of the extent of crime; and second, self-reports which are a means of assessing the extent of crime by asking – in this case children and young people – directly whether they are perpetrators. Each of these sources has their strengths but they also have significant shortcomings. The most fundamental observation to be made about the official statistics is that they are both partial and socially constructed. First, for a criminal statistic to exist, a crime event has to be reported to the police by the public and this clearly does not happen in all cases for a variety of reasons (see Bottomley and Pease 1986). Second, even when an incident is reported to the police it will not count as crime unless it is recorded as such and there are again a multitude of reasons why this might not happen (see Walker 1983). Third, changes in patterns of law enforcement – and thus what is to be regarded as criminal and recordable as such – make it very difficult to compare levels of youth criminality during different time periods. Muncie (1999a: 17-18) observes that:

> Self evidently, changes in legislation and in the number of arrests and sentences do not represent actual changes in the amount of crime, but changes in the capacity of the criminal justice system to process individual cases. More police and prisons coupled with the political will and resources to support law enforcement have an infinite ability to increase the amount of recorded crime.

Self-report studies have been widely used for over half a century to gain a more accurate picture of both the prevalence of criminality and exactly why people become involved. They also have significant shortcomings. First, they depend on the willingness of those being interviewed to admit their 'criminality' to researchers. Second, they are invariably administered through the use of questionnaires which have a notoriously low completion rate, in particular among ethnic minority groups (Coleman and Moynihan 1996). Third, they tend to ignore some significant hidden crimes such as domestic violence and corporate criminality.

Self-report studies have tended to continuously confirm the notion that a great many young people have committed a crime at some point in their lives and that involvement in criminality is in some way part of a normal transition to adulthood. Belson (1975) found in his study of London schoolboys that 98 per cent admitted offences of some kind, with 70 per cent having stolen from a shop. Rutter and Giller (1983), in a large-scale review of self-report studies, made similar findings. A decade later Anderson *et al.* (1994) found – in a study of young people conducted in Edinburgh – that two-thirds admitted to having committed a crime during the previous nine months.

Three influential reports during the mid-1990s found offending by children and young people to be extremely widespread and expensive to society. First, a study conducted for the Home Office supported the evidence of previous research and showed that one in two males and one in three females aged between 14 and 25 years admitted to having committed a criminal offence, with a similar ratio admitting the use of illegal drugs (Graham and Bowling 1995). Second, the Audit Commission Report *Misspent Youth: Young People and Crime* (Audit Commission 1996) estimated that people under 18 years of age commit seven million offences a year against individuals, retailers and manufacturers, with public services spending over £1billion a year in response to offending by children and young people.[2] Third, Nacro (1998) estimated the average response cost in dealing with the behaviour of a young offender to be around £52,000 (made up of prosecution, incarceration and supervision costs as well as family intervention and care). The direct cost of offending to the community was found to average around £22,700 per young offender. Thus, in short, these three influential reports found that many young people commit criminal offences at a great cost to society and this recognition was to be considered indicative of a significant social problem worthy of rigorous government intervention.

The costs of youth offending to the economy should nevertheless be put into some context. For example, it has been estimated that in the USA, the economic losses from various white-collar crimes are about ten times those from 'ordinary' economic crime (Conklin 1977), with corporate crime killing and maiming more than any violence committed by the poor or the young (Liazos 1972). Corporate crime receives little publicity in the mass media – in contrast to often low-level offences committed by young people – unless there has been fraud on a massive scale. Examples in the UK include the collapse of the investment managers Barlow Clowes in 1998, which left 17,000 small investors owed a total £200 million; the Guinness-Distillers Affair of 1990; the disclosure in 1991 that the late Robert Maxwell had appropriated £500 million from his employee's pension fund; and the collapse of Asdil Nadir's 'Polly Peck' empire in 1993 with the disappearance of £450 million. The latter subsequently jumped bail and fled the country (Jones 2001). Croall (1992, 2001) observes that the activities of the corporate criminal are not only greater in impact than those of the ordinary offender, but they are also longer-lasting in effect. The view taken in this book, however, is that offending behaviour by children and young people is still a highly significant issue which requires a rigorous and appropriate intervention where this is deemed both necessary and appropriate.

It is important to recognise that young offenders are not a homogenous group. The great majority of young people who commit offences do so infrequently and are predominantly responsible for less serious property crimes. It is this group that tends to grow out of their offending behaviour at a relatively young age, which can be diverted from their activities by a warning from the authorities, and they are extremely unlikely to become regular drug users. The influential Audit Commission Report (1996) readily acknowledged that the great majority of young people who offend do so infrequently, but at the same time, noted the existence of a substantially more problematic, small hard core, of persistent offenders who apparently fail to respond to attempts to divert them from their activities and who are responsible for a disproportionate amount of crime. Research conducted by the Home Office thus found that about 3 per cent of young offenders aged 14–25 commit 22 per cent of youth crime (Flood-Page *et al.* 2000) with 0.2 per cent of males having made six or more court appearances by age 17 and accounting for 28 per cent of the total for that age group (Home Office 2001). Crimes committed ranged from minor anti-social behaviour to more serious offending.

Defining persistent young offenders

The Home Office (1997) defines a persistent young offender as:

A young person aged 10–17 years who has been sentenced by any criminal court in the UK on three or more occasions for one or more recordable offences and within three years of the last sentencing occasion is subsequently arrested or has information laid against him for further recordable offence.

The Youth Lifestyles Survey – carried out in England and Wales between October 1998 and January 1999 – offers a simpler alternative definition of a persistent young offender 'as someone who, in the last year, had committed three or more offences' (Campbell and Harrington 2000). Among those aged 12–17 who fitted into this category the survey found that 23 per cent had been sanctioned (cautioned or taken to court) in the previous 12 months (24 per cent of male and 21 per cent of female persistent offenders). Younger persistent offenders – those under the age of 18 – were more likely to have been sanctioned (23 per cent) than those who were older (14 per cent). This could be because they had committed more offences – the average number of offences committed by persistent offenders under 18 was five compared to four for those aged 18 to 30 – or because younger offenders tend to commit more commonly detected offences (for example, criminal damage or shoplifting) whereas older persistent offenders are more involved in fraud and theft from the workplace, which are less likely to result in sanction or even detection. With this recognition, the whole notion of 'growing out of crime' is itself suspect.

There are significant methodological issues which make it impossible to both accurately estimate the full extent of current persistent or non-persistent offending behaviour and legitimately compare it with any other time period (Campbell and Harrington 2002). Thus, those who are not caught by the police – or those who receive informal warnings rather than recorded cautions – are not included in the crime figures. Current low police clear-up rates suggest that many offences and offenders go undetected and the published figures are thus serious underestimations.[3] Moreover, policies that have been introduced at different times to divert young offenders from the criminal justice system – through measures such as informal cautions[4] – will have the effect of reducing the number sanctioned and who are therefore recorded in the crime statistics.

5

Prevalence, concentration and location of offending

Males commit the great majority of offences committed by young people. Official statistics show that 142,600 males aged between 10 and 17 years were convicted or cautioned in 1996 and only 34,400 females in the same age group (Home Office 1997). Self-report data suggest a more ambiguous situation. The Youth Lifestyles Survey showed that among those aged 12 to 13 a similar proportion of boys and girls offend (and used drugs and drank regularly) but after the age of 14 the difference between boys and girls becomes marked. Over age 17, male offenders outnumber women offenders by a ratio of about 3:1. Graham and Bowling (1995) found the ratio extends to 11:1 for those aged between 22 and 25.

Youth justice policy in the latter part of the twentieth century had become increasingly founded on the assumption that young people will grow out of their offending behaviour. Or at least they fail to come to the attention of the authorities as their transgressions progress from highly visible 'street' activities to the relative invisibility of offences such as theft from work and the handling of stolen goods. Research evidence, nevertheless, suggests that any 'desistance' is highly class and gender dependent. For young men, particularly those situated in the lowest socio-economic classes, those positive effects of personal and social development which help insulate the young person against temptations to become involved in criminality – crucially, completing their education, getting a job, leaving home, settling down with a partner – tend to be outweighed by the more powerful influences of the peer group and siblings (Graham and Bowling 1995; Audit Commission 1996). We will find that these are highly significant findings.

The Youth Lifestyles Survey shows marked differences in the nature of crime committed by males and females at different ages. Among females, criminal damage, shoplifting, buying stolen goods and fighting are the most common offences committed by those less than 16 years of age. Over 16, girls commit less criminal damage and shoplifting but become increasingly involved in fraud and buying stolen goods. Over 21, all types of offending decrease, with fraud or buying stolen goods the most often admitted offences. Among males, comparatively high rates of offending by 14- to 15-year-olds reflect their involvement in fights (assaults), buying stolen goods, other theft and criminal damage. It was found that approximately one in eight boys from this age group admitted to each of these offences. Those aged 16 to 17 were less involved in buying stolen goods, 'other theft' and criminal damage, with over a third of offences committed involved fighting. At 18–21, fighting increases, shoplifting and criminal damage decline, and involvement in fraud and workplace theft commences.

Flood-Page *et al.* (2000) followed their predecessors and found that the great majority of young people who commit offences do so infrequently, but the authors also confirm the previous findings that a small hard core of persistent young offenders are responsible for a disproportionate amount of crime. They found that while nearly 50 per cent of those young people who said that they had offended in the previous year had admitted one or two offences – and these tended to be relatively minor, for example, criminal damage and or buying stolen goods – the most prolific 10 per cent of offenders were responsible for nearly half of all crimes committed by the sample.

Geographical location is also significant in the pattern of youth offending with both recorded crime figures and victimisation surveys showing higher crime rates in inner-city areas and poor local authority housing estates. Flood-Page *et al.* (2000), for example, found there were twice the proportion of males aged 12–30 living in inner-city areas who were persistent or serious offenders than in rural areas.

Risk of offending

Research conducted in recent years has sought to provide evidence of risk factors, which, if present in the life of a young person, increase the likelihood of becoming involved in offending or at least coming to the attention of the authorities. Flood-Page *et al.* (2000) found four key risk factors to be closely associated with persistent or serious offending among 12–17-year-old males. First, the use of drugs in the previous year was the strongest predictor, with boys in this age category five times more likely to offend than non-drug users. Second, those boys who were disaffected from school or were persistent truants had a higher risk of persistent or serious offending than those who did not. Third, those young people who were less highly supervised by their parents or who had friends or acquaintances that had been in trouble with the police were more at risk. Fourth, boys who hung around in public places were more likely to be offenders than those who did not. Because of the small number of persistent or serious female offenders in the survey, detailed analysis was not considered appropriate but the indications are that risk factors which are important for males generally apply to females (Flood Page *et al.* 2000).

A significant characteristic of serious or persistent young offenders has been found to be their lack of education and skills. Young people who truant from school are three times more likely to offend than those who do not and there is similarly a strong correlation between school exclusions and offending (Graham and Bowling 1995). Nearly 60 per cent of convicted young people aged 16 or 17 convicted during 1995 were found to be unemployed and not in training at the time they were sentenced (Audit Commission 1996). Nearly a decade later that figure had been substantially reduced, with less than a quarter of young offenders not in education, training and employment in 2004 (Youth Justice Board 2004). Stephenson (2007) observes that the more problematic young offenders continue to experience educational underachievement, particularly with respect to literacy and numeracy, a detachment and disengagement from mainstream education exacerbated by the impact of custodial sentences and periods in local authority care, plus the inability of the school organisation to provide adequately for their needs.

Mental health problems are relatively common among children and adolescents and these may act as a significant risk factor for criminal behaviour. Up to 20 per cent of children require help at some time and a survey of 5–15 year olds conducted in Great Britain found that 5 per cent had significant conduct disorders (aggressive and anti-social behaviour), 4 per cent had emotional disorders (anxiety or depression) and 1 per cent were found to be hyperactive. Severe mental illnesses such as schizophrenia were found to be very rare but their prevalence began to rise in adolescence (Meltzer 2000). A report by the Office for National Statistics found that nine in ten young offenders aged 16–20 years old showed evidence of mental illness (Larder 2000).

Children who have poor relationships with their parents have been found twice as likely to offend (Farrington 1978) and research has shown that 42 per cent of young people with low or medium levels of parental supervision admit to having committed criminal offences, in comparison with only 20 per cent of those with high levels of supervision (Graham and Bowling 1995). Children and young people in local authority care are however among the most disadvantaged and socially excluded populations. Their low educational attainment increases their chances of being unemployed, becoming homeless and the likelihood they will engage in anti-social behaviour and crime (Utting 1997). This finding is reflected in statistics that show that 26 per cent of all prisoners and 40 per cent of prisoners under 21 have been in care at some stage in their lives (National Prison Survey 1992).

Multiple risk factors

The Youth Lifestyles Survey found that the greater the number of risk factors there are in the life of the young person, the greater the chances are of them becoming an offender. Thus, although only 6 per cent of boys under 18 had at least four risk factors, over three-quarters (85 per cent) had committed at least one offence at some point in their lives, and more than half (57 per cent) were currently persistent or serious offenders (Campbell and Harrington 2000). A study of persistent offenders by Liddle and Solanki (2000) appears to confirm the cumulative effect of risk factors, with the presence of nearly six risk factors found to be present in the lives of each of those in the sample.

Young people as victims of crime

Young people are not only involved in criminal behaviour but also suffer from it excessively. The vast majority of research on children, young people and crime in the UK has, nevertheless, tended to focus on their offending behaviour rather than their victimisation. Mawby (1979) conducted a study of children in two Sheffield schools and found that 67 per cent had been victims of crime, but it was the Edinburgh study (Anderson *et al.* 1994) that exposed the 'alarming frequency' to which children and young people become victims, with over half their sample having been the victims of violence during a nine-month period. Hartless *et al.* (1995) reported a similar situation in Glasgow the following year, with 82 per cent of their sample stating that they had been victims during the past year.

Analysis of the 1992 British Crime Survey on the experiences of 12–15-year-olds showed that young people in this category were more likely to be victims of personal crime than adults (Aye Maung 1995; see also Audit Commission 1996). The MORI Youth Survey (2000) conducted on behalf of the Youth Justice Board found that 54 per cent of all school pupils had experienced crime victimisation during the previous 12 months, with 30 per cent having had items of personal property stolen, 30 per cent having been threatened by others, 11 per cent physically attacked, 5 per cent racially abused and 2 per cent racially attacked.[5]

The British Crime Survey 2000 shows that young people are generally at greater risk of all types of violence than older people (Kershaw *et al.* 2000). Violent offences – including robbery and snatch theft – are predominantly crimes committed against victims in their teens or early twenties and more often against males than females.

Almost 21 per cent of men aged 16–24 were victims of violent crime, as against 9 per cent of men aged 25 and above. 9 per cent of women aged 16–24 years old were victims of some kind of violent crime, but less than 8 per cent of women aged 25 or above.

The purpose and structure of this book

This book is about the involvement of young people in criminality and the subsequent response of the authorities to their activities. It has its origins in a third-level undergraduate module – now with the same title as this text – that has been developed by the author during the past ten years at Nottingham Trent University. It is a very popular option module with students on three courses, not least the highly respected BA Criminology. The book is thus loosely based on the themes to be encountered in that module but has developed these further in a more detailed socio-economic context. It provides a comprehensive and detailed introduction to these themes but it is intended for a primary target audience of second- or third-level undergraduates or those commencing postgraduate studies in this area. Certain assumptions are thus made about prior knowledge and there is an expectation that a student at this level encountering material which is new to them and/or wishes to develop a further understanding will use this text as a starting point for delving into issues in more depth elsewhere. This is the purpose of the book.

While this book provides an extensive examination of young people, crime and justice, it is not a fully exhaustive account and thus omissions may well be noted by the reader. Moreover, while the introductory nature of the text requires fair discussion of different perspectives, the author makes no apology for presenting his own viewpoint and favoured theoretical perspective. This approach is intended to be challenging and the student who does not accept the perspective adopted is clearly invited to read further in order refute the stance taken here. This is the nature of traditional liberal education and it is well worth preserving albeit in a tarnished post-age of reason.

Many academic texts on young people, crime and justice are written from at least an implicit – but often an explicit – critical criminology perspective. Such accounts highlight the reality that many young people predominantly – but by no means exclusively – those from the lower reaches of the working classes have a troublesome transition from childhood to adulthood which involves some offending behaviour and observe that, left to their own devices, they will invariably grow out of it. It is moreover invariably observed – following in the labelling tradition discussed later in this book – that state intervention merely exacerbates the problem (see, for example, Muncie 2004). This book is not unsympathetic to the critical criminological agenda. It is clear that many children or young people 'offend' in some way, not least because of the seductions of crime and the pleasures and the normality of participation in such behaviours as recreational drug use (see Katz 1986; Presdee 2000). The 'schizophrenia of crime' thesis moreover recognises an adult moral ambiguity towards criminality whereupon the very same people who may be involved in some, possibly low-level, criminal activity are at the very same time likely to be espousing a commitment to a rigorous popular law-and-order discourse (Hopkins Burke 2005, 2007). Furthermore, these very same morally ambivalent adults are very likely to be heavily represented among the ranks of those critical of 'young people today'.

Thus, involvement in offending behaviour is for many a merely transitional stage in life to a later predominantly law-abiding and materially satisfactory existence, regardless of how ambiguous and tenuous commitment to that legitimacy might be for the many enjoying risqué 'second lives' attracted to the activities and pleasures provided by the deviant and illicit which encourage periodical diversions from our core existence (see Presdee 2000). For a small minority of young people involvement in ongoing offending behaviour is, on the other hand, a real and serious problem. It is a problem that requires some form of intervention to protect, not just society from their troublesome activities, but which is also in their best interests. For left alone these young people face a life of social exclusion, serious offending, probable lengthy periods of incarceration and the likelihood of being involved in the raising of a further generation in their own image. Of course many of these young males may have only a tangential role in parenting their own children.

This text thus departs from the orthodox critical criminological account of young people, crime and youth justice and adopts a left realist perspective (see Lea and Young 1984; Matthews and Young 1986, 1992; Young 1986, 1994). This approach recognises the need to deal with the problematic actions of individuals and the conditions which encourage those behaviours not least for the good of the young person involved. It is a text thus compatible but far from uncritical of the contemporary youth justice system.

The book is divided into three parts. The first part, 'Young people, criminality and criminal justice', traces the development of young people from their social construction as children and adolescents, considers attempts to educate, discipline, control and construct them in the interests of a myriad different interest groups, not least industrial capitalism, and examines their deviance, 'offending behaviour' and the consequential societal response, from the beginnings of industrial modernity, via the morally certain modern era at its most confident, to the present-day morally uncertain, fragmented, non-confident modernity or postmodern condition.

Chapter 2, 'Children, young people and modernity', discusses the social construction of childhood and youth, industrialisation, modernity and the essential requirement for the first time in the history of humanity for an abundant fit and healthy population. The process of discipline, industrial schools, reformatories and more generic educative methods that came to construct this population as functional, or simply useful, for the needs of industrial society, and the different theoretical perspectives which seek to explain why these developments occurred, and in whose interests, are discussed.

Chapter 3, 'From justice to welfare', tells the story of juvenile justice from its inception, and its gradual transition from a justice model with unequivocal theoretical foundations in the rational actor model of crime and criminal behaviour, to the triumph of a fatally flawed welfarism with its theoretical foundations in both the predestined and victimised actor models, and epitomised by the Children and Young Persons Act 1969. The chapter concludes by considering the apparent failure of welfarism and the crucial issue of net-widening that brought into the parameters of a newly expanded well-meaning criminal justice system a whole raft of previously non-problematic young people.

Chapter 4, 'Youth justice and the new conservatism', considers the ambiguous story of youth justice during the Conservative administrations 1979–97 with its 'short, sharp shocks', bifurcation or twin-track approach, enthusiasm for diversionary schemes, new managerialism and for some a surprising substantial reduction in the youth incarceration population but with a nevertheless parallel growth in social exclusion and poverty for a substantial minority (Hopkins Burke 1999).

The second part of the book, 'Explaining youth criminal behaviour', considers the various criminological explanations – and the relevant empirical evidence to support these – of why it is that young people offend. Chapter 5, 'Youth offending as rational behaviour', considers rational actor model theories which propose criminal behaviour to be very much like any other activity with involvement simply a matter of choice. While it has long been recognised that children and young people are incapable of making the same rational decisions as adults, the rational actor model has, nevertheless, been revitalised during the past 30 years and it is now widely recognised that rationality can be 'bounded' or limited and thus young people do make decisions which are rational for them but in the context of the life circumstances in which find themselves (Clarke 1980, 1987, 1999; Clarke and Mayhew 1980; Cornish and Clarke 1986; Mayhew *et al.* 1976; Wilson and Herrnstein 1985). The contemporary youth justice system has significantly come to incorporate notions from this revised variant of the rational actor model, not least in the proposition that young people should take responsibility for their actions.

The theories discussed in the following three chapters are fundamentally underpinned by the predestined actor model, which proposes that criminal behaviour is to be explained in terms of factors, either internal or external to the human being, that cause or determine them to act in ways over which they have little or no control. Chapter 6, 'Biological explanations of youth crime', considers first those theories that propose young offending to be simply a product of some physiological defect in the individual which has been inherited in some way from their biological predecessors (see Shah and Roth 1974). There follows discussion of two contemporary variants of the model. First, there is the notion of altered biological states which considers the very contemporary issues of alcohol (Collins 1988; Fagan 1990) and drug use (Fishbein and Pease 1990; Pihl and Peterson 1993) as being the instigations or accentuations of young offending. Second, there is an examination of socio-biological theories which propose that biological predispositions are triggered in very different ways in different environmental conditions often dependent on the socialised upbringing of the young person (Jeffery 1979; Mednick 1977, 1987).

Chapter 7, 'Psychological explanations of youth crime', examines those theories which consider youth offending behaviour to be the product of a criminal personality or mind. First, there is the influential psychodynamic approach with its roots in the notion of psychosexual development (Freud 1920, 1927), developed through latent delinquency theory (Aichhorn 1925; Healy and Bronner 1936), maternal deprivation theory (Bowlby 1952), child rearing practices (Glueck and Glueck 1950; McCord 1959; Bandura and Walters 1959; Hoffman and Saltzstein 1967) and 'broken family' theories (Burt 1945; Mannheim 1948; Wootton 1959; West 1969; Pitts 1986; Kolvin *et al.* 1990; Farringdon 1992). Second, behavioural learning theories propose that offenders subconsciously learn and develop abnormal, inadequate, or specifically criminal personalities or personality traits that differentiate them from non-offenders and which can be isolated, measured and their offending behaviour predicted (Eysenck 1970, 1977; Smith and Smith 1977; McEwan 1983; McGurk and McDougall 1981; Farrington 1984). Third, cognitive theories propose that behaviour is learned through watching what happens to other people and then making choices to behave in a particular way (Sutherland 1947; Akers 1979, 1985, 1992), an approach that significantly moves psychology away from its roots in the predestined actor model to incorporate notions of choice from the rational actor model.

Chapter 8, 'Sociological explanations of youth crime', considers theories where offending is attributed in some way to the social environment in which the young person grows up. Earlier versions clearly have their foundations in the predestined actor model and propose that offending behaviour is transmitted to others – and later generations – by frequent contact with criminal traditions which have developed over time in disorganised urban areas (Durkheim 1964; Shaw and McKay 1972). Subsequent anomie or strain theories propose that most members of society share a common value system that teaches us both the things we should strive for in life and the approved way in which we can achieve them; however, without reasonable access to the socially approved means, people will attempt to find alternative ways, including criminality, to resolve the societal pressure to achieve (Merton 1938).

Delinquent subculture theories develop anomie theory further by observing that lower-class values serve to create young male behaviours that are delinquent by middle-class standards but which are both normal and useful in the social context in which young people find themselves. Thus, youth offending is considered a consequence of the efforts of lower-class youth to attain goals and respect valued within their own subcultural social world (Cohen 1955; Miller 1958; Cloward and Ohlin 1960; Spergel 1964; Wolfgang and Ferracuti 1967; Mays 1954; Morris 1957; Downes 1956; Wilmott 1966; Krisberg 1974; Parker 1974; Curtis 1975; Pryce 1979, Williams 1989; Anderson 1990; Maxon and Klein 1990; Miller 1990; Taylor 1990; Moore 1991; Wilson 1991; Hagedorn 1992). From this perspective, offending behaviour by young people in gangs and subcultures is simply 'cool' and enables the individual to gain appropriate respect from their peers. Matza (1964) subsequently provides an influential link with the non-determinist tradition by noting that young people are capable of making rational choices but these are limited by structural constraints, and thus provides an explanation as to why it is that most young offenders 'grow out' of offending not least because most of them had little commitment to deviancy in the first place and they no longer consider involvement to be 'cool'.

A later radical variant of deviant subculture theory adopts a neo-Marxist perspective, proposing that involvement in particular youth subcultures – whether these be 'mainstream' (Willis 1977; Corrigan 1979) or 'spectacular' (Hebdige 1976, 1979; Brake 1980, 1985) – is determined by specific economic factors that arise at particular historical moments; while postmodern approaches recognise the coexistence of different youth cultures that reflect the differential experience of the rapid socio-economic changes that have occurred during the past 30 years (Hopkins Burke and Sunley 1996, 1998).

Social control theories provide a significant explanatory component within the contemporary youth justice system and are based on the fundamental assumption that criminal acts take place when an individual has weakened or broken bonds with society (Hirschi 1969). Later researchers have sought to integrate control theory with other perspectives: thus, Elliot *et al.* (1979) expand and synthesise anomie, social learning and control theories; Box (1981, 1987) integrates control theory with a labelling/conflict perspective; Braithwaite (1989) integrates elements of control, labelling, anomie and subcultural theory; and Gottfredson and Hirschi (1990) combine rational actor notions of crime with a predestined actor model (control) theory of criminality.

Later sociological theories can be at least partially located in the victimised actor model, which proposes that offenders are themselves the victims of an unjust and unequal society which targets and criminalises the behaviour and activities of disadvantaged sections of society. Thus, the labelling tradition proposes that no behaviour is inherently deviant or criminal, but only comes to be considered so when others label it as such. Hence, being found out and stigmatised may encourage an individual to become involved in further deviance and seek solace from others so involved (Lemert 1951; Becker 1963). The labelling perspective has also been applied at a group level where it is argued that media campaigns instigate a frenzy of popular societal indignation – or a 'moral panic' – about particular activities or groups of young people who are seen to threaten the very fabric of civilisation (Hopkins Burke and Sunley 1996, 1998). Critical and radical criminologists have developed the labelling thesis to draw our attention to the capacity for powerful groups to make laws to their advantage and to the disadvantage of the poor (Vold 1958; Turk

1969; Quinney 1970; Taylor *et al.* 1973; Chambliss 1977; Hall *et al.* 1978), while critical criminologists have more recently revitalised that tradition by observing that it is members of the less powerful social groups who are the most likely to suffer the weight of oppressive social relations (Cohen 1980; Box 1983; Scraton 1985; Sim *et al.* 1987; Scraton and Chadwick 1996).

Left realism is an eclectic perspective with strong sociological theoretical foundations which recognises that many criminological theories have – at least some – validity in the appropriate circumstances. It is recognised that crime is a real problem that seriously impinges on the quality of life of many poor people and that it must be challenged and a comprehensive solution to the crime problem or a 'balance of intervention' is thus proposed (Lea and Young 1984; Matthews and Young 1986, 1992; Young 1994, 1997). On the one hand, crime must be tackled and offenders are required to take some responsibility for their actions; on the other hand, the social conditions that encourage crime must also be confronted. It is this approach that has been very influential with 'New' Labour governments in the UK since 1997 and is fundamental to the contemporary youth justice system (Hopkins Burke 2001, 2005). There follows discussion of the formation and rise to prominence of a socially excluded 'underclass' from a behavioural perspective (Murray 1990, 1994), a structural perspective (Dahrendorf 1985; Campbell 1993; Jordan 1996; Crowther 1998) and a left realist – or process model – perspective (Hopkins Burke 1999a, 2005).

The third part of the book, 'The contemporary youth justice system and its critics', examines the origins, foundations, implementation and parameters of the contemporary youth justice system. Chapter 9, 'New Labour and the new youth justice', considers the origins the new system and commences with the emergence of New Labour as an electoral force during the mid-1990s and its commitment to the philosophy of communitarianism which is founded on the notion that the traditional liberal provision of individual rights should equally involve responsibilities to society (Etzioni 1993); the risk society thesis, which observes a new governmental style focusing on the control of 'criminogenic situations' and the assessment and management of risk (Feeley and Simon 1994; Ericson and Haggerty 1997; Barry *et al.* 1996); the new public management, which has seen the incorporation of private-sector management techniques into the public arena long criticised for its financial ineptitude and incompetence (Manning 2005); transparent quality assurance systems and processes (Charlton 1999) which are all part of the audit society (Power 1997); and effective and evidence-based practice which requires access to sound critical knowledge and evidence to provide the basis of successful practice (Stephenson *et al.* 2007).

Chapter 10, 'The contemporary youth justice system', introduces and examines the parameters of the contemporary youth justice system and the concerns of academics and other commentators at the outset and in the aftermath of its establishment. Thus concerns are identified relating to the speedy establishment of a new system which involved a self-acknowledged rupture with the previous juvenile justice system that was perceived to have failed, with its apparent successes now seemingly ignored (Cavadino 1997; Didduck 1999; Jackson 1999; Newburn 1998; Padfield 1998; Campbell 1999; Goldson 1999, 2000a; Hogg 1999; Muncie 1999b; Walsh 1999; Harvey 2000; Pickford 2000; Jones 2001; Smith 2007).

Chapter 11, 'Effective youth justice in practice', considers the operation of the contemporary youth justice system with its foundations in effective and evidence-based practice. There is thus an examination of the role and significance of identified key areas of effective practice in a multi-agency youth justice system with the central aim of reducing youth offending. First, assessment, planning and supervision are all considered essential elements of practice with young people at all stages of the youth justice system and guide and shape all work conducted within the system. Second, the likelihood of individual children and young people becoming involved in offending behaviour has been crucially linked to the number of risk factors present in their lives and the key areas of effective practice for identifying and responding to these risk and protective factors are seen to be parenting (Farrington 1995; Coleman and Roker 2001); education, training and employment (Parsons and Howlett 2002; substance misuse (DPAS and SCODA 2000; Nacro 2000; Hammersley *et al.* 2003) and mental health problems (Hagell 2002). A third category addresses the lives of apprehended young offenders and thus offender behaviour programmes which have been shown to make a significant contribution to reducing criminality (Lipsey 1995; Dowden and Andrews 1999); neighbourhood prevention schemes targeted at young people living in areas of high deprivation and criminal activity (Honey and Mumford 1986; Hawkins and Catalans 1992; Patterson and Yoerger 1997); mentoring (Brewer *et al.* 1995; Styles and Morrow 1992; Fo and O'Donnell 1974; Tierney and Grossman, with Resch 1995); restorative justice interventions which seek the integration of the young person back into mainstream society (Marshall 1998); intensive supervision and surveillance programmes which target that small minority of offenders who are responsible for a disproportionately large number of offences (Andrews *et al. 1990*; Graham and Bowling 1995; Waters *et al.* 2003); remand management and settlement services which exist primarily to divert appropriate young people from unnecessary custodial remands and to manage those awaiting trial or sentence (Woolf 1991; Cavadino and Gibson 1993; Her Majesty's Inspectorate of Prisons 1997; Moore and Smith 2001); and resettlement which in an ideal world would include the cessation of – or at least reduced – offending and engagement in employment, education or training activities on release from a custodial sentence (Hagell and Newburn 1994; Loeber and Farrington 1998; Rutter *et al.* 1998).

Chapter 12, 'The contemporary youth justice system reconsidered', critically reconsiders the introduction of New Labour youth justice policy and the implementation of the contemporary youth justice system in a wider structural context. Thus, there is a reconsideration of the notions of evidence-based practice (Nutley *et al.* 2000; Sanderson 2002; Wilcox 2003); the management of contemporary youth crime (Communities that Care 2002; Flood-Page *et al.* 2000; MORI 2001 2002, 2003); risk-based contemporary youth justice where it is observed that this new orthodoxy appears to have provided the legitimation for increased state intervention in the governance of children, families, schools and designated problematic communities (Armstrong 2005); the issue of social exclusion and reintegrative tutelage where it is observed that the legitimacy of such a project is founded on a significantly unequal division of labour (Furlong and Cartmel 1997; Fergusson *et al.* 2000; and the legitimacy of restorative justice strategies introduced in communities characterised by social injustice and inequality (Braithwaite and Daly 1994; Strang 1995; Crawford and Clear 2003; Gray 2005).

This concluding chapter then considers the future of the contemporary youth justice system at a time when there are concerns that the rigour of the New Labour neo-communitarianism project might simply have gone too far (Jamieson 2005). The proposed structural solution is the development of a genuine moral communitarianism founded on notions of consensual interdependency with others and a concurrent need for a new research agenda which reconsiders notions of risk and how we – and young people in particular – understand it (Armstrong 2005). There follows a consideration of future possibilities for the contemporary youth justice system and where it is observed that a good starting point would be the de-politicisation and the independence from government of the Youth Justice Board (Pitts 2003). It is argued nevertheless that the contemporary system will not obtain proper independence from government until it has gained the trust of the public and government to deliver on its key aims of cost-effective reductions in offending by children and young people.

Notes

1 See also Simon (2000) and Garland (2001).
2 £660m was spent on the police; £42m on legal aid; £24m on the Crown Prosecution Service; £13m on the courts; £200m on social services; £12m on the Probation Service and £40m on prisons.
3 For example, police detection rates for offences of burglary are as low as 9 per cent in some geographical locations (Hopkins Burke 2005).
4 There are two kinds of police caution – formal and informal. The informal one is an oral warning given by a police officer and does not count towards a criminal record and is not included in the crime statistics.
5 Nine per cent lived in families which had their car stolen and 7 per cent had their home burgled (MORI Youth Survey 2000).

Part 1

Young People, Criminality and Criminal Justice

Chapter 2

Children, young people and modernity

The first part of this book traces the social construction[1] of young people in the modern era in terms of the concepts of childhood and adolescence and examines the strategies that were introduced to educate, discipline and control this increasingly important section of the population – ultimately in the interests of a capitalist economy and its agents – and it then proceeds to trace the history of what was to become a specialist juvenile justice system designed to deal with those individuals who came to deviate from, and transgress against, the legal and social norms established by the child tutelage strategies of modern society.

Chapter 3 tells the story of the juvenile justice from its inception and its gradual transition from a justice model, with its theoretical foundations clearly located in the rational actor model of criminal behaviour, to the triumph of an imperfect welfarism with its theoretical foundations located in both the predestined and victimised actor models. It then proceeds to consider the apparent failure of welfarism as a youth justice model of intervention and examines the critiques that were to emerge from right across the political spectrum. Chapter 4 considers the later ambiguous story of youth justice during the Conservative administrations in the years 1979–97 and the subsequent transition to New Labour in 1997 and the establishment of the contemporary youth justice system.

This chapter discusses the child tutelage strategies employed by which children and young people came to be constructed as an important and essential element of the population during the period of industrial modernity. For it was with the emergence of the modern

23

era that there came for the first time in history a requirement for an ample, fit, healthy, increasingly educated and skilled but always obedient population. We will start by considering how modern societies differed from their pre-modern societies and how the role, status and behavioural requirements of young people were to be significantly different from those in the previous socio-economic era. This is an important analysis because it helps us to establish the reality that the lives of people – both young and old – what they might expect from life and what is required from them is always closely linked to the requirements of the economy. This is a significant point to which we will return throughout this book.

The emergence and consolidation of modern societies

In pre-modern societies the role and status of children and young people were ambiguous and because of the nature of the pre-industrial capitalist economy they were of little significance or importance and often a drain on limited material resources. It was a world where a large population was invariably a disadvantage rather than an advantage. It was, nevertheless, a situation that was to be significantly reversed with the emergence of modern industrial societies where for the first time in history an abundant, fit, healthy populace was to become essential.

Pre-modern societies were predominantly rural and agrarian, with the great majority of people living a virtual subsistence existence in the countryside where any significant increase in population would put an enormous pressure on very limited resources, with the outcome being periodic famine and starvation. Thomas Malthus (1959) had famously argued during the nineteenth century that, if unchecked, population would grow geometrically while, at the same time, agricultural product would increase only arithmetically. Disaster, it was argued, had only been averted by the three periodical population controls of famine, plague and war and, therefore, in such a world children – or more accurately, little people – were of little intrinsic value to society and invariably an economic liability.

Malthus was a political economist and was concerned with what he perceived to be the decline of living conditions in an England which was becoming rapidly industrialised and urbanised with consistently appalling living conditions for the vast majority of poor working people who had emigrated to the new towns and cities from the countryside. Malthus blamed this decline on three elements: first, the now overproduction of children; second, the consequential inability of resources to keep up with the fast-growing human population; and, third, the irresponsibility of the lower classes in producing this unsustainable populace. He therefore proposed that the family size of the lower classes should be regulated so that the poor did not produce more children than they could support.

But modern industrial societies were fundamentally different from their predecessors and required an ever-increasing population and Malthus was unappreciative of this new reality. In this new world, children were now an asset and increasingly they were to be nurtured, pampered and disciplined in the interests of a society that needed them. A discussion of the processes by which children and adolescents were to be constructed as a significant component of society needs thus to be located in the context of the transition from pre-modern, medieval, invariably feudal societies to industrialised modern societies. It will be worthwhile, therefore, first reflecting on the ways in which these societies significantly differed.

'Modernity' or 'modernism' are terms used to describe the development of a secular, scientifically rational, increasingly industrialised and urban tradition with its origins in the seventeenth-century scientific revolution and the eighteenth-century philosophical Enlightenment and which had come to replace the previous feudal and medieval tradition in Western Europe. The principal defining features of subsequent mature modern societies can be identified in the areas of economics, politics and culture (Hopkins Burke 1998, 2005). Economically, there was the development of a market economy with the growth of production for profit rather than the predominantly immediate local use that had characterised subsistence-existence rural communities. Wage labour now became the principal form of employment with the development of industrial technology and the extension of the division of labour and specialisation, although poor people were significantly to lose their long-term rights to land that they had in feudal societies. Politically, there was to be the growth and consolidation of the centralised nation state with formalised boundaries and frontiers, the growth and extension of state institutions with their bureaucratic forms of administration and myriad officials, ever-increasing systematic forms of surveillance and control and the development of representative democracy and political party systems. Culturally, there was a challenge to the previously dominant local folk traditions in the name of rationality, which stressed the virtues of scientific and technical knowledge as being superior to any other form (see Harvey 1989; Nelken 1994, Morrison 1995, Hopkins Burke 1998).

Modern societies are mass societies characterised by mass production and consumption, corporate capital, organised labour and importantly an extensive large demand for workers (Harvey 1989; Hopkins Burke 1999 2001). In such societies a fast-growing population is essential and crucial to a successful industrial economy and in such changed circumstances, children and young people were now seen as important economic assets because they would grow up to be the next generation of productive workers – or indeed military personnel – on which the economic strength and defence of the modern state was to become heavily dependent. There were to be, nevertheless, frequently reoccurring concerns about the quality of that population with a corresponding increasing demand for state intervention in the rearing and socialisation of young people, not least when their behaviour was problematic, or indeed criminal. The discussion continues by examining the increasing and varied attempts to control and shape that young population and, indeed, to ensure that their parents carried out their duty to socialise a compliant, disciplined, obedient and law-abiding populace which was appropriate to the needs of the economy.

The social control of childhood and adolescence

The way childhood is viewed today in the twenty-first century is very much the product of modern societies and modernist modes of thought. In pre-modern times childhood had not been seen as a distinct period of development in the way it is now (Aries 1962). Young children dressed like adults were viewed in the same way as their elders and participated fully in adult life, including the drinking of alcohol (Aries 1962; Hoyles and Evans 1989). Moreover, in the pre-modern era, the child mortality rate often exceeded 75 per cent during the first five years of life (Hoyles and Evans 1989) and it would have made very little sense to have developed emotional attachments to your children in the way we do today, let alone start making plans for their future.

Our modern conception of childhood began to develop in Western Europe during the sixteenth century with the emergence of a small recognisable middle class and its demand for a formalised education for its sons (Aries 1962). Previously, the apprenticeship system had been the main form of education and preparation for adult life had involved children from all social groups being sent into the homes of other families of equal social status. The idea of education now began to embrace formal schooling, a shift that reflected increasing attachment to the child, with middle-class parents choosing to keep their children close to them (Aries 1962; Hoyles and Evans 1989). Furthermore, during the eighteenth century, the contemporary conception of a house emerged and became established among the wealthier classes with the establishment of separate and specialised rooms (Aries 1962) and it was at this time that the child came to be seen as an irreplaceable and unique individual, the centre of the family and who started to assume great importance in society (Hoyles and Evans 1989). It is important to recognise nevertheless that this evolution in the concept of childhood occurred mainly in the statistically tiny upper and middle classes. The poor – who made up the substantial proportion of the population – continued to live like medieval families into the early nineteenth century (Aries 1962). However, it was these newly emergent middle-class attitudes to childhood that were to provide the dominant template of acceptable – and increasingly enforceable – child socialisation from the nineteenth century onwards.

Muller (1973), a Canadian academic but with an analysis still appropriate to generic Western European society, argues that the development of our modern conception of childhood – and thus the increasingly compulsory introduction of bourgeois childrearing socialisation mores into the lower social classes – can be divided into four phases, each distinguished by trends in birth and death rates. The first identified phase – which had clear foundations in pre-modern socio-economic conditions and values – was to end around 1750 with the beginnings of mass industrialisation and urbanisation. It was a period when birth and death rates were both very high but quite similar, with the outcome being a reasonably stable population size. Thus, with a high rate of childhood mortality and an average life expectancy of only 25 years, children were seen as fragile, easily replaceable, and of little importance (Muller 1973; Hoyles and Evans 1989). Childhood was merely a necessary evil on the way to productive adulthood.

The second phase encompassed the period between 1750, and the beginnings of the Industrial Revolution, and the final triumph of industrial capitalism and urbanisation around 1880 when infant mortality dropped drastically without a corresponding drop in the birth rate, with the outcome being the population boom which was to so concern Malthus.[2] This rise in population combined with rapid industrialisation and urban expansion was largely responsible for the widespread use of child labour. Children were simply a cheap,

27

plentiful and available source of labour and were often small enough to perform jobs that full-grown adults could not, such as crawling under machines to repair them. Societal support for child labour, moreover, spread far beyond the obvious interests of entrepreneurial, capitalist mill and mine owners. As late as 1866, the International Alliance of Workers – an early prototype trade union organisation – proclaimed child labour to be 'a legitimate and logical step forward ... In a rational society, every child over the age of nine years should be a productive worker' (cited in Muller 1973: 6).

The third phase was the period 1880 to 1930, which saw the birth rate go down and, at that time, children came to assume central importance in the family of all social classes. The French Enlightenment philosopher Jean-Jacques Rousseau had proposed childhood to be a desirable state of innocence and had argued that society needed to protect the child against adult corruption and although this idea had begun to gain in popularity among the upper and middle classes during the late eighteenth century, it was during this third phase that the idea crossed class boundaries and became significant in the socialisation of the mass of working-class children (Muller 1973). Several factors were important in this process of transition and the often-enforced introduction of bourgeois child socialisation mores into a sometimes resistant working class. First, with the arrival of compulsory education and the raising of the minimum age of employment, children began to be financial burdens on their parents rather than sources of income. Second, with increasing urbanisation, the family lost its status as an economic unit that produced food and other necessary commodities and took on the role of a consumer. Third, with the decline in the birth rate, there was a reduction in the size of families. Not only were fewer children being born but extended family households were becoming less common. Children of all social classes now came to assume a central place in the family; they had much more contact with their parents and became increasingly dependent upon them to provide the necessities of life. Increased contact nevertheless meant more discipline and punishment, as the idea that children were innocent but easily corrupted grew in popularity. In general, children were expensive but emotionally invaluable because they were seen as an avenue for upward mobility and a guarantee that their parents would be taken care of later in life. The idea that the family should not only be held responsible for the appropriate socialisation and discipline of their children but was also to be considered responsible when the child deviated from enforced social mores and transgressed against the rules of society became increasingly accepted during this period.

The fourth phase is the period from 1930 to the present day and is also child-centred but in a different way from the previous phase. The contemporary goal is care, understanding, and respect for the needs of the child, rather than the needs of the parents but if this all goes wrong and the child socialisation process fails to deliver an acceptable product, then the parents become increasingly responsible and – certainly since the introduction of the contemporary youth justice system post-1998 – accountable for that failure.

We have thus seen that childhood, since its 'discovery' in the seventeenth century, has been increasingly viewed as a time of innocence and dependence, when protection, training and appropriate socialisation are paramount. Youth, in contrast, is expected to be an age of deviance, disruption and wickedness (Brown 1998) and this expectation has been strongly linked to the historical discovery of the pseudo-scientific notion of adolescence. Many researchers (Gillis 1974; Hendricks 1990a, 1990b; Jenks 1996; Brown 1998) follow Aries (1962) and argue that adolescence was 'discovered' during the Victorian era and from that time onwards it became identified as a cause of delinquency (Gillis 1974: 171). Prior to that time when there was little differentiation between children and adults, the problem of youth or adolescent offending simply could not exist.

It was the rapid growth of industrial modernity in the early nineteenth century – at the same time as the emerging distinction between child and adult – that led eventually to fewer young people in the workplace and, with more spare time on their hands, they took to hanging out together on the streets. The social construction of the notions of adolescence, acceptable youthful behaviour, juvenile delinquency or 'hooliganism' (see Pearson 1983) became increasingly apparent from that time onwards. The social commentators of the time had their own middle-class conceptions of what should constitute acceptable youthful behaviour and the incremental criminalisation of working-class youth began as early as 1815 with the creation of the Society for Investigating the Causes of the Alarming Increase of Juvenile Delinquency in the Metropolis (Pinchbeck and Hewitt 1981; Muncie 1999).

Hendricks (1990b) discusses the emergence of the social and scientific term 'adolescence' that was constructed by the professional middle classes in accordance with the work of the child study movement and especially the highly influential G. Stanley Hall, who described this stage of development in biologically determinist terms as one of 'storm and stress' in which instability and fluctuation were normal and to be expected (Hall 1905, cited in Hendricks 1990b). Hall ominously based his notion of 'normal adolescent demeanour' on the 'unspontaneous, conformist and confident' white middle- class youths he observed and it was this model that was soon to be prescribed as desirable for young people of all social classes (Griffin 1997). Thus, the marginalisation of whole cross-sections of young people – especially, the working class, girls and ethnic minority groups – became implicit with the social construction of a notion of adolescence acceptable to middle-class sensibilities.[3] Although theories of 'delinquency' were to broaden their approach during the twentieth century, the ways in which adolescence is conceived remain heavily influenced by the 'storm and stress' model (Newburn 2002).

A historical perspective on youth justice is essential in helping us understand contemporary perceptions of offending by children and young people. Throughout history we can find references to the escalating problems of youth crime (West 1967; Pearson 1983). Moreover, we can trace historical debates and discourses surrounding the nature of youth crime and political solutions which are remarkably similar to contemporary political debates. Historical studies show us that fears about the rising trends in youth crime are repeated throughout British social history with the present continuously compared unfavourably with the halcyon days of the past, thus signalling a moral decline (Humphries 1981; Pearson 1983). While these studies also inform the reader that this golden age, where youth was unproblematic, has never actually existed, it is a conclusion that does not appear to be widely recognised or understood by either the general public or their political representatives.

Young people, social control and discipline

Our discussion to date suggests that the concepts of childhood and adolescence appear to have emerged with the rise of industrial modernity and the capitalist system of production (Thane 1981) although no simple relationship between the two can be identified (Springhall 1986). Within pre-industrial European economies children were working in the home – or around it – by about the age of four or five and were thus quickly absorbed into the productive process and would mix with adults in both work and social situations (Pollock 1983). They were thus easily subject to adult control and discipline. As the middle and upper classes came to understand childhood as a time of innocence and preparation for adulthood, the technical demands of the economy produced the need for ever-longer periods of training and apprenticeship. Children and young people, therefore, came increasingly to spend time in their own company and with their peers on the street while decreasingly being under the control and tutelage of their elders. We have here the origins of contemporary notions of 'peer group' pressure and the formation of the deviant youth subcultures that are so central to legitimate explanations of youth offending in the late twentieth century and beyond and which we explore in detail during the second part of this book. It is, moreover, with the growing concerns about the behaviour of youths on the streets of Victorian England that we see the creation of a range of interventions and legislation aimed at the discipline and tutelage of working-class youth in the image of middle-class sensibilities and ensuring that they are fit for purpose in a capitalist industrial economy. The concept of adolescence was to be central to this process of tutelage.

The development of compulsory schooling and changes in the economy were, therefore, the two interlinked elements crucial to the widespread application of the concept of adolescence to working-class young people (Walvin 1982), the outcome being the creation of a time of delay and discontinuity which could be seen as a peculiar property of youth. Throughout the nineteenth century schooling expanded, first in voluntary and then, following the 1870 Education Act, in state schools. By 1893 the school leaving age was 11 and by 1899 it had risen to 12. Compulsory schooling combined with efforts to enforce attendance had a considerable impact: first, children were pulled off the streets and the problem of their control was transferred to the classroom (Humphries 1981); second, they had their access to the symbols and material benefits of adult economic life postponed, while their importance to the labour market became marginal.[4]

The outcome was a 'moral panic' prompted by the large numbers of children and young people on the streets (Pearson 1983), a situation that was made worse in the last decade of the nineteenth century by a major economic recession which led to widespread unemployment among all age groups. At the same time, the accuracy of national statistics concerning juvenile crime improved substantially and these changes were mistakenly used as evidence of a massive increase in crime. The outcome was increased action taken against certain types of visible 'crime' on the streets, for example, drunkenness, gambling, malicious mischief, loitering, begging and dangerous play, which criminalised further groups of young people (Muncie 1984: 40).

At the same time, young women were observed to be involved in a street problem of a different kind with prostitution – often involving children – flourishing in the larger cities and towns. There was consequently widespread public demand for the resultant legislative response, the Criminal Law Amendment Act 1885, which increased the age of sexual consent to 16 and this has remained so to this day. A significant motivation for involvement in prostitution was clearly the appalling social and financial position of many working-class families and the limited economic opportunities available to working-class young women themselves.

A number of middle-class women were also worried about the conditions faced by young women in domestic service, the factories and sweated labour shops. Still others were appalled by the experiences of young women in the domestic home where many worked hard for many hours a day looking after their families hidden from the public eye. They did not, however, pose the openly visible problem posed by young men because they had always been controlled and supervised in the home (Nava 1984). Home life was nevertheless undergoing a process of restructuring. The separation of the home from work, the changing rhythms of working life and demands for different forms of skill all had an impact upon the shape of household life. Some of the changes were consciously promoted by the middle class who through their economic and political power were able to influence significantly the shape of, and power relations within, the family, and their ideals and beliefs came to dominate nineteenth-century legislation and ideology (Gittins 1985).

Gittins observes that this was not just a family, but a gender ideology, and part of a careful and deliberate attempt to reorganise the relations between the sexes according to bourgeois norms and values. These changes both affected the way in which young men and women experienced these institutions and how young people were perceived by adults, or at least by middle-class adults. The outcome was that young men and women were both now viewed as problematic and they had to be fitted into the new social and industrial order that the reformers wanted. Those who were undisciplined, dangerously independent and precocious were a matter of grave concern (Hendricks 1986). The family was thus to play its part, with women undertaking the major productive role therein and providing the conditions for the activities of men in the world while providing a reserve army of labour, to be called upon as and when the economy required their services.

Central to the changed nature of the experiences of youth were developments in the nature of leisure provision which by the second half of the nineteenth century had begun to take a form we would recognise today. Cunningham (1980) identifies four factors which influenced this development. First, there were the market forces of supply and demand where in response to the growing relative affluence of the working class there developed a considerable commercial sector which included the growth of various forms of variety theatres and 'penny gaffs', public houses, travel opportunities, such as day excursions, popular literature, such as the 'penny dreadfuls', and sports of various kinds. Second, these market forces were modified by the attachment of the working class to forms of leisure created in the first half of the nineteenth century, and before, which included loyalty to various games and sports and to the public house. Third, there was increased provision by government and charity organisations in the name of 'rational recreation' which had led to the spread of public parks, libraries, wash houses and museums. Fourth, there were growing concerns about the dangers of leisure that were expressed in calls to control various activities including some in the home.

The middle class already had a degree of control over the working-class experience of employment, schooling and other forms of incarceration, including hospitals, poor houses and prisons, with considerable effort expended in an attempt to cultivate correct attitudes and behaviour within the churches. What appeared to elude the middle class was any influence over the private world of the working-class home and the 'dangerous' pastimes enjoyed therein. There was widespread abhorrence of 'brutal' sports, cheap entertainments, drinking and gambling, all of which were seen to be ungodly, as posing a threat to social order and as a reflection of the moral failure of the working classes. Leisure was simply that dangerous time between leaving work and going to bed when many of the worst fears of the middle classes about the working-class young were readily apparent and were therefore to be singled out for attention (Hendricks 1986). At the same time, there was considerable growing concern about working-class unrest and political activity.

The growth of working-class political organisation was seen by many in the middle class as heralding a period of intensified class conflict, with socialism perceived as a threat to stability (Simon 1965). Crucially, it can be argued that something akin to a remaking of the working class – based on solidarity and organisational strength – took place in the years between 1870 and 1900 (Stedman Jones 1984) and these developments indicate a transformation in the central forms of working-class activity, and the dangers were not lost upon the middle class, with young people being seen as particularly susceptible to the appeals of extremism (Rosenthal 1986).

There were also concerns about the ability of Britain to maintain the Empire and it was argued that this had particular implications for domestic stability and wealth (Ramdin 1987: 63) while the South African war of the 1890s revealed the poor physical condition of young working-class recruits, where over a third of volunteers were not fit for military duty (Springhall 1977: 14). Moreover, there was the emergence of other industrial and trading nations – in particular the USA and Germany – and the possibility of 'economic defeat'. There was, therefore, a demand for state and voluntary welfare measures designed to increase 'national efficiency' among influential social groups who previously had been hostile or indifferent to social issues (Thane 1982: 61).

Middle-class reformers already had access to common-sense explanations of the problems faced by young people but there now appeared scientific justifications to explain why they lacked the potential for intellectual and emotional development. Dyhouse (1981) observes that the concept of adolescence provided a significant means by which a pathological picture of working-class young people could be sustained. Significantly, the way in which a number of behaviours were attributed to a phase of physiological and psychological development helped to shift attention away from material inequality as a way of explaining the position of young people. Juvenile delinquency thus came to be explained as the 'natural attribute of adolescence' and the terms a 'lack of parental guidance' combined with 'troublesome adolescence' were to remain the dominant form of explaining youth offending until at least the 1950s.

It was, nevertheless, working-class adolescents, in particular, who were thought to be the most likely to display delinquent and rebellious characteristics during this 'storm and stress' period in the life cycle because it was widely assumed that their parents exercised inadequate control over their brutal adolescent instincts (Humphries 1981). The new concept of 'adolescence' was, therefore, considerably enhanced by the efforts of psychologists and those who saw it as their duty – or job – to intervene in the lives of young people and who now had a suitable vocabulary of scientific terms with which to carry forward their intentions.

Equipped with the new language of social science – and stimulated by fears of social disruption and imperial decline – significant elements of the expanding newly affluent middle classes devoted time and energy to charitable work (Stedman Jones 1984). Much of this charitable effort was centred in the large cities where there was a significant middle-class presence in close proximity to the forms of deprivation and 'problems' that so alarmed their sensibilities. London, especially the East End, became the site for many forms of philanthropic intervention. The composition of the middle class in London was skewed towards professions such as law, medicine, the church, the military and the civil service, groups which were of considerable importance in determining the formation of characteristic attitudes towards the problem of poverty. The absence of substantial, direct economic links between these particular groupings of the rich and the poor – as for example between employer and employee – can be seen as explaining the importance of charitable activity in London, 'both as a mode of interpreting the behaviour of the poor and as a means of attempting to control them' (Stedman Jones 1984: 240).

There does appear to be something of a change of attitude among key groups to the notion of intervention, particularly in the case of the 'casual poor'. The London dock strike of 1889 and the riots three years previously, along with the concerns already outlined earlier, provoked the 'intellectual assault which began to be mounted against laissez faire both from the right and the left in the 1880s' (Stedman Jones 1984: 297). Nevertheless, while the extent of government action concerning perceived social problems undoubtedly increased from 1870 to 1900, it was limited when compared with the demands for action and the nature of the problems themselves. The state, both local and central, was envisaged as providing a 'safety net', a net which operated to a large extent through the Poor Law. Beyond this there were incursions into welfare, such as in education, but by and large such works were to be left to voluntary organisation and it was thus in the 1880s that the first 'youth organisation', the Young Men's Christian Association (YMCA), began to make a mass impact (Simon 1965).

From the mid-nineteenth century, youth work came to assume many guises, although with the passing of the Education Act 1870 and the gradual introduction of other welfare legislation, there was a significant shift in style and emphasis. With schools apparently now offering basic instruction and other agencies material and welfare assistance, many clubs and youth organisations turned overwhelmingly to 'the inculcation of intangible social and spiritual values amongst their clients rather than in improving their material well-being' (Jeffs 1979: 4). Youth work can therefore be understood not as an effort to further the natural intellectual development of the individual but as a means of producing subjectivity (Donald 1985). The problem was how young people were to be attracted by the sponsors and workers to these places of improvement in their 'own' time. The answer to that conundrum was to be recreation, that is, in return for an opportunity for some amusement, young people would have to submit themselves for 'improvement' and if they were to be 'improved' then they would have to be taken out of the home, off the street, or away from any other environment that contributed to that which was offensive to middle-class values. The two apparently antagonistic elements of amusement and improvement were eventually to come together in the notion of 'improving amusement' with, for example, many of the London boys' clubs putting the emphasis on sport (Simon 1965).

The effectiveness of the new youth provision was, however, somewhat limited. For while clubs sought to exploit the demand for recreation among working-class adolescents and, at the same time, subtly combine the provision of sport with the sponsorship of conservative ideology, they did not necessarily attract large numbers (White 1980). There was simply resistance among many working-class young people to the various attempts to improve them (Dawes 1975; White 1980).

Other more structured forms of intervention with young people were, nevertheless, emerging during the 1980s. The Boys' Brigade was the first to mix drill, athleticism and the wearing of a uniform, and it was later followed by a number of similar organisations during the last decade of the nineteenth century, with the outdoor healthiness and social imperialism of scouting appearing in the following decade. Blanch (1979) proposes three main strands of nationalist attitudes which link these early male organisations and demonstrate their significance for the bourgeois child tutelage project. First, there was the idea of national efficiency in the drive to mental and physical fitness which was rooted in drill and discipline. Second, there was the idea of model authority, for within these organisations we find a highly organised hierarchical system of authority by ranks and levels and it was seen by their proponents as providing a model for social organisation and leadership. Third, there was the 'enemy outside'.

Young people at least knew what they were joining and what was expected of them. There was some resistance to drill, military manoeuvres and uniforms but members were attracted by sport, the band and the annual camp (Humphries 1981). Furthermore, there were significant differences between the Boys' Brigades and the Scouts. From the outset the latter were independent of one particular religious organisation and they utilised a rather different concept of discipline (seen as an inner quality, rather than something that had to be externally drilled) (Jeffs 1979).

These organisations nevertheless failed to reform the behaviour and attitudes of those who the reformers saw as 'being at risk', namely the working-class young. First, the uniformed organisations were predominantly pre-adolescent. Second, the majority of working-class young people were in effect excluded from such organisations either because of the cost of membership and their uniforms or because it was alien to their culture (Springhall 1977). Third, there was resistance from a significant proportion of those who did join. Nevertheless, to some extent, such youth movements did allow the assimilation of upper-working-class and lower-middle-class boys into the new social order (Springhall 1977).

Those young men who wanted to advance within the existing socio-economic system were therefore provided with a means of preparing themselves in a way which was acceptable to those who presided over entry into desired jobs and social organisations. Those who did not wish to advance on these terms could at least be offered some recreation in the hope of containment. Work with girls and young women nevertheless tended to emphasise a different type of 'getting on', and suggests there were serious limits to this process. It was feared that the involvement of young women in the labour market and, consequently, their acquisition of independent spending power, would tempt girls away from their allotted roles of wife and mother. If young women were 'upwardly aspiring', then what such organisations could provide them with was an experience in the 'womanly arts' so that they might influence their men (Dyhouse 1981).

The middle-class improvers could, however, only offer a limited social mobility between classes for both young men and women. They supported and operated within a capitalist socio-economic system which required a particular division of labour with a predominant need for manual labour and would have considerable difficulties in accommodating large numbers of young people wanting significant advancement. While the rhetoric of individual achievement came easy, it had to be contained within particular class, gender, racial and age structures. The place of a woman was in the home; to be British was to be best, betters were to be honoured and youth had to earn advancement and to wait its turn.

Much early youth work was directed at young people in the same class as the providers but the organisations were themselves controlled by members of the middle class who carried with them specific themes – in particular an attack on working-class cultures – and developed forms recognisable in present-day practice and sought to engage the services of particular 'types' of adult. In this respect they had much in common with the notions of rational recreation that formed the initial development of the working men's clubs (Jeffs and Smith 1988a).

The middle class that was so prominent in the above accounts of the subtle – and sometimes not quite so subtle – control, discipline and tutelage of young people was itself the product of a socio-economic system with its own dynamic. Many of the concerns that were expressed by the early sponsors of youth work were reflections of the requirements of the economic system but the relationship between the latter and the nature of intervention is ambiguous (Jeffs and Smith 1988a). At one level, many of the efforts of the 'improvers' were directed at the containment and reformation of elements of the system, yet without doubt, these early workers and philanthropists were sincere in their belief that they were acting in the best interests of the young, that the values and institutions they saw threatened were there for the good of all rather than the benefit of the few. Their viewpoint was nevertheless formed within a particular social class which in turn was both the creation and beneficiary of capitalism. Similarly, the organisations they created had to act within that system and inevitably took on the values and ways of operating which made sense within that system. In particular, because youth organisations were, and still are, in the market economy, they have to respond to its dynamics much like commercial operations (Jeffs and Smith 1988a). Those advocating rational recreation and improvement were thus in competition for the bodies and minds of the young people with commercial forms of entertainment, in particular, the public house and the music hall.

Youth work could be clearly located as part of the nineteenth-century bourgeois child tutelage project. First, it aimed to assist with the maintenance and development of the social and economic order envisaged by key members of the middle class. Second, it adopted and confirmed distinctively bourgeois forms and values which were often drawn from the experience of public schooling and military service or represented paradigms of middle-class leisure. Indeed, the notion of adolescence as it was articulated – and as we have seen – was largely a bourgeois construction. Third, it acted to alleviate middle-class consciences by enabling them to feel they were doing something about the worst excesses of capitalism. The very fact that they were providing help, and others were defined as not, also allowed them to justify their pre-eminent position. Fraser (1973) argues that it was both a way of confirming superiority and status and of receiving thanks and gratitude. Lastly, this work provided a range of opportunities for 'meaningful' endeavour for those members of the middle class who were denied entry or were unable to enter both the labour market and the representative political arena.

The social control, discipline and tutelage of working-class children and adolescents was, therefore, a significant strategy of middle-class 'moral entrepreneurs' (see Becker 1963) sometimes working consciously in bourgeois or capitalist interests but invariably unaware of the real significance of their work. Central to much of this work was increasingly the surveillance and training of parents to ensure that they carried out the requirements of the tutelage project.

The centrality of parenting

The emphasis on parenting in the contemporary youth justice system that we will encounter in the third part of this book is again nothing new. The notion that 'the family' is in 'crisis', and/or that parents are 'failing', comprises a 'cyclical phenomenon with a very long history' (Day-Sclater and Piper 2000: 135), and the 'parenting theme' (Gelsthorpe 1999) has enjoyed, and continues to enjoy, a certain prominence within debates surrounding youth crime and youth justice. Indeed, the 'improper conduct of parents' was identified as one of the 'principal causes' of 'juvenile delinquency' by the Committee for Investigating the Causes of the Alarming Increase of Juvenile Delinquency in the Metropolis 1816, which was first public inquiry into youth crime. The Committee proposed that 'neglect of parental authority', 'improper conduct', 'disproportionate severity', 'undue indulgence', 'permitting absence from school', 'weakness', 'laxity of morals' and other 'parenting deficits' combined to 'cause delinquency' (Goldson and Jamieson 2002: 83).

This influential discourse developed and consolidated throughout the nineteenth century and beyond as it accumulated an increasingly 'scientific' support. In the 1850s a Parliamentary Select Committee on 'Criminal and Destitute Juveniles' reported that no parent should be allowed to bring up a child 'in such a way as to almost secure his becoming a criminal' (cited in May 1973: 111). Moreover, Mary

Carpenter, an extremely influential moral entrepreneur of the time, defined a threefold classification of 'delinquency' within which the notion of 'inadequate' parenting was unequivocally stated:

> The first class consists of daring, hardened young offenders, who are already outlaws from society ... We need hardly ask what has been their previous history; it is certain that they have had an undisciplined childhood, over which no moral or religious influence has been shed ... The second class is, if possible, more dangerous to society than the first ... these are youths who are regularly trained by their parents or others in courses of professional dishonesty ... A third class, and perhaps a still more numerous one, consists of children who are not as hardened or daring as the first, or as trained in crime as the second, but who, from the culpable neglect of their parents, and an entire want of all religious and moral influence at home, have gradually acquired, while quite young, habits of petty thieving, which are connived at, rather than punished, by their parents.

> (Carpenter 1853: 23, cited in Goldson
> and Jamieson 2002: 83–4)

Goldson and Jamieson (2002: 84) further observe that 'the developing agenda – invariably informed by constructions of (ir)responsibility, (im)morality and (in)discipline – was one in which the legitimacy of state intervention in respect of "malfunctioning" or "dysfunctional" families was increasingly expressed'. Equally, it was not simply the principle of state intervention that emerged, but also the question of sanction and punishment. Thus, during the 1870s and 1880s, various Acts of Parliament were passed that required parents to carry out certain duties, with the threat of a penalty or even the loss of the child if they failed (Morris and Giller 1987).

'The family' was thus a key focus of the Victorian interest in locating the basis of social order (Donajgrodzki 1977) and this legacy was sustained and further developed during early decades of the twentieth century when the 'delinquency' discourse began to claim scientific legitimacy not least from academic psychologists. Although the crime rate had decreased during the war years (1914–18), it had started to rise during the Great Depression period of the 1920s, but despite an almost logical demand for a commonsense link between poverty and crime, the dominant emphasis was placed at the micro level of parent–child relations and individual personality. Biological-psychological explanations became very influential with the work of Cyril Burt (1925), who characterised the family backgrounds of 'delinquents' in terms of 'defective family relationships' and 'defective discipline', and he argued that parents were primarily responsible for the offending conduct of their children. These arguments influenced key government committees and, in turn, had a major impact on legislation. Perhaps most significantly, a Home Office Departmental Committee on the Treatment of Young Offenders (the Molony Committee) was established in January 1925, and many of its recommendations formed the basis of the Children and Young Persons Act 1933. This legislation was a significant youth justice policy milestone which had the effect of making the courtroom 'a site for adjudicating on matters of family socialisation and parental behaviour' (Muncie 1984: 45).

The following two chapters take up the story of the changing nature of state intervention in the lives of children and young people who offend, from the beginnings of a particular juvenile justice system to the election of New Labour in 1997 and the creation of the contemporary youth justice system. We will first reflect further on the developments we have encountered above.

Social progress, exploitation or something more complex

In this chapter we have seen how contemporary notions of childhood and adolescence were socially constructed at the outset of industrial modernity and how children and more often their families were disciplined and controlled, apparently in the interests of an industrial capitalism which required a fit, healthy, increasingly educated, trained, but always obedient workforce. The neo-Marxist accounts cited above testify to a reality that was nevertheless more complex; while an orthodox social progress perspective, which considers these developments to be merely an account of how motivated entrepreneurial philanthropists with genuine concerns about poor urban children and young people at risk of the numerous dangers on the streets, including criminality and a failure to find God, is even more simplistic, although it is clear that many if not most acted with the best benevolent intentions without always fully understanding the consequences of their actions. Howard Becker's (1963) concept of the 'moral entrepreneur' helps us to not only understand further the motivated philanthropist but also the consequences – intentional or unintentional – of their actions.

Becker argues that rules of conduct – including criminal laws – are made by people with power and enforced upon people without power. Thus, rules are made by the old for the young, by men for women, by whites for blacks, by the middle class for the working class. These rules are invariably imposed upon their recipients against their will and own best interests. Moreover, the rules are legitimised by an ideology that is transmitted to the less powerful in the course of primary and secondary socialisation and as a result of this process, most people internalise and obey the rules without realising – or questioning – the extent to which their behaviour is being decided for them.

Becker argues that some rules may be cynically designed to keep the less powerful in their place but others have simply been introduced as the outcome of a sincere – albeit irrational and mistaken – belief on the part of high-status individuals that the creation of a new rule will be beneficial for its intended subjects. Becker termed the people who create new rules for the 'benefit' of the less fortunate, as we have we have seen above, 'moral entrepreneurs'.

Becker was writing about the mid-twentieth century USA but his account has resonance with the story of how philanthropic entrepreneurs came to define categories of children and youth as acceptable and non-acceptable and at the same time developed strategies to ensure their surveillance, control, discipline and tutelage with the intention of reconstructing the non-acceptable in the form of the acceptable. Yet, again this account is too simplistic. It is clear that not only did many of these philanthropists have little idea of the actual or potential consequences of their actions but they might well have become disturbed with the recognition of that final reality. It also fails to take into account the complexities of power and the outcomes of strategies promoted by agencies at the mezzo level of the institution that often enjoy autonomy from the political centre and implemented by those working at the micro level of the frontline who often enjoy considerable discretion in their work with children and young people. Helpful in understanding that situation is the notion of the carceral surveillance society devised by Michel Foucault (1980) and developed notably by Jacques Donzelot (1980), Stanley Cohen (1985) and David Garland (2001).

From this Foucauldian perspective power is not simply conceptualised as the privilege of an all-powerful state although the power that it does both possess and wield is clearly significant. Strategies of power are in reality pervasive throughout society, with the state only one location of the points of control and resistance.

Foucault (1971 1976) observes that particular areas of the social world – and he uses the examples of, law, medicine, sexuality, but youth justice neatly fits his analysis – are colonised and defined by the norms and control strategies a variety of institutions and experts devise and abide by. He argues that these networks of power and control are governed as much by the knowledge and concepts that define them as by the definite intentions of groups.

The state, for its part, is implicated in this matrix of power-knowledge, but it is only part of the story, for in this vein it has been argued that within civil society there are numerous 'semi-autonomous' realms and relations – such as communities, occupations, organisations, families – where surveillance and control are present but where the state administration is technically absent. These semi-autonomous arenas within society are often appropriately negotiated and resisted by their participants in ways that, even now, the state has little jurisdiction.

This text favours a variation on that Foucauldian orthodoxy which has been developed previously elsewhere (Hopkins Burke 2004a, 2004c). It is readily accepted from this perspective that disciplinary strategies are often implemented by philanthropists, moral entrepreneurs, professional agents and practitioners who invariably have little or no idea how their often but sometimes less humble discourse contributes to the grand overall disciplinary control matrix. The bourgeois child tutelage project of the nineteenth and early twentieth century can clearly be viewed in that context and the accounts of two scholars of crime, young people and justice – Anthony Platt and Victor Bailey – help support this thesis.

Platt's (1969) study of the child saving movement in the USA in the late nineteenth century was concerned with the ways in which certain types of youthful behaviour came to be defined as 'delinquent' and argued that 'the child savers ... brought attention to ... and, in doing so, invented – new categories of youthful behavior which had been hitherto unappreciated' (1969: 3–4). Platt argues that the movement was related to the changing role of middle-class women who were attempting to rebuild the moral fabric of society. While the changes were of instrumental significance in that they legitimated new career opportunities for these women, they were also symbolic in that they preserved their prestige in a rapidly changing society and institutionalised certain values and ways of life for women, children and the family. Platt characterises the 'child savers' as disinterested reformers because they regarded their cause as a matter of conscience and morality, and not one which would improve their economic or class interests even though their subjective actions contributed to that objective reality.

Bailey (1987) is concerned with developments in juvenile justice in the period between the creation of the juvenile courts in 1908 and the Criminal Justice Act 1948 and which are discussed in the following chapter. Although much of Bailey's book involves a detailed scholarly account of legislative and institutional change, it also reconstructs the social and ideological background of those who promoted reform. He therefore describes how, in the 1920s, a consensus of opinion emerged around the issue of the causes of young offending, which brought together 'social workers, magistrates, penal reform groups, associations of penal practitioners, and the administrators and inspectors of the Children's Branch' who collectively favoured 'the social conception of delinquency' (Bailey 1987: 66). This consensus for reform could nevertheless be located in deeper socio-political conditions, not least the new welfarist brand of liberalism which had flourished at the turn of the twentieth century. This, he observes, was a generation of middle-class men and women whose ideas had formed the social policies of the Liberal governments of 1906–14 and they, therefore, inherited not only a social philosophy which recognised social inequalities and their structural roots, but also a political and legal framework in which the scope for state intervention and administrative action was considerably extended and which again contributed almost subconsciously to the increasing disciplinary control matrix.

The variation on the carceral society thesis presented here proposes that there are further interests involved in the creation of that disciplinary control matrix and those significantly are ours and in this context our predecessors. This hybrid – or left realist – perspective accepts that all the above accounts – neo-Marxist or social progress – are to some extent legitimate for there were and are a multitude of motivations for both implementing and accepting the increasing surveillance and control of young people on the streets and elsewhere. For the moralising mission of the entrepreneurial philanthropists and the reforming zeal of the liberal politician and administrator corresponded conveniently with those of the mill and mine owners and a government which wanted a fit, healthy fighting force, but it also coincides with the ever-increasing enthusiasm for self-betterment among the great majority of the working class that has been described from differing sociological perspectives as 'embourgeoisement' (Goldthorpe 1968–9) and 'the civilising process' (Elias 1978, 1982). Those who were resistant to that moralising and disciplinary mission – the 'rough working' class of the Victorian era – have subsequently been reinvented in academic and popular discourse as the socially excluded underclass of contemporary society, with the moral panics of today a reflection of those of the past and demands for action remarkably similar.

Neo-Marxist accounts nevertheless demand prominence in this hybrid explanation for significantly young people – and indeed all of us – were in the nineteenth century and are certainly today subject to the requirements and demands of the economy. Attempts at self-improvement or embourgeoisement always were constrained and restricted by the opportunities provided by the economy – healthy or otherwise – and this will always be the case, as we shall discover later in this book. Children and young people were increasingly disciplined and controlled through the nineteenth and first half of the twentieth century in a form that was functional and appropriate to the needs of mass modern society and an industrial capitalism which required an abundant, healthy and increasingly skilled workforce. With the fragmentation of that modernity and the subsequent retreat from mass industrialism that was to occur in the last quarter of the twentieth century, the requirements for young people were to change accordingly, as we shall discover later in this book.

Notes

1 A social construction or social construct is any institutionalised entity or object in a social system 'invented' or 'constructed' by participants in a particular culture or society that exists because people agree to behave as if it exists or follow certain conventional rules. Social status is an example of a social construct (see Clarke and Cochrane 1998).
2 The most likely explanation for this decrease in the infant death rate was the invention of the microscope and the discovery of bacteria (Hoyles and Evans 1989).
3 Hall's interpretation of adolescence was founded on biological notions but problematically no definitive age could be placed upon this transitional phase, or importantly upon the completion of the transition and the onset of adulthood. The various rites of passage that may be seen to constitute a period of adolescence are clearly delineated by societal reaction to the biological individual. Thus, for example, a young person may be sexually mature by the age of 13, but not until 16 can they legally have sexual intercourse with a consenting adult and thus become a parent, yet inexplicably, they cannot drive a motorcar on a public road until they are 17 years old (Coleman and Warren-Adamson 1992).

4 Changes in technology and in the economy did nevertheless give rise to different types of employment opportunities for young people, particularly in urban areas with large numbers of young men finding employment in the various occupations that emerged with the growing complex of distributive and administrative functions. Frequently these jobs were 'reserved' for those in their teens who in turn were required to leave such employment when they became older and too expensive to employ.

Chapter 3

From justice to welfare and its malcontents

The previous chapter discussed the social construction of childhood and adolescence in the context of the needs of an emerging, developing and consolidating mass society modernity and attempts to control the socialisation and discipline of this problematic population not least in the interests of industrial capitalism. This chapter tells the story of the creation of a juvenile justice response to those young people who had transgressed against the law of the land. It is ostensibly the story of a transition from a criminal justice response, which operated predominantly in accordance with rational actor model criminological principles, to one prescribed by treatment-oriented predestined actor model principles. It is, significantly, a story told in the context of repeated societal concerns and panics about the extent of offending by children and young people and popular demands that something is done about it.

The origins of youth justice provision

Before the nineteenth century there was no special provision for young offenders, who were treated no differently than adults and could be sent to adult prisons, hanged or transported to the colonies. Children were considered to be adult above the age of seven and were held criminally responsible for their behaviour; thus, for example, on one day alone in 1814 five children between the ages of 8 and 12 were hanged alongside each other for offences of petty theft (Pinchbeck and Hewitt 1973: 352) and this event was by no means exceptional.

This harsh treatment of juveniles, nevertheless, makes perfect sense in the context of the discussion in the previous chapter where we saw that childhood was not viewed as a particularly important stage of life in the eyes of working-class parents, employers or the law. Throughout the nineteenth century children were, however, gradually singled out from adults as a distinctive category in relation to both criminal behaviour and legal control, and again, there were a multitude of different motivations for implementing these changes. For example, the Society for the Improvement of Prison Discipline and the Reformation of Juvenile Offenders 1817 was convinced of the need to separate the young offender from the hardened adult criminal and avoid the moral contamination of the former; while refinements in prisoner classification brought the particular case of the younger offender to the fore. In 1823 a separate convict hulk (prison ship) was, therefore, introduced for young offenders and 15 years later the first penal institution solely for juveniles was opened at Parkhurst, although it should be noted that conditions were no less repressive than in an adult prison (Weiner 1990). It was to be the arrival of the first official crime statistics for offences committed by children and younger people during the 1830s that suggested a sizeable and appreciably growing problem and this was to accelerate widespread demands from a whole range of interest groups for a more rigorous intervention.

The need for a distinctive criminal justice process for young offenders was actually first proposed by liberal-minded magistrates who questioned the validity of sending children to prison while awaiting trial for minor offences. Thus, legislation was first introduced into Parliament in 1840 that would have enabled magistrates to deal with children under 12 immediately, act as the moral guardians of destitute and delinquent juveniles and advocate training and discipline in industrial schools rather than imprisonment. The House of Lords rejected the legislation, however, because it denied children the right to a jury trial and was deemed contrary to the existing dominant criminal justice orthodoxy of justice/punishment summarised in Table 3.1. This is a significant point and a theme that recurs throughout the history of youth justice, for we shall see later in this chapter that a crucial concern of progressive critics of welfarism was the withdrawal of legal rights to children and their parents which is a cornerstone of the justice/punishment model.

Concerns about young offending were increasing rapidly, however, with a parallel widespread demand that something be done to reduce the problem. Voluntary reformatories for miscreant young

Table 3.1 The justice/punishment model of youth justice

- Based on rational actor model of criminal behaviour notions that young people have free-will and choose to offend.
- Offenders should be held responsible for their actions and punished if they transgress.
- The level of punishment inflicted should be commensurate with the seriousness of the offence committed.
- Offenders should be punished for the offence committed and not on the basis of whom they are or the social conditions in which they live.

---

people had been opened by the Philanthropic Society and by private founders in the early nineteenth century, but with increasing concerns about youthful legal violations, a select committee of the House of Lords was established in the 1840s and the outcome was the Youth Offenders Act 1854. This legislation required the Home Office to certify certain recognised institutions and these came to be known as Certified Reformatories and Certified Industrial Schools, and boys and girls aged under 16 who had spent time in adult prisons could be transferred there to complete their sentences. These specifically juvenile institutions came to replace prison terms for many young offenders, and gave boys and girls a basic education plus a trade. There were also several reformatory ship schools or industrial training ships certified in the late 1850s, although they became shore-based in the twentieth century.

The Industrial Schools Act 1857 was aimed at making better provision for the care and education of vagrant, destitute and disorderly children who, it was thought, were in danger of becoming criminals (Newburn 1995). This Act and following legislation in 1860–61 enabled magistrates to commit certain young offenders directly to the industrial schools – without a prior spell in prison or a house of correction – and there were 30 such establishments in existence by the end of 1865. The legislation also made provision for the religious persuasion of the child to be taken into account in the choice of a school. Denominational (non-Church of England) industrial schools also existed after 1866, including some for Catholic children, and these were supported by local taxation. The Education Act 1870 led to the founding of industrial day schools and truant schools and by the beginning of the First World War in 1914, there were 208 schools for juvenile delinquents, and 132 of these were residential industrial schools.

There were again widespread motivations for change and in particular pressure from politically powerful religious, philanthropic and penal reform groups concerned with the brutality of conditions in adult prisons and their impact on young offenders was to increase throughout the nineteenth century. Pitts (2003) notes that towards the end of the century these concerns had spread to the general public, not least because of media campaigns against a perceived 'crisis of control' in the industrial cities, and the apparent inability of the authorities to control problem groups of what can be considered the first modern subcultures (Davis 1990), such as the 'scuttlers' and 'peaky blinders', on the streets (Humphries 1981; Pearson 1983). These developments raised concerns about the apparently declining standards of parenting and the family socialisation process – which are so familiar today – and which were said to be responsible for the social disorganisation epitomised by drunkenness, violence, immorality and criminality that characterised the Victorian urban landscape.

It was the Summary Jurisdiction Act 1879 that substantially reduced the number of children in prison. They were now to be tried by magistrates rather than at higher courts, available penalties were reduced, and those aged under 16 were tried summarily for nearly all indictable offences. Throughout the nineteenth century destitute and delinquent children were to be treated in the same way while, at the same time, there was little legal recognition given to the differences in cause and kind between adult and juvenile crime.

The Gladstone Committee and the Lushington Committee were established in the mid-1890s and these were to advocate a welfare/treatment model intervention rather than a justice/punishment model intervention with young offenders and the introduction of alternatives to custody. Pitts (2003: 73) observes that:

> Then, as now, it was a self proclaimed 'modernising' government that acted on these recommendations, and then, as now, this government argued that the new measures were 'evidence-based', informed by the new sciences of paediatrics, child psychology, criminology and penology and responsibility for this new form of youth justice was placed in the hands of a new legal and administrative reality, the juvenile court.

This focus on the 'welfare' of young offenders and the 'treatment' necessary to reform them is in accordance with the welfare/treatment model of youth justice which summarised in Table 3.2.

Table 3.2 The welfare/treatment model of youth justice

- Based on predestined actor model of criminal behaviour notions that young people are not fully responsible for their actions because of biological, psychological and social factors.
- Treatment and rehabilitation are advocated rather than punishment.
- Cases are to be dealt with by welfare professionals and experts and not the criminal justice system.
- Later variants of the model recommend limited or non-intervention in accordance with the principles of the victimised actor model of criminal behaviour.

Newburn (2002) observes that by the turn of the twentieth century, young people in the new cities and manufacturing towns were experiencing increasing independence and leisure time and it was at this time that new heightened concerns about delinquency and hooliganism emerged. Pearson (1983) has noted that this close association between 'youth' and 'crime' has remained virtually undisturbed ever since in the minds of the public, while this discovery has been paralleled by continued nostalgic yearnings for a lost 'golden age' of tranquillity and calm that in reality never existed.

It was in this socio-economic context that the Children Act 1908 established specialised juvenile courts which were given powers to deal with both the delinquent and destitute, albeit differently from adults. There was, however, to be a mixture of welfare and punitive strategies and this can be noted in the comment of Herbert Samuel, the minister responsible for introducing the legislation, who stated that 'courts should be the agencies for the rescue as well as the punishment of juveniles' (cited in Gelsthorpe and Morris 1994: 951). Morris *et al.* (1980) subsequently note that juvenile courts remained essentially criminal courts and the idea that the child was a wrongdoer was the dominant orthodoxy.

Platt (1969) has observed that the arrival of the juvenile court was to herald the arrival of another social construction of youthful humanity, the 'juvenile delinquent'. Previously, there had been simply 'young offenders', to whom varying degrees of responsibility could be ascribed in accordance with the dominant rational actor model philosophy. Juvenile delinquents – according to the newly emerging predestined actor model orthodoxy – were significantly perceived to be different from their non-delinquent peers. Pitts (2003: 73) observes that:

It was not simply that they behaved differently: they were different in the way they thought, how they felt, in the beliefs and attitudes they held and, indeed, in their very biogenetic constitution. Thus, the juvenile court did not simply assume powers to sentence children and young people to a new, distinctively juvenile, range of penalties and facilities; it also shaped its disposals in accordance with the relationships the new sciences of human behaviour had proposed between the present demeanour of the delinquent and their future needs.

Platt (1969), moreover, argues that we need to look beyond the rhetoric of benevolence and the concerns of the 'child savers' for 'salvation', 'innocence' and 'protection' that were undoubtedly the motivations of the middle-class women involved. The ideologies of welfare, nevertheless, enabled constant and pervasive supervision of children and young people and allowed the state to intervene directly into any elements of the working class that were considered to be immoral or unruly. Regardless of the benevolent original intentions of the 'child savers', the outcome was that troublesome adolescents could now be defined by the new 'professional' bodies of experts – psychiatrists, social workers and the philanthropists – as 'sick' or 'pathological' with the outcome that young people came to be imprisoned 'for their own good', had very limited legal rights and were subjected to lengthy periods of incarceration. Morris and Giller (1987: 32) note that most reforms were either implicitly or explicitly coercive and that in reality 'humanitarianism and coercion are essentially two sides of the same coin'.

The development of the juvenile justice system

The Probation of Offenders Act 1907 introduced community supervision as an alternative to custody and by 1920 approximately 8,000 of the 10,000 people being supervised by probation officers were aged between 8 and 18 years (Pitts 2003). The following year the use of imprisonment for children under the age of 14 was ended but the Prevention of Crime Act 1908 established specialised detention centres where rigid discipline and work training could be provided in a secure environment. The first of these was at Borstal in Kent, which gave its name to numerous similar establishments.

The borstal system emphasised a mixture of discipline and training with some placing an emphasis on education, being strongly imbued with the values and traditions of English public-school education, and later some even adopted a therapeutic approach (see, for example, Hood 1965). By the early 1920s there was nevertheless some public disquiet following allegations of brutality in a number of borstal institutions (Humphries 1981; Crimmens and Pitts 2000). The subsequent committee of inquiry (the Molony Committee) investigated the treatment of young offenders under 21 and in particular those who were considered to be in need of 'protection and training'. The focus was on the 'welfare' of young offenders and the 'treatment' necessary to reform them.

Pitts (2003) observes that the immediate consequences of the 1907/08 reforms were contradictory. On the one hand, the probation order – a new non-custodial sentence – simply failed to reduce the incarceration of young offenders. From that time onwards, the number of youngsters dispatched to juvenile reformatories and Borstals increased significantly with the numbers exceeding 20,000 by the early 1920s. On the other hand – and this is very much the case today with the contemporary youth justice system discussed in the third part of this book – the introduction of a new and apparently more positive secure estate was to persuade some sentencers to take advantage of their supposed benefits. Thus, a system which had been established to create 'alternatives to custody' was in reality imposing greater custodial control on a larger number of less problematic subjects. This significant theme of the 'spreading of social control' (Cohen 1980) is another one to which we return later in this chapter and elsewhere in this book.

This twin expansion of institutional and community sanctions occurred, nevertheless, at the same time as a declining crime rate during the first 20 years of the century. Pitts (2003) observes different explanations for this decline. On the one hand, the political right – epitomised by Charles Murray (1990 1994) – has, subsequently, pointed to the increased role of incarceration in helping to bring about this decrease in criminality, although we should note that the significant reductions in the prison population in the 1930s occurred at the same time that the UK was experiencing the lowest crime rates of the twentieth century (Pitts 2003). On the other hand, John Lea (1999) – a left realist – has proposed that these low crime rates were related to the growth of unionised democratic socialism and the development of a 'social contract' which provided rights to healthcare, housing, education and material security. The outcome was an increasingly reliable workforce, low divorce rates, 'stable' families and 'respectable', law-abiding working-class communities with criminality now consigned to the social margins.

David Garland (2001) has argued that these economic, political and social changes in the early part of the twentieth century were to create the conditions for the emergence of what he has termed 'penal modernism'. The new social democratic politics viewed offenders as socially and economically disadvantaged, or poorly socialised, and thus sought to improve these perceived crime-producing conditions through the judicious use of social and criminal justice policy. Pitts (2003) notes that these policies attracted cross-party political support because of a widespread belief and confidence in the capacity of social science – and its application by experts and professionals – to solve social problems. He argues that penal modernism found its fullest expression in the 'child-centred' youth justice policies that emerged between 1933 and 1969.

The welfare/treatment model was further emphasised by the Children and Young Persons Act 1933. An earlier limited practice of having a specially selected panel of magistrates to hear juvenile cases was adopted as uniform for the whole country, restrictions were placed on the reporting of cases in newspapers, the age of criminal responsibility was raised from seven to eight and, above all, magistrates were directed to take primary account of the welfare of the child. This latter clause, while heralded as an important victory for the welfare lobby, nevertheless highlighted a fundamental contradiction in youth justice policy that has continued to the present day. The justice/punishment and welfare/treatment models appear to be inevitably incompatible with the former emphasising full criminal responsibility and punishment and the latter the needs of the individual child and welfare treatment. The Act also abolished capital punishment for those aged under 18 and the nineteenth-century reformatories and industrial schools were consolidated into a national system of approved schools for the treatment of young offenders aged 10–15.

Most indicators suggest that the levels of juvenile crime rose fairly steadily throughout the 1930s and were to rise sharply – albeit with some variations – during the Second World War (Newburn 2002). Seismic wartime social conditions were highly significant in the formative years of development in the lives of a generation of young people. The 'black-out', evacuation where children were taken from their families in the city and sent to rural areas, the closure of schools and youth clubs, were all blamed for much delinquency (Bailey 1987) and this notion of family disruption or dysfunction remains a dominant approach to explaining criminality among children and young people to the present day.

The period between 1945 and the early 1970s was to witness the high point in the confidence of industrial modernity although for some observers this was built on unstable foundations. There was to be a process of deskilling for many in the industrial working class from the early 1950s (Cohen 1972) while full employment during this period of the long economic boom was closely linked with greatly increased enrolment in higher education institutions and recruitment into the military (see Taylor 1997). The period was, nevertheless, epitomised by an unwritten social contract between the government and their citizens which was fundamentally based on the provision of full employment and the fallback position of a relatively generous welfare state (including social security benefits, free education, healthcare and cheap, reasonable quality state-sponsored housing). For the first decade following the end of the war youth offending figures were not to return to the expected pre-war levels.

The Criminal Justice Act 1948 was thus introduced in the context of the creation of the welfare state. It placed a number of restrictions on the use of imprisonment but – although it marked the beginning of a trend restricting the use of custody for young offenders (Newburn 2002) – introduced detention centres and attendance centres which appeared to reflect a more punitive approach (Morris and Giller 1987). Detention centres were institutions in which young offenders could be sentenced to a short period of custody, in a regime intended to be tough and disciplinary with an emphasis on physical education although there were also elements of education and training. Attendance centre orders required a young person to attend a centre, run mainly by the police, for a number of hours per week, often on a Saturday afternoon. Discipline was a key feature of early attendance centres which mixed elements of physical education with more practical pursuits. Concern about the 'welfare' of juveniles was also evident with the passing of the Children Act 1948, which sought to end the placement of neglected children in approved schools alongside offenders. Local authority children's departments were also established with their own resources for residential care and trained staff to oversee fostering and adoption (Harris and Webb 1987).

Pitts (2003) observes that the reforms of 1907/08 had established the right of young offenders to be dealt with differently from adults while the reforms of 1933 and 1948 were concerned with elaborating the nature of that difference. He notes that subsequent policies were infused with ideas about child development with their origins in the Freudian psychoanalytic tradition – which we will encounter in the second part of this book – but also the significant effects of poverty and inequality on the healthy development of the child. The new political consensus favoured the prescriptions of the welfare/treatment model of intervention and because the 'welfare' of young offenders was considered to be paramount it was proposed that the issue should be dealt with, wherever possible, by experts in the care and protection of children and young people. There was, however, resistance to this shift in youth justice emphasis from Conservative politicians, senior police officers, magistrates and judges, who wished to retain a strong element of retribution in the youth justice system and who favoured the prescriptions of the justice/punishment model of intervention.

Bailey (1987) moreover observes the ambiguities of welfarism itself and it is here possible to identify the beginnings of the progressive critique that was to be become so significant during the 1970s and which we encounter below. The influential 'social conception of delinquency' which had become so influential during the inter-war period had made good sense to the many administrators and reformers with experience of boys' clubs or settlement work. From this perspective offending behaviour was seen as a symptom of wider social and personal conditions, in particular, weak parental control, poor character training and a lack of opportunity. Furthermore, such explanations suggested practical solutions to the problem – a change of environment, exercises in self-control, occupational training, or the personal influence of suitable adult role models – all of which could be provided through an improved borstal system and probation services. In themselves, they were a series of explanations, justifications and solutions that were in future years to encourage periodic crackdowns on wayward youth and the introduction of 'short, sharp, shocks' to direct them back to the path of righteousness.

The argument between the proponents of the two apparently different models of intervention was to continue into a post-war period which was to be characterised by a continued rise in recorded youth crime and where it was increasingly suggested that the approved school system was unable to cope with some of the hardened young offenders that were appearing before the courts (Newburn 1995). Windlesham (1993: 76) observes that from this point onwards 'the twin claws of the pincer that was to hold the development of penal policy in its grip were the remorseless increase in the incidence of crime, and the overcrowding in the prisons'. This seemingly endless increase in the crime rate from 1955 onwards was to become increasingly influential in criminal justice policy formulation and is worthy of further examination.

Consumer society and criminal youth

Those born and raised in the UK during the mid-to-late twentieth century would be familiar with apocryphal stories of how in the 'good old days' – or 'before the [Second World] War' – people left their doors open and neighbours entered unannounced to borrow a cup of sugar. These accounts of community and working-class solidarity were also a staple of classical sociological texts (see Dennis *et al.* 1956). In all probability, there was little else to borrow. The defining characteristic of the lives of the great majority of people in those days was poverty and that was the case whether in work or not. The extent of ambition for most people was to earn sufficient money to feed, clothe and keep a roof over the heads of their families. There was no television, limited radio, no videos or DVDs, no motor cars for the vast majority of the population and certainly no overseas holidays. Most people were poor, had limited ambitions and aspirations beyond basic survival and, in reality, most were rather unsophisticated in comparison with people in a similar social position today. Significantly, there was a relatively high level of social consensus and group solidarity because people had very similar life experiences.

In the language of the French sociologist Emile Durkheim a century ago, the lives of ordinary working people – regardless of whether they lived in the great mass industrial areas or the rural countryside – were characterised by high levels of mechanical solidarity. They had similar beliefs, understandings and life experiences which encouraged feelings of group solidarity and community which discouraged widespread involvement in criminal activity (Durkheim 1964). Pearson (1983), nevertheless and significantly, warns us against simplistic, popularly held 'common-sense' notions that criminal activity by children and young people is a relatively recent phenomenon but, at the same time, crime was quantitatively and qualitatively different in a society characterised by relative poverty and very limited aspirations. Poor people undoubtedly did steal from each other but the level of economic gain would have been small. Theft from a neighbour would have been relatively unlikely in the areas with the greatest group solidarity and the least money.

We should not really be surprised that crime levels rose so much – and so regularly – from 1955, however, because the nature of British society was itself to change radically in the intervening years. Wartime rationing finally ended in 1955 and the bright, brash consumer society that was to produce an educated, relatively sophisticated, affluent population of people with diverse knowledge, skills and experiences of life, was born. In the language of Durkheim, the lives of people were to become increasingly characterised by high levels of organic solidarity where there is less dependence on the maintenance of uniformity between individuals, and more emphasis on the management of the diverse functions of different groups (Durkheim 1964).

Perhaps the most important development in the half-century following the establishment of the consumer society has been the reality that the UK has become substantially more prosperous than at any time in its history. The annual GDP figures show that the output of the economy has risen by approximately 50 per cent since 1970 (Northcott 1991). But significantly this growth in prosperity has not been equally shared. The skilled industrial worker – largely male – was to virtually disappear and be replaced by casualised, low-paid, temporary, part-time workers ('McJobs'),[1] a growing proportion of them female. Increased material affluence has often been the outcome of a shift towards dual-income families, where both parents work but also spend less time with their children, and lone parenthood, with its associated significant social consequences (Rowntree Foundation 1995). Perhaps, most significantly, the qualitative experience of poverty and unemployment today is substantially different than in the past.

Life in the 1920s and the 1930s was characterised by a generalised, shared working-class experience of poverty, whether in work or not. Today, the level of home ownership is substantially higher than in the past, and car ownership and holidays in increasingly more exotic overseas locations are becoming far more widespread. The workless and homeless, nevertheless, live alongside, or at least not far from, the relatively affluent. The wonders and delights of the consumer society are aggressively advertised during the low-budget television programmes churned out 24 hours a day to entertain the 'new leisure classes'.[2] Moreover, the contemporary economically dispossessed have very different aspirations than their predecessors 60 years ago. Many aspire to the products they see in the television commercials and they are not easily distracted from these ambitions. They do not accept long-term unemployment and poverty in the same stoic fashion as their predecessors. They have legitimate aspirations to a share in the 'good life'. It is these socio-economic changes that have provided the cultural context for the huge explosion in recorded crime that has occurred during the past 50 plus years.

Four closely interconnected explanations have been offered from various sources – some more contested than others – to explain this huge increase in crime (Hopkins Burke 1998). First, relatively non-contentiously, there has been a huge increase in opportunity provided by the growth of the consumer society and it is instructive that 94 per cent of all modifiable offences recorded by the police are against property (Barclay 1995) and of course ownership of consumer durables is very widespread.[3] Second, a further more contested explanation points to the 'breakdown in informal social controls' that has occurred in society, with commentators drawing attention to the decline in the traditional nuclear family, the rise of the single-parent family and the 'parenting deficit' (Dennis and Erdos 1992). Third, a less widely voiced explanation observes the disintegration of the traditional collective working-class culture and the triumph of competitiveness and entrepreneurialism.[4] The 'go for it' philosophy of the enterprise culture has penetrated the whole social structure, from the boardrooms of big business to youths carrying out robberies on the street or committing burglaries. Everyone is an entrepreneur now and the boundaries between many legitimate and illegitimate business activities are increasingly blurred (see Hobbs 1994, 1988) and morality is indeed ambiguous (Hopkins Burke 2007). Fourth, the mass working-class culture of modernity was based on the similarity of existence described earlier. In contrast, the increasingly diverse and fragmented consumer society has brought spending power, opportunities, and with it new and diverse groups with subjective and varied interests which have often set them against the traditions of their parent communities. Young people, of course, have been in the vanguard of this change and the development of a group identity through an association with others who share a particular taste in music and clothes has been an important part of the transition to adulthood for many young people since the beginnings of the consumer society. It was against this background that crime levels were to increase substantially over the past half century, with parallel concerns as to how the authorities should respond to an apparently growing problem. We will consider the various explanations as to why young people become involved in offending behaviour in some detail in the second part of this book. We now return to the development of the juvenile justice system and the apparent triumph of welfarism during the 1960s.

The triumph of welfarism

The Ingleby Report of 1960 endorsed the structure of the juvenile court and rejected any merger of approved schools with other residential accommodation, or the removal of responsibility for these institutions from the Home Office. The major focus of the report centred on the conflict that it felt existed between the judicial and welfare functions of the juvenile court. Newburn (1995) observes that this resulted in:

> ... a child being charged with a petty theft or other wrongful act for which most people would say that no great penalty should be imposed, and the case apparently ending in a disproportionate sentence. For when the court causes enquiries to be made ... the court may determine that the welfare of the child requires some very substantial interference which may amount to taking the child away from his home for a prolonged period.

The proposed solution was to be an immediate increase in the age of criminal responsibility from 8 to 12 – with the possibility of a rise to 13 or 14 – and below that age only welfare proceedings were to be brought (Morris and Giller 1987). The Children and Young Persons Act 1963, by way of compromise, increased the age of criminal responsibility to 10. The argument that there is little point in punishing children or young people whose offending behaviour may be related to family or other problems was nevertheless to continue to influence policy. Some went as far as to suggest that children and young people should be removed from the criminal justice process altogether, and dealt with by a family council or tribunal which would deal with all children with family or social problems (Cavadino and Dignan 1997).

These debates were central to the introduction of the Children and Young Persons Act 1969, which advocated a rise in the age of criminal responsibility to 14, and sought alternatives to detention by way of treatment, non-criminal care proceedings and care orders. The benefits of diversionary policies were stressed and one of its aims was that all offenders under 14 should be dealt with through care and protection proceedings rather than the juvenile court. The police were encouraged to use cautions for juvenile offenders and only refer them to court following consultation with the social services. The expanding role of the social worker was also reflected in provision for care orders, which, after being given by magistrates, were to be implemented by social workers. Social workers rather than magistrates would, therefore, make the key decision as to whether the young person would be sent to a residential institution or left at home. Community homes, which were to house all children in care whether or not they had committed an offence, replaced the approved schools which dealt only with offenders. It was, moreover, intended to phase out borstals and detention centres and to replace them with a sentence of intermediate treatment – again to be run by social services.

The Children and Young Persons Act 1969 was heralded by its pro-welfare treatment model supporters as a decisive instance of 'decriminalising' penal policy but it was never to be fully implemented. Crucial opposition came from the Conservative government elected in 1970, magistrates, the police and some sections of the probation service, on the grounds that it undermined 'the due process of law' by relying too heavily on the discretion of social workers. The outcome was that the social welfare philosophy of the legislation was consistently undermined; for example, it had been the intention to keep juveniles out of the criminal justice system but the 1970s were to be characterised by substantial increases in the number of custodial sentences given to young people.

Two central features of twentieth-century youth justice policy were to culminate in the 1969 Act. First, increasing attention was to be given to assessing the suitability of the family situation of the offender when seeking causes of delinquency. Second, the distinction between the delinquent and the neglected child was to become increasingly obscured. The notion of the 'responsible individual' enshrined in the justice/punishment model of intervention was, moreover, replaced by the concept of the 'responsible family' and the juvenile court was empowered to play the part of the responsible parent by establishing child welfare as the primary principle of intervention. There was thus to be an increasing state intervention in family life and socialisation under the guise of protecting children who were considered to be living in 'undesirable' surroundings.

These welfare/treatment model developments appear at first sight to be progressive and humane but came to be criticised from various standpoints right across the political spectrum. Clarke (1975) argued – from a radical criminological perspective – that we were simply witnessing a continuation of dominant nineteenth-century concerns to ensure the stable reproduction of future generations of labour power. The only change was that this process would now be achieved by the reformation of whole families rather than by isolating their 'wayward' children. Morris et al. (1980) and Taylor et al. (1979) criticised the treatment philosophy and the family pathology model of the causes of delinquency inherent in the 1969 Act as justifications for exercising greater coercive intervention in the lives of 'delinquent' children and their families. They argued that a social work understanding of delinquency, given its dominant grounding in psychoanalytical theories, would only reinforce the principle of individual pathology and ignore the material and social inequality inherent in society. Taylor *et al.* (1979), observing that more children were incarcerated during the 1970s than ever before, argued that the rights of children would be better upheld by returning to principles of eighteenth-century liberal criminal justice. It is argued from this perspective that a welfare-orientated juvenile justice system based on the discretion of social work and medical 'experts' erodes the rights of children to natural justice.

In some respects such arguments mark a return to early nineteenth-century rational actor principles of viewing the juvenile as a young adult and, from this perspective, it is argued, that children are the best judges of their own interests and should be free to exercise their own choice from the age of ten years on. Such legalistic arguments for the concept of 'juvenile responsibility for law-breaking' were also ideologically effective in the arguments for order and control promoted by the Conservative government that came to power in 1979 and this is discussed in the following chapter.

Juvenile justice during the 1970s was characterised by dramatic increases in the use of custody and this was in direct contradiction to the intentions of the 1969 legislation. This drift towards custody was primarily an outcome of a combination of three factors. First, there was a popular belief that the 1970s witnessed a rapid growth in youth crime, characterised by a hard core of 'vicious young criminals' (Pearson 1983). Second, there was a tendency on the part of magistrates to give custodial sentences for almost all types of offence. Third, there was the net-widening propensity of welfarism in drawing young people into the juvenile justice process at an increasingly earlier age. These unintended consequences of the implementation of the Children and Young Persons Act 1969 therefore acted collectively to accelerate the rate at which young people moved through the sentencing tariff. The number of indictable offences recorded for young offenders remained statistically constant throughout the 1970s – with a slight rise in burglaries and a reduction in violent and sexual offences (Pitts 1982: 8) – but the number of custodial orders nevertheless rose dramatically. A Department of Health and Social

Security (DHSS) Report concluded that the number of juveniles sent to borstal and detention centres had increased fivefold between 1965 and 1980 and this increase in incarceration was believed to reflect a growing tendency on the part of courts to be more punitive (DHSS 1981).

At the same time, social workers were extending their preventive work with the families of the 'pre-delinquent'. Rohrer (1982) observed that this development meant many more children were under surveillance, the market for the court was extended and more offenders were placed in local authority care for relatively trivial offences. Preventive work thus meant that children were being sent to institutions at a younger age. Thorpe *et al.* (1980: 8) identify a judicial backlash against the liberalism of the 1969 Act in which popular wisdom about youth justice and its actual practice had become totally estranged:

> The tragedy that has occurred since can best be described as a situation in which the worst of all possible worlds came into existence – people have been persistently led to believe that the juvenile criminal justice system has become softer and softer, while the reality has been that it has become harder and harder.

Pitts (2003) observes that welfare/treatment model thinking during the 1960s was founded on the notion that crime committed by children and young people was an outcome of poverty and the social and psychological damage that arises from this. He notes that this proposition is easily dismissed by its critics, who draw our attention to all those socially excluded young people – to use the contemporary terminology – who come from these difficult socio-economic circumstances but do not transgress against the law, work hard and against the odds become successful law-abiding citizens. But the proponents of the welfare/treatment model realised that there is a tiny of minority of young people – that 3 to 4 per cent we identified in the first chapter of this book – who do not grow out of crime. Pitts (2003b) notes that it is these seriously problematic young people with deep-seated socio-psychological problems who are the real focus of attention for any youth justice system that also go on to become homeless, teenage prostitutes and serious drug users before graduating to adult prisons and psychiatric institutions.

Conclusions

This chapter has told the story of an apparently gradual transition from a criminal justice/punishment-based model of intervention in the lives of children and young people who offend, towards a more welfare/treatment-based perspective. In reality, from the nineteenth century, when the troubled and troublesome among the youth population was first thought to require a different response to that afforded adults, the history of youth justice has been riddled with confusion, ambiguity and unintended consequences. The transition from a justice/punishment to welfare/treatment-based model of intervention was never straightforward and a tension between the two models was always there and this continues to be the case until the present day. Moreover, the persistent critique of welfarism is that its rhetoric of benevolence and humanitarianism often blinds us to its denial of legal rights, its discretionary non-accountable procedures and its ability to impose greater intervention than would have been merited on the basis of conduct alone. These issues persist in the next chapter where we resume the story of youth justice from the election of a Conservative government in 1979 until the subsequent election of New Labour in 1997 and the creation of the contemporary youth justice system.

Notes

1 'McJobs': 'A low-pay, low-prestige, low-dignity, low-benefit, no-future job in the service sector. Frequently considered a satisfying career choice by people who have never held one' (Coupland 1992).

2 Some years ago Central TV was the first UK television company to introduce 24-hour viewing on the grounds that the unemployed had no reason to go to bed early. For what other reason would the company regularly broadcast a programme entitled 'Central Job Finder' at 4.30 am?

3 Whereas motor vehicles were in very short supply 40 years ago they now account for upwards of one-quarter of all recorded crime.

4 This is a process usually associated with the various Conservative governments led by Margaret Thatcher and John Major. However, the trend has been very much in place since the 1950s. Their economic policies and legitimating philosophy merely accelerated the process.

Chapter 4

Youth justice and the new conservatism

The previous chapter discussed the history of the youth justice system from its origins with clear foundations in a criminal justice/ punishment model of intervention to the apparent high point of the welfare treatment model epitomised by the Children and Young Persons Act 1969. That transition between justice and welfarism was never straightforward and a significant tension continues to the present day in the contemporary youth justice system between these apparently polar opposites.

This chapter resumes that narrative with the election of a Conservative government in 1979 which presented itself to the electorate as being prepared to take a vigorous stance against crime. Conservative intellectual Sir Keith Joseph made explicit reference to the need to reject 'fashionable socialist opinion' and in particular focused attention on a perceived need to amend the Children and Young Persons Act 1969. The outgoing Labour government was depicted as being anti-police, condoning law-breaking, and as having ineffective policies for crime control. After the election the Home Secretary expanded places in detention centres for young 'thugs' and introduced a regime of 'short, sharp, shocks'. A subsequent White Paper – *Young Offenders* (Home Office 1980) – and the resulting legislation, the Criminal Justice Act 1982, attacked the welfare approach of the Children and Young Persons Act 1969 and there was a significant move away from predestined actor notions of treatment and lack of personal responsibility and a return to rational actor notions of punishment and individual and parental responsibility. In accordance with this rediscovery of the rational actor model, there was also a significant move away from executive decision-making (social workers) and a return to judicial decision-making (courts) and away from the belief in the 'child in need' to what Tutt (1981) termed 'the rediscovery of the delinquent'. The Criminal Justice Act 1982 was nevertheless 'not an unremittingly punitive statute' (Cavadino and Dignan 1997) for it essentially introduced restrictions on the use of custody for all those under 21 and this in itself was an indication of the ambiguity of Conservative government youth justice policy and its outcomes during the following years.

In many ways youth justice policy in the 1980s and 1990s was underpinned by contradictions and inconsistencies. For example, the Criminal Justice Act 1991 espoused an 'anti-custody' ethos, while the government announced the introduction of 'new' secure training units in 1993 and the Criminal Justice and Public Order Act 1994 introduced new tougher sentences for young offenders. Some observed these apparently contradictory measures to be the response of a government that had lost confidence in the ability of the 'experts' to find solutions to the problem of youth offending and it was merely reacting to crises as they arose. On the other hand, it is possible to identify an increasing and consistent tendency to deal with young people as adults. Others took a more optimistic view. Gelsthorpe and Morris observed that:

> The arguments are clearly no longer about 'welfare', 'crime control', or 'justice'. The new philosophies cannot be allied to the political right or left as they once could. Indeed, there is every indication that there is a new political consensus on criminal justice in the 1990s.
>
> (Gelsthorpe and Morris 1994: 984)

Conservative youth justice policy during the 1980s and 1990s clearly provided significant foundations that have been built on in the development of the contemporary youth justice system – regardless of a change in political leadership and the self-proclaimed rupture with the past – and these are considered in this chapter.

The retreat from welfarism

During the 1980s, the 'welfare' approach to youth justice came under increasing attack, not just from the aforementioned right-wing political, law-and-order lobby influenced by 'right realist' criminological thinking and the rediscovery of the rational actor model discussed in the following chapter, but also from proponents of a 'progressive' 'back to justice' policy. In particular, faith in the ability of the social worker to diagnose the causes of delinquency and to treat these with non-punitive methods was increasingly questioned. Empirical justification for this viewpoint came with the publication of an influential paper by Robert Martinson (1974) which purported to show that rehabilitation programmes in prison simply 'do not work' and thus the whole rationale for the existence of welfare-oriented intervention strategies was called into question. Moreover, the discretion of social work judgements was criticised as a form of arbitrary power with many young people, it was argued, the subject of apparently non-accountable state procedures with their liberty often unjustifiably denied (Davies 1982: 33). It was further argued that the investigation of social background is an imposition and social work involvement not only preserves explanations of individual pathology but also undermines the right to natural justice. We are here reminded of the first attempt to introduce legislation into Parliament in 1840 that would have enabled magistrates to act as moral guardians of destitute and delinquent juveniles but was, nevertheless, rejected by the House of Lords because it denied children the right to a jury trial in accordance with the then rational actor model of criminal behaviour and which was discussed in the previous chapter. Such an approach, it was now argued, might place the child or young person in double jeopardy and unintentionally accelerate movement up the tariff.

With the experience of the 1970s, in which the numbers of custodial sentences increased dramatically in the aftermath of the implementation of an at least nominal welfare treatment system, the progressive new justice proponents argued for a return to notions of 'due process' and 'just deserts' along with moves to decriminalise certain (for example, victimless) offences and a general shift towards using alternatives to custody (Rutherford 1978). As Taylor *et al.* (1979: 22–3) observe:

> Under English law the child enjoys very few of the rights taken for granted by adults under the principles of natural justice. The law's reference to the child's 'best interests' reflects the benevolent paternalism of its approach. Essentially as far as the courts are concerned, the 'best interests' principle empowers social workers, psychologists, psychiatrists and others to define on the basis of their opinions what is good for the child ... [The

law] does not require that the experts should substantiate their opinions or prove to the court that any course of action they propose will be more effective in promoting the best interests of the child than those taken by the parent or by the child acting on his own behalf ... A child may find that his/her arguments against being committed to care are perceived as evidence of their need for treatment, as a sign, for example, that they have 'authority problems'.

A classic justice/punishment model solution was thus proposed with a return to the use of determinate sentences based on the seriousness of the offence rather than the profile of individual offenders. This, it was argued, would be seen as 'fair' and 'just' by young people themselves. Moreover, a greater use of cautions by the police for minor offences would help to keep young people out of the courts, but when in court, closer control over social inquiry reports would in turn ensure that intermediate treatment, care orders or other forms of 'community correction' would only be used in the most serious of cases as an alternative to custody, thus helping to avoid the 'net-widening' potential inherent within the system.

While it was recognised that this approach would help overcome some of the ambiguities of a system dogged by the dual concern to both 'care and control' and apprehensions about the 'arbitrary discretion' of social service professionals, the 'back to justice' movement was not without its own critics. Pitts (1996) notes that this renewed faith in legalism was advocated at precisely the same time as 'youth' was yet again the subject of a major moral panic and was thus seen as requiring greater degrees of containment. There is nevertheless little doubt that such debates had considerable influence on, and helped to legitimate, government policy throughout the populist Conservative years between 1979 and 1997.

Populist conservatism and youth justice

The Criminal Justice Act 1982 involved a fundamental attack on the social welfare perspective introduced by the Children and Young Persons Act 1969, with a significant move away from the welfare/treatment model of youth justice towards the justice/punishment model and this was epitomised by new powers of disposal made available to magistrates. Criteria were introduced to restrict the use of care and custodial orders and juveniles were now to be legally represented. Moreover, custodial orders were to be made only in cases where it could be established that the offender had failed to respond to non-custodial measures, where custody was seen as unavoidable for the protection of the public, or where the offence was serious. Offenders had previously been sentenced to an indeterminate period of borstal training with the date of release – which could be up to three years – decided by those running the system. Borstals were now abolished, thus removing any element of indeterminacy from the system, and replaced by a fixed-term youth custody order, and the use of imprisonment was abolished for offenders under the age of 21.

There appeared to be little consistency as different sentences were repeatedly introduced and then abolished. Thus, from 1983 a determinate sentence of youth custody was introduced for offenders aged 15 and under 21 with a maximum sentence for those aged under 17 of 12 months. A sentence of custody for life was introduced as the equivalent to life imprisonment when the offender was aged 17 and under 21, while detention sentence orders for males were changed so that the usual sentence ranged from 21 days to four months instead of three to six months.

The Criminal Justice Act 1982 appears at first sight to provide clear evidence of the ambiguity and inconsistency of Conservative youth justice policy during the 1980s. It was clearly introduced with the objective of helping to 'restore the rule of law' (Pitts 1996) but at the same time placed significant restrictions on the use of custody for young people. This apparent inconsistency can nevertheless be explained with reference to a significant legislative strategy which Bottoms (1974) terms 'bifurcation' and which involves separating the treatment of serious offenders from that of minor offenders with the outcome being that the former are dealt with by overtly punitive means and the latter are dealt with much more leniently.

Pitts (1988) observes that the introduction of shorter detention centre sentences – or 'short, sharp shocks' as they became known – was supplemented by considerable government-instigated publicity, or what is now termed 'spin', which sought to assure the public that while young offenders were being subjected to shorter periods of incarceration, the deterrent effect of these tougher regimes would nevertheless be greater in accordance with the contemporary rational actor model philosophy we will encounter in the following chapter. Many of those designated less serious offenders would now be dealt with by a significant expansion of the Department of Health and Social Security (DHSS) Intermediate Treatment Initiative which was to provide 4,500 'alternatives to custody'. Pitts (1996: 266) observes the somewhat ironic consequences of these policies:

> The government was seeking to persuade magistrates to sentence larger numbers of less problematic children and young people, whom they described as 'hooligans', to a brief and relatively inexpensive spell 'inside'. They were also trying to persuade magistrates to divert simultaneously a similar number of more serious young offenders, who attracted much longer and much more expensive custodial sentences (and who, since the mid 1970s, had constituted an important element in the crisis of overcrowding in British prisons) to alternatives to custody, in the community.

> However, the government had given magistrates a mixed message. The Home Secretary, as a politician, had said that we must 'get tough', but the Home Secretary as a penal administrator had said that we must limit the use of custody. The bench, by and large, had listened to the first and ignored the second.

Muncie (1990) observes that the outcome was that the youth custody centre population increased by 65 per cent in the 12 months ending in May 1984, while that of the new-style 'short, sharp shock' detention centres was to actually decline during the same period. Pitts (1996) observes that a policy which had sought to both 'get tough' with a minority of serious and persistent young offenders while, at the same time, actually reducing the incarcerated population had quite simply failed. A successful bifurcation strategy was still sought.

By the mid-1980s the Home Office had enthusiastically discovered and adopted the new public management philosophy that we will encounter in the third part of this book, and had come to pursue a rational cost-effective youth justice process:

> Describing their 'mission' in terms of 'targets', 'minimum standards' and 'performance indicators', they were anti-union, anti-professional and pro-privatisation. This was 'full-blown' Thatcherism and it set itself against restrictive practices in the police, the law and the Prison Service.
>
> (Pitts 1996: 267)

The late 1980s nevertheless came to be proclaimed a 'successful revolution' in youth justice policy not least because the numbers of young people incarcerated was reduced substantially during the period. The numbers aged 17 or under convicted or cautioned decreased from 230,000 in 1981 to 149,000 in 1991 (Hagell and Newburn 1994), while the number of juveniles given custodial sentences was also significantly reduced: 6,700 juveniles were sentenced to custody in 1984, compared with 3,400 in 1988, 2,000 in 1991 and 1,700 in 1992 (Hagell and Newburn 1994). It was the projects developed within the DHSS Intermediate Treatment (IT) Initiative that were seen as a key factor in this reduction although we should also note that there was a quite substantial 18 per cent drop in the population of 14- to 16-year-old males during the period 1981–8 (Newburn 2002).

The DHSS Intermediate Treatment Initiative of 1983 financed the establishment of 110 intensive schemes in 62 local authority areas to provide alternatives to custody and practitioners were required to evolve a 'new style of working' with less focus on the emotional and social needs of juveniles and more on the nature of the offence. It was through such means that magistrates were to be persuaded that IT was no longer a 'soft option', but a 'high tariff' disposal and this was achieved, in practice, by the development of inter-agency juvenile panels which by the 1980s existed in most local authorities in England and Wales. The panels, comprising of representatives from the welfare agencies, the youth service, the police and education departments, reviewed the cases of apprehended children and young people entering the youth justice system and, where possible, they were diverted away from court.

Perhaps the most significant development throughout the 1980s was the repeatedly affirmed government commitment to the concept of community-based diversionary schemes for young offenders. Diversion had increased in the years following the introduction of the Children and Young Persons Act 1969 with an enormous rise in the numbers cautioned by the Juvenile Liaison Bureaux established by the police, but by the 1980s there was a growing recognition of the limitations of custodial or institutional treatment. Custody was extremely expensive – with detention invariably costing considerably more than fee-paying boarding schools – but the vast majority of young offenders coming out of such institutions went on to reoffend (Cavadino and Dignan 1997). Many argued that such institutions acted like schools of crime where offenders perpetuated a delinquent or criminal subculture based on violence and bullying (Hopkins Burke and Hopkins Burke 1995). Treatment in the community was, therefore, considered preferable and no less effective in terms of reconviction rates (Cavadino and Dignan 1997).

Diversionary policies were to continue throughout the 1980s. Consultative documents, circulars to the police, and the Code of Practice for Prosecutors emphasised that prosecution should be used only as a last resort, with a greater use of cautioning encouraged to avoid net-widening (Gelsthorpe and Morris 1994). Moreover, the use of cautions for second and third offences was encouraged along with the development in some areas of caution-plus schemes, which included some form of supervised activity in the community.

Thus, explanations of decarceration probably lie more in efforts to divert juveniles from court (through increased use of informal cautioning, rather than court appearance) than in diversion from custody once in court (as the intensive IT schemes were designed to do). Home Office Circular 14/1985, for example, encouraged the use of 'no further action' or 'informal warnings' instead of formal action and from then (up to a reversal of the policy in 1994) the number of juveniles brought into the system did decline. Again the practice varied regionally, but in Northampton, in 1985, for example, 86 per cent of juveniles who came to the notice of the police were either prosecuted or formally cautioned; however, by 1989 this figure had been reduced to 30 per cent (McLaughlin and Muncie 1994).

A major theme running through all such developments appears to be a reduction in court processing and custody on the grounds of expense and effectiveness. In 1990–1, it was estimated that keeping an offender in custody for three weeks was more expensive than 12 months of supervision or community service. In addition, 83 per cent of young men leaving youth custody were reconvicted within two years, with the reconviction rate for those participating in community-based schemes substantially lower (McLaughlin and Muncie 1994). A less politically motivated approach to offending therefore appeared to be in prospect when the Criminal Justice Act 1988 introduced further restrictions on immediate custody and finally acknowledged the failure of 'short, sharp shock' regimes by merging detention centre orders and youth custody sentences into a single custodial sentence to be served in a 'young offender institution'.

Pratt (1989) now proposed that the 'welfare' and 'justice' models which had always provided the theoretical foundations and justifications of the youth justice system had been superseded by a depoliticised 'corporatist model' in which a partnership of social workers, youth workers, police and magistrates co-operated to produce a cost-effective mechanism for the effective processing of adjudicated offenders. Youth justice workers were also developing working relationships with local juvenile court magistrates in an attempt to encourage them to divert young offenders away from custody and into 'alternatives to custody' programmes. It was the growing confidence of magistrates in the common-sense 'hard-headedness' of these programmes, and the competence of the workers who staffed them, that were seen as the most important factors in the success of the Intermediate Treatment Initiative.

The process was furthered by the Criminal Justice Act 1991, the provisions of which were enacted in October 1992. This legislation was heralded as a significant policy move away from custody in that it attempted to provide a national consistency to the success of local initiatives and to expand the use of diversionary strategies for juveniles to include young adults (17- to under-21-year-olds). The anti-custody ethos of the legislation was justified with the promise of more rigorous community disposals which were not alternatives to custody but disposals in their own right.

'Punishment in the community' was to be the favoured option but at the same time this required a significant change in focus for the juvenile court and the practices of probation and social work agencies. For the latter it meant a shift in emphasis away from the traditional approach of 'advise, assist and befriend' towards tightening up the conditions of community supervision and community service work; for the former it meant the abolition of the juvenile court (which had previously dealt with criminal and care cases) and the creation of youth courts and family courts (created by the Children Act 1989) to deal with such matters separately.

The youth court subsequently became operative in October 1992 and would deal only with criminal cases involving those up to and including those aged 17 years of age. Justice-based principles of proportionality in sentencing or 'just deserts' appeared to provide a more consistent, visible and accountable decision-making process, thus ending a confusion which had haunted the juvenile justice system since the inception of the juvenile justice courts in 1908 (Gibson 1994). Moreover, the rationale for dealing with young offenders was now more in accordance with that for dealing with adults.

The impact of decarcerative measures was nevertheless shown to be fragile when, in 1991, the Home Secretary hastily established a new offence of 'aggravated vehicle taking' carrying a maximum five-year sentence. Two years later, the establishment of 'new' secure training units (akin to the old approved schools) was announced amidst a furore of media and political debate about a small group of supposedly 'persistent young offenders', 'bail bandits' and to appease the public outcry following the James Bulger case where two ten-year-old children were found guilty of abducting and killing a two-year-old child. Prime Minister John Major insisted that 'we should understand a little less and condemn a little more' and comments from police, judges and MPs that official figures showing a decrease in juvenile offending were quite simply 'wrong' also signalled a renewed tough stance on the part of government and a repoliticisation of youth crime. As a result Home Office Circular 18/1994 advised the police to discourage the use of 'inappropriate' – and in particular, repeat – cautions and to pursue conviction instead. The Criminal Justice and Public Order Act 1994 subsequently introduced new sentences for juveniles aged 10–13 convicted of serious offences, secure training centres, and a doubling of the maximum sentence of detention in a young offender institution.

Thus, until the late 1980s the Conservative government pursued youth justice policies which sought cost-effective reductions in the incarcerated population in accordance with their reduced state-intervention philosophy. Pitts (1996) observes that this system of justice was to appear totally inadequate for dealing with an unprecedented real increase in the crime rate that was to occur on a significant scale in a socio-economic world devastated by an economic restructuring unprecedented since the great Industrial Revolution of the late eighteenth and early nineteenth centuries and the subsequent mass – invariably youth – unemployment. Pitts (1996: 276) observes support for a draconian intervention from right across the political spectrum:

> The then Home Secretary Kenneth Clarke announced the introduction of the secure training order. Tony Blair, then Labour Party shadow Home Secretary, demanded a regime of 'tough love', a phrase he had borrowed from US President Bill Clinton, in which containment and confrontation in secure units would be tempered by responsiveness to the needs of the offender. The Labour MP Ken Livingstone advocated longer prison sentences, and David Blunkett, then Shadow Health Secretary, called for the return of National Service. It suddenly appeared as if politicians across the entire political spectrum had felt for the last 10 years that things, particularly juvenile things, were 'getting out of hand'. The repoliticisation and remoralisation of youth justice was under way and this time the political Left and Centre were determined to wrest the political issue of 'law and order' from the grasp of the Tories if they possibly could.

Within weeks of becoming Home Secretary in 1993, Michael Howard, undoubtedly bolstered by apparent cross-party support, commenced a process of revising youth justice policy. Secure training centres were to be rethought along the lines of US-style 'boot camps' to provide tougher and more physically demanding regimes aimed at knocking criminal tendencies out of young offenders. Pitts (1996) observes that the retreat from the highpoint of welfarism exemplified by the Children and Young Persons Act 1969 was apparently now complete. At the same time most observers proposed that a return to the 'short, sharp shock' strategies of the recent past would be no more successful than previously when dealing with a new, potentially dangerous young underclass that had been created as an outcome of economic restructuring and whose formation is discussed in more detail at the conclusion of the second part of this book.

For some populist Conservative youth justice policies had amounted to a 'successful revolution' (Pitts 1996) but it is nonetheless a notion worthy of closer consideration. There was certainly no lack of enthusiasm for the apprehension and incapacitation of offenders with a distinct recognition that the latter need not mean imprisonment. Perhaps the most significant component was the policy and legislative strategy of 'bifurcation' (Bottoms 1977) discussed above. It was in reality a twin-track approach to justice that sought to identify those young people who had briefly stumbled in the pursuit of an 'upward option' of increased commitment to education and training (Cohen 1972) and provide them with the impetus and support to overcome their offending behaviour.

In a social world where the modernist project had been undermined by the emergence of what some social scientists have referred to as the postmodern condition (Lyotard 1984) or at least the fragmentation of modernity and social class (Hopkins Burke 1999) – which are discussed below – and where the old moral certainties seemed increasingly less appropriate, it is possible to identify discourses emerging from very different locations to justify the implementation of bifurcation strategies. First, from an unequivocal liberal standpoint, there was the enduring influence of labelling theory (see Becker 1963, 1967) and its policy implication of unduly avoiding the criminalisation of young people. Second, the 'punishment in the community' approach was more popular than previously with conservative-minded magistrates because it had been given some 'teeth' by the common-sense 'hard-headedness' of the new 'alternative to custody' programmes. Third, the strategy coincided neatly with the extremely influential anti-state spending discourse within the government that was happy to reduce court processing and custody on the grounds of expense (Pitts 1996). Fourth, there were those – usually probation officers and social workers – who questioned the very effectiveness of custody. During the period, 1990–1, 83 per cent of young men leaving youth custody were reconvicted within two years; the reconviction rate for those participating in community-based schemes was, on the other hand, substantially lower (McLaughlin and Muncie 1994). In short, there was a considerable range of support for a bifurcation strategy.

The persistent and more serious offenders considered more worthy of a punitive intervention could easily be identified as predominantly belonging to those sections of working-class youth who had failed to take advantage of the economic changes that had transformed Britain during the previous 20 years and had objectively taken a 'downward option', ignoring the need for – or unable to take advantage of – improved education and training (Cohen 1972), and had thus drifted into a non-skilled, unemployable underclass location. At the peak of industrial modernity there had been informal mechanisms whereby these offenders had been reintegrated back into the fold, as Pitts (1996: 280) pertinently observes:

> In the 1960s it was not uncommon for young people in trouble to avoid a custodial sentence by joining the armed forces. For their part, probation officers would often cite the rehabilitative powers of 'going steady', which usually involved getting a 'steady' job in order to 'save up to get married' and 'put a few things away in the bottom drawer'.

Excluded now from legitimate employment opportunities and presenting themselves as unattractive propositions to young women as partners in long-term relationships, these young men found themselves 'frozen in a state of persistent adolescence' (Pitts 1996: 281). This had important implications for their involvement in crime because the evidence suggests that 'growing up' means growing out of crime (Rutherford 1992) and, stripped of legitimate access to adulthood, these young men now found themselves trapped in a limbo world somewhere between childhood and adulthood long after the 'developmental tasks' of adolescence had been completed (Pitts 1996). Having failed to heed the warnings provided by the welfare and youth justice system, persistent and more serious young offenders were, therefore, to be targeted with a much harsher intervention than those who had been labelled non-problematic.

The new multi-agency forum managerialism was without doubt about identifying the two categories of young miscreants we have identified earlier in this book and setting in motion a twin-track response. On the one hand, there was the great majority who could be diverted from further offending behaviour and reintegrated back into the fold; on the other hand, there was the small minority for whom harsher treatment was inevitable. The notion of a new political consensus is, nevertheless, more suspect. Conservatives and Labour were in agreement over the need for realism but there was a substantial difference in their interpretation of that reality (Hopkins Burke 1999).

Conservative youth justice policy during the 1980s and 1990s had been for many young people particularly strong on 'the stick' but rather weak on 'the carrot'. There were many complexities and ambiguities to government policy during the period where the closely connected twin concerns of political expediency and pragmatism had led repeatedly to apparent changes in direction but in summary the perceived solution to the problem of offending by children and young people was to catch more of them, send out a clear message to them that they would get caught and be punished, although this did not have to mean incarceration or, indeed, serious punishment. However, this did not mean that all children and young people would be treated the same. Populist Conservative youth justice policy during the period again, and indeed where possible, involved a twin-track approach that differentiated between those who were deemed to have briefly transgressed and could be provided with the support to overcome their offending behaviour (and thus were to receive a minor punishment) and the persistent and more serious offenders who were deemed to be far more of a problem and considered more worthy of a punitive intervention (and thus were to receive a more severe punishment). The purpose of 'the stick' was to make young people take responsibility for their actions and become fully aware of the consequences of any illegal transgressions. The latter group of persistent and more serious offenders were, however, seriously over-represented among the ranks of those sections of working-class youth who had drifted into a non-skilled, unemployable underclass location. For a fundamental outcome of *laissez-faire* economic and social policy during that period had been the creation of a socially excluded underclass. Youth justice policies, in particular, and welfare policies, in general, had, at best, done nothing to alleviate that situation, and, at worst, had managed to exacerbate the problem. I have thus elsewhere termed this the 'excluded tutelage' model of youth justice (Hopkins Burke 1999) and it is summarised in Table 4.1.

Table 4.1   The excluded tutelage model of youth justice

- The solution to the crime problem involves catching more offenders in order to deter others.
- It involves a twin-track approach to justice that differentiates between those who have briefly transgressed and can be provided with the support to overcome their offending behaviour, and the more persistent and serious offenders considered more worthy of a punitive intervention.
- The latter group predominantly consists of members of those sections of working-class youth who have drifted into a non-skilled, unemployable underclass location.
- A failure of government non-interventionist socio-economic policies to significantly address the social exclusion of this group of young people.

Vivian Stern of NACRO, writing in 1996, points out that while other European countries favoured the reintegration of offenders back into the community as being central to social and criminal justice policy, Home Office press releases and Conservative government ministers:

> Use the language of conflict, contempt, and hatred ... doing good is a term of derision, and seeking to help offenders means that you do not care about the pain and suffering of victims.
>
> (Stern, cited in Brown 1998: 74)

Central to the criminal justice strategy of the New Labour government elected in 1997, therefore, were to be significant attempts to reintegrate this socially excluded underclass back into inclusive society. It is this notion of reintegration into the community that enables us to explain the approach to youth justice favoured by the Labour government elected in 1997 and which enables us to distinguish its policies from those of its populist Conservative predecessors. It is a distinctive approach that was to be part of a wider set of government strategies that sought to reintegrate those sections of the population that had become increasingly socially and economically excluded during the previous 20 years. I have termed this unwritten and unspoken government strategy 'reintegrative tutelage' and this is summarised in Table 4.2.

The reintegrative tutelage model is discussed further in the third part of the book, which extensively considers the origins and workings of the contemporary youth justice system introduced by New Labour via its flagship criminal justice legislation, the Crime and Disorder Act 1998.

Table 4.2 The reintegrative tutelage model of youth justice

* Based on the left-realist notion that crime requires a comprehensive solution and there must be a 'balance of intervention'.
* Young people who commit crime must face up to the consequences of their actions and take responsibility (rational actor model of criminal behaviour).
* An effective intervention needs to address the causes of offending as well as punishing the offender (predestined and rational actor model).
* Part of a wider set of educative and welfare strategies that seek to reintegrate socially and economically sections of society.

Postscript: young people and the postmodern condition

This first part of the book has discussed the social construction of children and adolescents, considered strategies to educate, discipline and control them in the interests of myriad different interest groups, including industrial capitalism, middle-class philanthropists, and the respectable working classes who themselves had a significant self-interest in improved life chances and protection from 'the rabble' or 'rough' working classes in their midst. There followed a discussion of the official, increasingly legislative and institutional response to the deviance and offending behaviour of children and young people from the beginnings of industrial modernity via the rational actor-inspired justice model and the predestined actor-inspired treatment model to scientific managerialism, corporatism and the election of New Labour in 1997. It is, however, an account rooted in notions of modernity and modern society.

We have seen that modern societies at their most confident were fundamentally mass societies with a very high demand for workers and military personnel (Harvey 1989; Hopkins Burke 1999, 2001). In such societies people were, therefore, an important commodity, with children and young people perceived to be economic assets worthy of nurture and protection. There were, however, frequent concerns about the quality of that population with the outcome being increasing state intervention in the socialisation of children and young people and especially their re-socialisation when their behaviour became problematic or indeed criminal. The young nevertheless continued to be at least potential societal assets regardless of the level and extent of their bad behaviour and were always worthy of reintegration into mainstream society. Jock Young (1999) observes this process of societal reintegration to be the overriding welfare and social work strategy of modernity. The situation was to change significantly with the fragmentation of that modernity (Hopkins Burke 1999) and the arrival of what some social scientists have termed the postmodern condition (Lyotard 1984).

From at least the last three decades of the twentieth century substantial doubts started to emerge – and again from disparate sources – about the sustainability of the modernist project in an increasingly fragmented social world. The collapse of the post-war socio-political consensus and an intensifying lack of enthusiasm for large-scale state intervention in the socio-economic sphere coincided with a decreasing enthusiasm for grand theoretical explanations in the social sciences. Underlying this disintegration of confidence was the beginning of an economic and political transformation accelerated by the oil crisis of the early 1970s, an abandonment of full employment policies with a decline in economic competitiveness, and a restructuring of the world economy with the rise in the productive capacity of the nations of the Pacific Rim. At the same time, increasingly diverse and fragmented social structures began to emerge in the economic, political and cultural spheres. In the economic sphere, there was a rejection of mass production-line technology in favour of flexible working patterns and a flexible labour force. This involved a weakening of trade unions, greater reliance on peripheral and secondary labour markets, the development of a low-paid and part-time, often female, labour force, and the shift towards a service, rather than manufacturing, economy. Politically, there was the dismantling of elaborate state planning and provision in the fields of welfare. Meanwhile, most conventional representative democratic systems were proving increasingly inadequate to the task of representing myriad interest groups as diverse as major industrialists and financiers, small business proprietors, the unemployed and dispossessed, wide ranging gender and sexual preference interests, environmentalists, the homeless and the unemployed (Giddens 1994).

It had been with the emergence of modernity and the needs of a mass industrial economy that children and young people had become an asset rather than a liability to society. The modern epoch was thus epitomised by strategies to control the activities of children and young people via education and discipline with the implicit objective of integration into an inclusive and productive, albeit unequal, society. The period of high modernity – circa 1945–74 – was distinguished by an unwritten social contract secured between government and the people based on full employment and a relatively generous welfare state. The subcultural mechanisms whereby unskilled working-class youth came to accept and reproduce their role within that socially unequal industrial modernity are discussed at the conclusion of the second part of this book.

It was with the fragmentation of that modernity that whole tracts of the former industrial working class now appeared superfluous to the requirements of society and the consequences – either intended or unintended – of subsequent government policies were to lead to growing social exclusion for this group. The unwritten social contact of high modernity had collapsed. The total transformation of the UK economy that occurred during the 1980s brought with it perhaps the last chance for a now far from confident modern mass society. Mass unemployment had now arrived:

> On official figures ... unemployment increased from 4.1 percent of the labour force in 1972 to 10.3 percent in 1981. Official figures suggest that the highest level of unemployment in the 1980s in Britain was 12.4 percent in 1983, declining to 6.8 in 1990, returning to 11 percent (three million) in 1992, and declining again to 8 percent in 1996.
>
> (Taylor 1997: 281)

The end of full employment as a social and political project led to increasing social exclusion for the residual group of low-skilled workers identified above and discussed in more detail later in this book. With the arrival of long-term unemployment many became absorbed into what some cultural and sociological commentators have referred to as a socially excluded, uneducated and unskilled 'underclass' with little value or use to contemporary society. The following part of this book will consider the various explanations – or criminological theories – that have been proposed at various times during the modernist era to explain why it is that young people offend, and it will conclude with a critical discussion of the creation of the socially excluded underclass.

Part II

Explaining Youth Criminal Behaviour

Chapter 5

Youth offending as rational behaviour

The first part of this book discussed the social construction of childhood and adolescence as particular categories of human development and the various methods utilised and developed over time for the socialisation and disciplining of young people as a group functional to the requirements of industrial modernity. The final two chapters discussed the development of increasingly sophisticated attempts to respond and intervene in the lives of children and young people who had deviated from defined acceptable norms of behaviour.

Throughout the first part of the book reference was made to explanations of why young people deviate from norms of society and become involved in offending behaviour. This second part of the book discusses the different explanations – or criminological theories – that have been proposed at different times during the era of industrial modernity to explain offending behaviour by children and young people. It provides a discussion which is complementary to the author's *Introduction to Criminological Theory* (Hopkins Burke 2001, 2005) and uses the same explanatory models of crime and criminal behaviour introduced and developed in those texts. Thus, this chapter discusses youth offending in terms of the rational actor model, which proposes that involvement in criminal behaviour is very much a matter of choice. The explanations discussed in the following three chapters are, on the other hand, fundamentally underpinned by both the predestined actor model, which proposes that criminality can be explained in terms of factors, either internal or external to the human being that cause or determine them to act in ways over which they have little or no control, and the victimised actor model, which proposes offenders to be themselves the victims of an unjust and unequal society which targets and criminalises the behaviour and activities of disadvantaged sections of society. It will nevertheless become increasingly obvious to the reader that these three models are not mutually exclusive. Young people do make choices but those available to them are significantly constrained by the life circumstances in which they find themselves. We shall commence our discussion of the rational actor by locating the pre-modern context in which they originally emerged.

Pre-modern explanations of criminal behaviour

All human societies throughout history have sought to explain why it is that some of them break the rules of the group. The purpose is to identify the basis of social solidarity, reasons for disorder, and subsequently the implementation of sanctions against those who contravene the established norms of behaviour (Durkheim 1933, Hopkins Burke 2001, 2005). Many pre-modern explanations of criminal behaviour were grounded in spiritualism and naturalism; that is, involvement in criminality could be explained by an inappropriate relationship with supernatural powers. Offences were, therefore, spiritual 'sins' or crimes against the natural order and punishments were said to be carried out in accordance with nature or to be divinely sanctioned. This presumption of a linkage between order, disorder and non-human influences became part of the body of laws and traditions in many pre-modern societies, albeit with a number of cultural adaptations. Thus, two early theories of delinquency that were extremely influential in pre-modern medieval Western Europe were naturalism[1] and demonology.[2]

It was observed in the first part of this book that concepts of childhood, adolescence and juvenile delinquency are relatively recent social constructions, as is the notion of a separate juvenile or youth justice system. Pre-modern societies certainly considered young offenders to be nothing more than little versions of adult criminals and, very often, this approach was rooted in the presumption – offered by both naturalism and demonology – that explanations of criminal behaviour are indistinguishable from criminal causation, and therefore all such behaviour should be similarly punished. From a perspective where criminal behaviour was the outcome of an inappropriate relationship with natural or supernatural phenomena it made perfect sense to respond to contaminated individuals in the same way, which invariably meant the termination of their ungodly lives. Differential responses to different categories of people in such circumstances would simply have been irrational.

With the rise of modernity in Western Europe explanations of offending behaviour came to focus on the personal responsibility of individuals. These new theories simply rejected naturalism and demonology as explanations of delinquency and criminality and were heavily influenced by the rationality and humanitarianism which was the basis of European Enlightenment philosophy (Hopkins Burke 2001, 2005).

The rational actor model of criminal behaviour

Hopkins Burke (2001, 2005) identifies three models – or traditions – of explaining criminal behaviour: the rational actor, the predestined actor and the victimised actor models. Variants of the latter two models are discussed in the following three chapters while the former is the focus of this one. The rational actor model has its origins in the classical school of the late eighteenth century and proposes that criminal behavior is the outcome of individual rational choice and has its theoretical foundations in the human desire for the pursuit of pleasure and aversion to pain. Because of this emphasis on human rationality, it is argued that offenders should be held personally accountable for criminal and delinquent acts and punished accordingly. Since the calculus for making this choice is the acquisition of a benefit from criminal behaviour (pleasure), it is argued that society must develop policies to increase the costs for this benefit (pain). Thus, punishment should become increasingly harsher as the extent of criminal behaviour becomes greater and more serious, and the costs of crime must, therefore, always outweigh the possible benefits that might be obtained from the criminal act. Table 5.1 summarises the main points of the rational actor model of criminal behaviour.

The classical school and its aftermath

It was the two key classical school theorists – Cesare Beccaria in Italy and Jeremy Bentham in Britain – writing in the late eighteenth century who established the essential components of the rational actor model. Beccaria considered that criminals owe a 'debt' to society, and

Table 5.1 The rational actor model of criminal behaviour

- Humans are fundamentally rational beings who enjoy free will.
- Crime is an outcome of rationality and free will.
- People choose to engage in criminal rather than conformist behaviour.
- Criminality is morally wrong and an affront against social order and the collective good of society.
- Civil society must necessarily punish criminals to deter individual wrongdoers and other would-be criminals.
- Punishment should be proportional to the nature of the criminal offence and never excessive.
- Punishment must also be a guaranteed response to criminal behaviour and delivered quickly.

---

he advocated the then radical proposition that punishment should be swift, certain and proportional to the seriousness of the crime. Beccaria provides the essential foundations of the rational actor model which is based on the concepts of free will and hedonism. He proposes that human behaviour is essentially purposive and based on the pleasure–pain principle and that punishment should reflect that principle: thus, fixed punishments for all offences must be written into the law and not be open to the interpretation, or the discretion, of judges; the law must be applied equally to all citizens, the sole function of the court is to determine guilt, there should be no mitigation and all that are guilty of a particular offence should suffer the same prescribed penalty.

The philosopher Jeremy Bentham promoted the ideas of Beccaria in late eighteenth- and early-nineteenth century England and argued that human beings rationally seek pleasure and avoid pain. Rational people can, therefore, be easily deterred from criminal deviance by the threat of punishment, but the criminally minded will conclude that the pleasure derived from crime outweighs the pain of punishment and are not easily dissuaded. Bentham went further, however, and argued that deterrence was far more likely to be achieved by the certainty of punishment and by making the severity of each punishment surpass any benefit derived from the crime.

This argument appears at first sight both plausible and even attractive but significantly these early rational actor theorists had deliberately and completely ignored differences between individuals. First offenders and recidivists were treated exactly alike, solely on the basis of the particular act that had been committed; children, the 'feeble-minded' and the insane were all treated as if they were fully rational and competent. Thus, the appearance in court of people who were unable to comprehend the proceedings against them did little to legitimise the new judicial orthodoxy and it became increasingly recognised that people were not equally responsible for their actions. The outcome was that a whole range of experts gradually came to be invited into the courts to pass opinion on the degree of reason that could be expected of the accused and judges were now able to vary sentences in accordance with the degree of individual culpability argued by these expert witnesses.

It was this theoretical compromise that led to the emergence of a modified criminological perspective that came to be termed the neo-classical school and which informs the justice/punishment model of youth justice outlined in Chapter 3. In this modified variant of the rational actor model, ordinary sane adults were still to be considered fully responsible for their actions, and all equally capable of either criminal or non-criminal behaviour, but it was now recognised that children – and in some circumstances, the elderly – were less capable of exercising free choice and were, therefore, less responsible for their actions. We have here early recognition that various innate predisposing factors may actually determine human behaviour: a perception that was to provide the foundation of the predestined actor model that is discussed in the following three chapters and which was to increasingly provide the basis of the welfare/treatment model of youth justice that was again outlined in Chapter 3.

It was significantly these revisions to the penal code that admitted into the courts for the first time non-legal 'experts' including doctors, psychiatrists and, later, social workers. These professionals were gradually introduced into the criminal justice system in order to identify the impact of individual biological, psychological and social differences and the purpose of this intervention was to determine the extent to which offenders were responsible for their actions. The outcome was that sentences became more individualised, dependent on the perceived degree of culpability of the offender and on mitigating circumstances. Moreover, it was now recognised that a particular punishment would have a differential effect on different people and consequently, punishment came increasingly to be expressed in terms of punishment appropriate to the rehabilitation of the individual.

Populist conservative criminology

The rational actor model was to go into increasing decline as an explanation of the offending behaviour of children and young people but was to return to favour with the rise of the 'new' political right – or populist conservatism – that came to political power in 1979 and which we encountered in Chapter 4. At that time conservative writers were mounting a vigorous moral campaign against various forms of 'deviance' and during the general election held during that year, the Conservative leader, Margaret Thatcher, made crime a major election issue for the first time in post-war Britain. Her general concern was to re-establish 'Victorian values' and to this end targeted the supposedly permissive society of the 1960s and its perceived legitimisation in 'soft' social science. In criminology, this perceived liberal indulgence was epitomised, first, by the predestined actor model of criminal behaviour – which had been the enduring dominant orthodoxy of criminological explanation in the twentieth century – with its focus on discovering the causes of crime and, having first located them, offering treatment and rehabilitation rather than punishment, but, second, even more so with the more radical variants of the 'victimised actor' model and their critique of an unfair and unequal society and their policy assumptions of understanding, forgiveness and non-intervention that were gaining increasing popularity with the idealistic but at that time still electorally viable political left.

Right-wing intellectuals observed that it was not merely that left-wing and liberal thought had simply failed to see the problems inherent in 'soft' approaches to crime, discipline and education but this so-called progressive theorising had itself provided a basis for the acceleration of the permissive syndromes in question. High levels of criminality and disorder were, therefore, blamed not only on the weakening sources of social authority, the family, schools, religion and other key institutions, but even more so on the corrosive influence of the surrounding culture with its emphasis on rights rather than obligations and the celebration of self-expression to the point of self-indulgence, instead of promoting self-control and self-constraint (Tzannetakis 2001). The populist conservatives thus argued that in such a de-moralising culture, it was clear that crime and violence would inevitably flourish. Real problems and sociological apologies alike had to be confronted, and an attempt made to reassert the virtue and necessity of authority, order and discipline (Scruton 1980, 1985).

In social policy in general (Morgan 1978) and in the area of crime and deviance in particular (Dale 1984), an assault was mounted on liberal and radical left trends. Empirical justification for this attack on the self-styled forces of socially progressive intervention came from the publication of an influential paper by Robert Martinson (1974) – discussed elsewhere in this book – which purported to show that rehabilitation programmes in prison simply 'do not work' and thus the whole rationale for the existence of a welfare-oriented probation service, in particular, was called into question. Consequently, we were to see the enthusiastic reintroduction of the idea of retributive punishment and arguments for the protection of society from danger. From this populist conservative perspective, punishment is essentially about devising penalties to fit the crime and ensuring that they are carried out, thus reinforcing social values. In short, this concern to treat the miscreant as an offender against social morality, and not as a candidate for reform, can be seen as a contemporary form of the rational actor model, but one with a distinctly retributive edge (Hopkins Burke 2005).

Contemporary rational actor theories

Three groups of contemporary rational actor model theories have come very much to prominence with the revival of the tradition: contemporary deterrence theories; rational choice theories; and routine activities theory.

Contemporary deterrence theories

Contemporary deterrence theories are founded on the twin principles that punishment must occur quickly after the offence has occurred and be certain to happen. Thus, if the punishment is sufficiently severe, certain and swift, it is argued that the rationally calculating individual will decide that there is more to be lost than there is to be gained from offending and not become involved (Zimring and Hawkins 1973; Gibbs 1975; Wright 1993). It is moreover proposed that the certainty of being caught and being processed by the criminal justice system is a significantly more effective deterrent than the severity of punishment imposed (Akers 1997).

There are two variations of the deterrence doctrine and it is proposed that these operate in different ways. In the case of 'general deterrence', the apprehension and punishment of offenders in society demonstrates clearly to the population as a whole what will happen to them if they break the law (Zimring and Hawkins 1973); while, in the case of 'specific deterrence', it is the apprehended and punished individual offender who learns from their specific experience the futility of involvement in criminality. The high rate of recidivism (or repeat offending) nevertheless challenges the effectiveness of deterrence as a crime control strategy. Reoffending rates for young people leaving custody are particularly high. Thus, for males aged 14–17, the rate of reconviction within two years of discharge from prison in 1998 was 84 per cent. Of those who were reconvicted, 36 per cent were again sentenced to custody for their first subsequent conviction (Nacro 2003). Moreover, there are clearly problems with the notion that even fully rational adults – if there are such people – accurately calculate the rewards and risks associated with crime but the notion is clearly more problematic in the case of immature children and young people who may have a limited sense of rationality and, therefore, cannot legitimately be held fully responsible for their actions. Contemporary rational choice theories help us explore this notion further.

Contemporary rational choice theories

The earlier and less sophisticated variants of rational choice theory tended to compare the decision-making process adopted by offenders with straightforward economic choice where the person chooses the activity – legal or illegal – that offers the best return (Becker 1968), very much in accordance with the pleasure/pain dichotomy of Bentham's hedonistic calculus. Thus, it was argued that offending could be prevented by reforming the law with the introduction of more rigorous and punitive punishment and the introduction of more effective criminal justice administration in order to alter the equation and make crime appear appreciably less attractive. Perhaps not surprising, this early variant was accused of implying too high a degree of rationality by comparing criminal choices too closely with marketplace decisions, and, at the same, failing to explain expressive non-economically motivated criminal activity such as vandalism (Trasler 1986). Certainly, it would appear an inappropriate theory for explaining the behaviour of children or adolescents who have long been recognised as possessing a less developed sense of rationality.

A more sophisticated, highly influential variant of rational choice theory was, however, developed by Clarke and Cornish, who define crime as 'the outcome of the offender's choices or decisions, however hasty or ill-considered these might be' (Clarke 1987: 118). Thus, from this perspective, offenders invariably act in terms of limited or bounded forms of rationality. They will not always obtain all the facts needed to make a wise decision and the information available will not necessarily be weighed carefully or appropriately, but they will make a decision that is rational in the context of their lives, experiences, cultural background and knowledge base. Clarke (1987) is, however, not entirely dismissive of the predestined actor model tradition that we will encounter in the following three chapters, and suggests that most of the factors seen as predisposing an individual to commit crime can be interpreted in terms of their influence on offender cognitive decision-making. It is, therefore, suggested that individuals respond to situations in different ways because they bring with them a different history of psychological conditioning. Thus, children and young people brought up in different social environments with different socialisation experiences are likely to make very different decisions when confronted with similar circumstances and criminal opportunities, which is a key concept for rational choice theorists. Significantly, a child brought up in a geographical location where criminality is common, their family and friends are actively involved in illicit activities that appear to bring them easily obtained material rewards, while access to legitimate opportunities appear both limited and implausible, could well consider criminal involvement to be a very rational choice for them.

Routine activities theory

Routine activities theory is, to some extent, a development of the rational choice theory key concept of criminal opportunity and this proposes that for a personal or property crime to occur there must be at the same time and place a perpetrator, a victim, and/or an object of property (Felson 1998). The criminal act can take place if there are persons or circumstances in the locality that encourage it to happen but, on the other hand, it can be prevented if the potential victim or another person is present who can take action to deter it.

Cohen and Felson (1979) have taken the elements of time, place, objects and persons to develop a 'routine activities' view of crime events and these have been placed into three categories of variables that increase or decrease the likelihood that persons will be victims of 'direct contact' predatory – personal or property – crime. The first variable is the presence in the locality of motivated offenders, those looking to commit offences or those who will do so if a reasonable criminal opportunity presents itself. Cohen and Felson observe – albeit in a US context but one which is easily transferable to the UK – that the great majority of motivated offenders walking the streets looking for criminal opportunities are young males. Second, it is necessary to have available suitable targets, either in the form of a person to rob or property to steal.[3] The third identified variable was the absence of 'capable guardians' against crime. Therefore, the probability that a crime will take place is enhanced when there are one or more persons in the locality who are motivated to commit a crime, a suitable available target or potential victim, and the absence of formal or informal guardians who could deter the potential offender.

Cohen and Felson argue that it is the fundamental changes in daily activities related to work, school and leisure that have occurred during the past 50 years that have placed more people in particular localities at particular times. This has both increased their accessibility as targets – or victims – of crime while at the same time they are away from home and unable to guard their own property and possessions.

Felson (1998) has more recently placed less emphasis on the significance of formal guardians – such as the police – because he has concluded that crime is a private phenomenon which is largely unaffected by state intervention. Natural crime prevention and deterrence are now emphasised and Felson argues that it is ordinary people, oneself, friends, family, or even strangers that are the most likely capable guardians. In this later work he has also applied routine activities theory to four crime categories other than the property variants:

- exploitative (robbery, rape)
- mutualistic (gambling, prostitution, selling and buying drugs)
- competitive (fighting)
- individualistic (individual drug use, suicide).

Felson has thus identified a fourth variable that enables a criminal event to take place – the absence of an 'intimate handler', a significant other; for example, a parent or girlfriend – that can impose informal social control on the offender. A potential offender must escape the 'intimate handler' then find a crime target without being under the surveillance of this 'capable guardian'.

Much routine activity theory research and discussion concentrates on the interlinked areas of crime targets and the lack of appropriate guardians. Thus, Cohen and Felson (1979) develop their concept of the 'household activity ratio', that is, the percentage of all households that are not husband–wife families or where the wife is employed outside the home, and argue that such households are more vulnerable because their members are away from home more and less able to function as guardians of their property. Cohen *et al.*

(1981) subsequently developed a more formalised version of routine activities theory which they named 'opportunity' theory and which considers the elements of exposure, proximity, guardianship and target attractiveness as variables that increase the risk of criminal victimisation. Others observe that routine activities theory is merely a way of explaining why people become victims of crime and that it fails to explain why it is that some people engage in criminal behaviour and others do not (Akers 1997). Thus, there is a taken-for-granted assumption that such people exist and that they commit crimes in certain places, at times when the opportunities and potential victims are available, but it tells us absolutely nothing about these people and their motivations.

The predestined actor model discussed in the following three chapters provides us with numerous suggestions for the identity of many motivated offenders. For as the evidence shows, it is often children and young people who are to be found wandering the streets during those times when adults are at work and who are motivated to offend, or at least are prepared to take advantage of crime opportunities when they arise, not least when they are in the company of likeminded others, in particular when they are truanting or excluded from school, or even when on their way home from school when, for example, they descend in groups on shopping malls. Or in the following years, having left school with inadequate educational qualifications, they often find themselves excluded from access to legitimate economic opportunities.

The rational actor model and the youth offender reconsidered

The original rational actor model theorists had emphasised the rationally calculating, reasoning, human being who could be deterred from choosing to commit criminal behaviour by the threat of a fair and proportionate punishment. Moreover, they had proposed that all citizens should be treated equally in terms of a codified and rationalised legal system. The purist version of that explanatory system nevertheless fell into decline because it became clear that not all people – and children and young people in particular – are capable of making purely rational decisions for which they can be held legitimately responsible. Thus, the revised version of the rational actor model, that came to the fore with the rise of the political 'new right' in the last quarter of the twentieth century, came to implicitly accept the predestined actor notion that there are different categories of human beings with different levels of reasoning. From this perspective, it is accepted that young people do make decisions which are rational for them in the circumstances in which they find themselves and in terms of their life experience and knowledge.

Notes

1 Naturalism refers to the ancient practice of linking human affairs to the natural world and inferring that human behavior is thus derived from the forces of nature. Just as the tides are affected by the sun and the moon, so too are human passions and fortunes. All that is necessary is for humans to become adept at understanding how the forces of nature work, and develop the ability to interpret these forces. Naturalism is therefore a deterministic theory of criminal causation, because it eliminates notions of individual responsibility and the ability to choose courses of action (Vold *et al.* 1998).

2 For many centuries, humans believed that evil creatures – demons or devils – wielded great influence over humans, sometimes possessing them and making them commit offences against the greater good. Criminal behaviour and delinquency were manifestations of conflict between creatures of evil and chaos against deities of goodness and order. Demonology is thus – like naturalism above – a deterministic theory of criminal causation where the individual has no choice in their behaviour (Hopkins Burke 2005).

3 The term 'target' has been used in preference to that of 'victim' because the acquisition of property or money was seen to be focus of the great majority of criminal behaviour.

Chapter 6

Biological explanations of youth offending

We saw in the previous chapter that the rational actor model of criminal behaviour proposes that human beings possess free will and are, therefore, free to choose the behaviour of their own choice. The predestined actor model, in contrast, rejects this emphasis on free will and replaces it with the doctrine of determinism which claims to account for criminality in terms of factors – either internal or external to the individual – which cause them to act in ways over which they have little or no control. The individual is, therefore, both predestined to be a criminal while being a different category of humanity than non-criminals. Table 6.1 summarises the main points of the predestined actor model of criminal behaviour.

There are three basic formulations of the predestined actor model: biological, psychological and sociological. All three variants, nevertheless, incorporate the same fundamental assumptions, and although each is discussed separately, they become increasingly non-exclusive; for example, biologists came to embrace sociological factors, while at times it is often difficult to differentiate between biological and psychological explanations. This chapter considers the biological variant of the predestined actor model and is divided into three sections. First, there is a consideration of those theories which propose that the young person has been born with a physiological predisposition to commit crime. Second, there is a discussion of altered biological states where criminal behaviour is at least influenced by the consumption of alcohol, drugs or poor diet. Third, there is an examination of socio-biological theories which propose that biological predispositions are activated in different ways in

Table 6.1 The predestined actor model of criminal behaviour

- The rational actor emphasis on free will is rejected and replaced with the doctrine of determinism.
- From this positivist standpoint, criminal behaviour is explained in terms of factors, either internal or external to the human being that cause – or determine – people to act in ways over which they have little or no control.
- The individual is thus in some way predestined to be a criminal.
- Criminals are in some way different from non-criminals.
- There are three basic formulations of the predestined actor model: biological, psychological and sociological.
- All three variants incorporate the same fundamental determinist assumptions.
- Treatment of the offender is proposed, rather than punishment.

---

diverse environmental conditions, often dependent on the socialised upbringing of the young person.

Physiological constituents and youth criminality

Early biological explanations of criminal behaviour have their origins in the work of the Italian school at the end of the nineteenth and the beginning of the twentieth centuries and although these theories were primitive by the standards of today, they significantly established an enduring research tradition that has persisted to this day. Cesare Lombroso (1876) argued that criminals are a physical type distinct from non-criminals with physical characteristics suggestive of earlier forms of evolution. It is an approach considered simplistic and naïve today yet Lombroso had made an important contribution to the development of criminological explanations by recognising in his later work the need for multi-factor accounts that include not only hereditary, but social, cultural and economic factors. These latter important factors were emphasised by his successors Enrico Ferri and Raffaele Garofalo.

Ferri (1895) argued that criminal behaviour can be explained by studying the interaction between physical, individual and social factors, influentially proposing that crime could be controlled by improving the social conditions of the poor, thus advocating the provision of subsidised housing, birth control and public recreation facilities. Garofalo (1914) returned to evolutionary arguments and proposed that some members of society have a higher than average sense of morality because they are superior, further evolved, members of the group, while conversely, true criminals lack properly developed altruistic sentiments and, moreover, have psychic or moral anomalies that they have inherited. From this perspective, criminals are a different category of humanity from non-criminals and this remains a key tenet of purist predestined actor model philosophy. Later biological explanations of criminal behaviour were to become increasingly more sophisticated but the notion of inherited criminal characteristics continues to be central with evidence to support this supposition obtained from three sources: criminal family studies; twin studies; and adopted children studies.

Criminal family studies

Criminal family studies have their origins in the work of Dugdale (1877), who traced 709 members of the Juke family and discovered that the great majority had been either criminals or paupers; Goddard (1914), who traced 480 members of the Kallikak family and found that a large number of them had been criminals; and Goring (1913), who conducted a study of 3,000 prisoners and found strong associations between the criminality of children, their parents and siblings, even if they had been separated from each other at an early age. Problematically, none of these studies was able to distinguish between biological and environmental factors in establishing criminal causality, a weakness that later twin and adoption studies sought to overcome but ultimately with limited success.

Lange (1930) examined a group of men with a prison record and found that in 77 per cent of cases involving identical twins, both brothers had such a record; however, in the case of non-identical twins, only 12 per cent of brothers both had a prison record; while only 8 per cent of ordinary brothers, near to each other in age, were both found to have records. Christiansen (1968) examined official registers over an extended time period and found that in the case of identical male twins where at least one brother had a criminal record, the same applied to 36 per cent of the other twins. This was only the case with 12 per cent of the non-identical twins.

A problem with twin studies is the lack of clarity about the sort of characteristics that are supposedly inherited as variations might reveal themselves in quite different forms of behaviour (Trasler 1967). For example, some pairs of twins in Lange's study had committed very different types of offences from each other and it could well be the case that a predisposition to offend is inherited but the actual form of offending is determined by other factors. Christiansen interestingly did not actually claim that inherited characteristics were the only, or even for that matter the dominant factor and proposed that twin studies could actually increase our understanding of the interaction between the environment and biological traits. It is, however, a significant criticism of twin studies that they cannot accurately assess the balance between the effects of inherited characteristics and those of the environment. Twins are more likely than ordinary siblings to share similar experiences in relation to family and peers and it is indeed possible that such similarities will be greater in the cases of identical twins.

More recent research conducted by Rowe and Rogers (1989) has supported both inherited characteristics and environmental explanations of criminality. Collecting data from self-report questionnaires involving 308 sets of twins in the Ohio State school system in the USA, they concluded that environment partly determines the similarity of behaviour of same-sex and identical twins and could lead them to develop similar offending behaviour. Moreover, as twins are usually brought up together, it becomes virtually impossible to reach any firm conclusion as to the role of inherited characteristics alone (Rowe 1990). It is adopted children studies that have sought to overcome this methodological predicament.

It would seem that in the case of adopted children – where contact with a criminal parent has obviously been limited – any association between criminal behaviour can be attributed to inherited characteristics with a greater degree of certainty. Thus, Hutchings and Mednick (1977) found that 48 per cent of young males with a criminal record and 37.7 per cent with a record of minor offences had a birth father with a criminal record. On the other hand, among young males without a criminal record, only 31.1 per cent had a birth father with a record. Interestingly, an adoptee was even more likely to have a record where both the birth and adoptive father had previous convictions.

A later wide-ranging study found a similar though slightly less strong correlation between birth parents and their adoptee children (Mednick *et al.* 1984). Again the most significant results were when both birth and adoptive parents were criminal and the researchers concluded that there was an inherited characteristic element that was transmitted from the criminal parents to their children that increased the likelihood of their offspring becoming involved in criminal behaviour. It should be noted, however, that adoption agencies try to place children in homes situated in similar environments to those from which they came and there remains a possibility that it is upbringing, not inherited characteristics, that 'causes' criminal behaviour. It might well be the case that some people are genetically endowed with characteristics that render them more likely to 'succumb to crime' (Hutchings and Mednick 1977: 140).

There have been attempts in more recent years to identify a link between the level of intelligence and criminal behaviour. Hirschi and Hindelang (1977) found that IQ, as a predictor of offending behaviour, is at least as good as any other major social variables and is also strongly related to social class and ethnic group. Thus, because offending behaviour is viewed as being the province of lower-class young people from ethnic minorities, this relationship implies that such people have lower IQs. It is an argument that has received a great deal of understandable criticism. For example, Menard and Morse (1984) argued that IQ is merely one of the ways in which young offenders are disadvantaged in society, citing societal and institutional response to these disadvantages as the real explanation for offending behaviour. In general, critics note that the way in which IQ tests are constructed provides advantages to those who are middle class and white and in reality do not measure innate intelligence, but rather some other ability, such as a facility in language or cultural concepts.

Genetic structure explanations

Genetic structure explanations of criminal behaviour consider abnormalities in the genetic structure of the offender with crucial identified defects being related to the sex chromosomes. People usually have 23 pairs of chromosomes, 46 in all, with the sex of a person determined by one of these pairs. The normal complement in a female is XX and in a male XY but in some men an extra chromosome has been found. Klinefelter *et al.* (1942) discovered that sterile males often display a marked degree of feminisation together, sometimes, with low intelligence and increased physical stature and it was later found that these men had an extra X chromosome. A later study conducted among Klinefelter males in psychiatric institutions discovered an abnormally high incidence of criminal behaviour among the research subjects which suggested they are overrepresented among homosexuals, transvestites and transsexuals.

Later studies examined incarcerated criminals and focused on men with an extra Y chromosome, in order to test the hypothesis that they might be characterised by extra maleness, and thus more aggressive. Casey in 1965 and Neilson in 1968 conducted the first major studies at the Rampton and Moss Side secure hospitals, respectively, and discovered that such men tended to be very tall, generally of low intelligence, often with EEG abnormalities and histories of criminal and aggressive behaviour, with theft and violent assault their characteristic offences.

Price and Whatmore (1967) noted that men with an extra Y chromosome tend to be convicted at an earlier age than other offenders, come from families with no history of criminality, have a tendency to be unstable and immature without displaying remorse, and have a marked tendency to commit a succession of apparently motiveless property crimes. Witkin *et al.* (1977) explained the overrepresentation of such men in institutions to be the result of their slight mental retardation.

A range of criticisms has been made of genetic structure theories. First, almost all the research has been concentrated on inmates in special hospitals and has revealed more evidence of psychiatric disorder than criminality. Second, there does not appear to be any fixed and identifiable XYY syndrome, which means the concept is not useful in predicting criminal behaviour. Third, the offending behaviour of some young males with an extra X chromosome may actually be due to anxiety in adolescence about an apparent lack of masculinity. Fourth, all the young male offenders with an identified extra Y chromosome have come from working-class backgrounds. It is possible that because they are tall and well built, they may be defined as 'dangerous' by judges and psychiatrists, and, therefore, more likely to be incarcerated than fined. Finally, and perhaps crucially, there are thousands of perfectly normal and harmless people in the general population who have either an extra X or Y chromosome.

Advances in genetic science in recent years have led to a revival of claims that aspects of criminality can be explained by genetic factors. Significantly, the discovery that some traits of personality can be explained by a genetic component (Jones 1993) does greatly strengthen the possibility that some criminal behaviour can be explained by a genetic susceptibility triggered by environmental factors. This is an observation to which we return later in this chapter.

Criminal body types

A further category of biological positivism has its foundations directly in the Italian school tradition of emphasising body type. Hooton (1939) thus concluded that criminals are organically inferior to other people and that low foreheads, in particular, were an indication of physiological inferiority, but his work was not surprisingly widely condemned for its racist overtones and failure to recognise that the prisoners studied represented only those who had been caught, convicted or imprisoned. Sheldon (1949) shifted attention to offending male youths, seeking to link different types of physique to temperament, intelligence and offending behaviour. He therefore categorised the physiques of the boys by measuring the degree to which they possessed a combination of three different body components: *endomorphs* tended to be soft, fat people; *mesomorphs* muscular and athletic; *ectomorphs* had a skinny, flat and fragile physique. Sheldon concluded that most offenders were mesomorphs and, moreover, because the youths came from parents who were offenders, the factors that produce criminal behaviour are inherited. Glueck and Glueck (1950) found offenders to have narrower faces, wider chests, larger and broader waists, bigger forearms and upper arms than non-offenders, with approximately 60 per cent mesomorphic. The researchers, like their predecessors in this tradition, nevertheless failed to establish whether the mesomorphs were offenders because of their build and disposition, because their physique and dispositions are socially conceived as being associated with offenders, or whether poverty and deprivation affected both their body build and offending behaviour.

Body type theories can be legitimately criticised for ignoring different aspects of the interaction between the physical characteristics of the person and their social circumstances. Thus, poor people tend to have an inferior diet and be small in stature; while young people in manual occupations are likely to acquire an athletic build. The overrepresentation of such people among convicted criminals may simply be explained by a variety of socio-cultural, rather than biological, factors. Gibbons (1970) argued that the high proportion of mesomorphs among offenders is due to a process of social selection and that the nature of their activities is such that deviants will be drawn from the more athletic members of that age group. Cortes and Gatti (1972), nevertheless, observe that such arguments falsely accuse biological explanations of being more determinist than they actually are. They propose that as physical factors are essential to the social selection process, human behaviour has both biological and social causes. This point is revisited later in this chapter.

Biochemistry explanations

Biochemical explanations of offending behaviour are similar to the altered biological state theories introduced below but differ in that the relevant substances are either already present in the body of the individual or are created by some internal physiological process.

It has long been recognised that male animals – of most species – are more aggressive than females and this has been linked to the male sex hormone, testosterone (Rose *et al.* 1974; Keverne *et al.* 1982). The relationship between sex hormones and human behaviour, however, appears to be more complex although testosterone has been linked with aggressive crime such as murder and rape. In most men, however, testosterone levels probably do not significantly affect levels of aggression (Persky *et al.* 1971; Scarmella and Brown 1978). Studies of violent male prisoners do however suggest that testosterone levels have an effect on aggressive behaviour (Kreuz and Rose 1972; Ehrenkranz *et al.* 1974).

Problematically, these studies have not differentiated between different forms of aggression but others have sought to address these problems. Olwens (1987) conducted a study of young men with no marked criminal record and found a clear link between testosterone and both verbal and physical aggression, with a further distinction between provoked and unprovoked aggressive behaviour. The former tended to be more verbal than physical and was in response to unfair or threatening behaviour by another person; the latter was violent, destructive and involved activities such as starting fights and making provocative comments. The relationship between testosterone and unprovoked violence was, nevertheless, found to be indirect and would depend on other factors such as how irritable the particular individual was. Schalling (1987) discovered that high testosterone levels in young males were associated with verbal aggression but not with actual physical aggression, which suggests a concern to protect their status by threats. Low-testosterone-level boys would tend not to protect their position, preferring to remain silent. Neither study suggests a direct link between testosterone and aggression, but in a provocative situation it is those with the highest levels of testosterone that are more likely to resort to violence.

Ellis and Coontz (1990) observe that testosterone levels peak during puberty and the early 20s and that this correlates with the highest crime rates. They claim that this finding provides persuasive evidence for a biological explanation of criminal behaviour and that it explains both aggressive and property crime, arguing that sociological researchers have failed to explain why it is that this distribution exists across all societies and cultures. There is, nevertheless, no evidence of a causal relationship between criminal behaviour and the level of testosterone. The link may be more tenuous, with testosterone merely providing the environment necessary for aggressive behaviour to take place.

Hypoglycaemia or low blood sugar levels – sometimes related to diabetes mellitus – may result in irritable, aggressive reactions, and may culminate in sexual offences, assaults and motiveless murder (see Shah and Roth 1974). Shoenthaler (1982) discovered that by lowering the daily sucrose intake of incarcerated young offenders it was possible to reduce the level of their anti-social behaviour. Virkkunen (1987) has, moreover, linked hypoglycaemia with other activities often defined as anti-social such as truancy, low verbal IQ, tattooing and stealing from home during childhood. Hypoglycaemia has also been linked with alcohol abuse; if consumed regularly and in large quantities, the ethanol produced can induce hypoglycaemia and increase aggression (Clapham 1989).

The relationship between adrenaline and aggressive behaviour is a similar area of study to that involving testosterone. Each involves the relationship between a hormonal level and aggressive anti-social behaviour. Schachter (cited in Shah and Roth 1974) found that injections of adrenaline made no difference to the behaviour of normal prisoners but a great difference to psychopaths. Hare (1982) found that when threatened with pain, criminals exhibit fewer signs of stress than other people. Mednick et al. (1982) discovered that not only do certain, particularly violent, criminals need stronger stimuli to arouse them, but also once they are in a stressed state they recover more slowly to their normal levels than do non-criminals. Eysenck (1959) had offered a logical explanation for this relationship some years previously, proposing that individuals with low stress levels are easily bored, become quickly disinterested in things around them, and crave exciting experiences. Thus, for such individuals normal stressful situations are not disturbing but they are exciting and enjoyable, something to be savoured and sought after.

Baldwin (1990) suggests that the link between age and crime rates can be partially explained by considering arousal rates, observing that children quickly become used to stimuli that had previously excited them and, therefore, seek ever more thrilling inputs. The stimulus received from criminal type activities also declines with age, as does the level of physical fitness, strength and agility required to perform many such activities. Baldwin interestingly explains both the learning of criminal behaviour and its subsequent decline in terms of stimuli in the environment. The question is then posed as to whether the production of adrenaline is biologically or socially dictated.

Altered biological state theories

Altered biological state theories are those that link behavioural changes in the individual with the introduction of an external chemical agent, and these can be divided into the following categories: allergies, diet, alcohol and other drugs.

Allergies and diet

There have been suggested links between irritability and aggression that may lead individuals in some circumstances to commit criminal assault, and allergic reactions to such things as pollen, inhalants, drugs and food. Research on the criminological implications of allergies is ongoing but studies indicate two main reactions in these patients: first, emotional immaturity characterised by temper tantrums, screaming episodes, whining and impatience; second, anti-social behaviour characterised by sulkiness and cruelty.

More recent research has sought to bring together earlier work on blood sugar levels, allergies and other biochemical imbalances and the basic premise of the resulting 'biochemical individuality' theory is that each person has an absolutely unique internal biochemistry. We all vary in our daily need for each of the 40-odd nutrients – minerals, vitamins, carbohydrates, etc. – required to stay alive and healthy. From this idea flows the concept of 'orthomolecular medicine' which proposes that many diseases are preventable and treatable by proper diagnosis, vitamin supplementation and avoidance of substances that would bring on an illness or preclude a cure. Prinz *et al.* (1980) propose that some foods, and in particular certain additives, have effects that may lead to hyperactivity and even criminality. A low level of cholesterol has often been linked with hypoglycaemia, particularly when alcohol use has been involved (see Virkkunen 1987).

At first sight, it might appear strange to link criminal behaviour with vitamin deficiency but there is, however, evidence for an active role for biochemical disturbance in some offences of violence and some quite impressive results have been obtained in the orthomolecular treatment of some mental disorders. For example, Vitamin B3 (niacin) has been used successfully to treat some forms of schizophrenia (see Lesser 1980; Pihl 1982; Raloff 1983); while there is evidence that addiction to both drugs and alcohol may be related to unmet individual biochemical needs.

Substance abuse is usually brought about by the intake of drugs in the widest generic sense. Some of these drugs are legal and freely available, such as alcohol, which is drunk, and glues and lighter fluids that are inhaled. The medical profession prescribes some, such as barbiturates, while others – such as cannabis, amphetamines, LSD, MDA or 'ecstasy', opiates (usually cocaine or heroin) – are only available illegally.

Alcohol, young people and criminality

Alcohol is more significant for criminality than any other drug, not least because it is legal and its extremely common usage makes it readily available. It has, moreover, long been associated with anti-social activity, crimes and criminality. Saunders (1984) calculated that alcohol was a significant factor in about 1,000 arrests per day or over 350,000 a year in the USA. Flanzer (1981) estimated that 80 per cent of all cases of family violence in the USA involved the consumption of alcohol, while De Luca (1981) estimated that almost a third of the cases of violence against children in the home were alcohol related. More general studies have discovered a strong link between alcohol and general levels of violence (Collins 1988; Fagan 1990).

Alcohol and young people are closely linked in the public mind in the contemporary UK although this has not always been the case. In the inter-war period young people aged 18–24 were the lightest drinkers in the adult population and the group most likely to abstain. Nor did alcohol play a significant part in the youth culture that came into existence in the 1950s, this being more likely to involve the coffee bar than the pub. It was not until the 1960s that pubs and drinking became an integral part of the youth scene. By the 1980s, those aged 18–24 years had become the heaviest drinkers in the population and the group least likely to abstain (Institute of Alcohol Studies 2005a).

By the year 2002, hazardous drinking, that is, drinking bringing the risk of physical or psychological harm now or in the future, was most prevalent in teenagers and young adults. Among females, hazardous drinking reached its peak in the age group 16–19, with just under one-third (32 per cent) having a hazardous drinking pattern. Among males, the peak was found in the 20–24 age group, with just under two-thirds (62 per cent) having a hazardous drinking pattern (Office for National Statistics 2001). These changes were, moreover, accompanied by a decline in the age of regular drinking. Thus, nowadays, most young people are drinking regularly – though not necessarily frequently – by the age of 14 or 15. One survey found that more than a quarter of boys aged 9–10 and a third a year older reported drinking alcohol at least once in the previous week, normally at home (Balding and Shelley 1993).

Most surveys suggest that there is a growing trend of drinking for effect and to intoxication. A related aspect is the partial merging of the alcohol and drug scenes in the context of youth culture, with alcohol being one of a range of psychoactive products now available on the recreational drug market. A large survey of teenagers in England, Wales and Scotland found that by the age 15–16 'binge drinking' is common, as is being 'seriously drunk' (Beinart et al. 2002). In this study, binge drinking was defined as consuming five or more alcoholic drinks in a single session. The growth in binge drinking may be regarded as particularly significant as there is evidence that drinking – and especially heavier drinking – in adolescence increases the likelihood of binge drinking continuing through adult life (Jefferis et al. 2005).

Alcohol is associated with a wide range of criminal offences – in addition to drink-driving and drunkenness – in which drinking or excessive consumption defines the offence. Alcohol-related crime has, therefore, become a matter of great public concern. In England and Wales, approximately 70 per cent of crime audits published in 1998 and 1999 identified alcohol as an issue, particularly in relation to public disorder (Home Office 2000).

The term 'alcohol-related crime' normally refers to offences: involving a combination of criminal damage offences, drunk and disorderly and other public disorder offences; involving young males, typically 18–30; and occurring in the entertainment areas of town and city centres. However, a whole range of offences are linked to alcohol and these do not necessarily occur in the context of the night-time economy and in 1997, Jack Straw, the then Shadow Home Secretary, pledged a New Labour government to 'call time' on drunken thugs:

> Every year, there are almost 1.5 million victims of violent attacks committed by people under the influence of drink (excluding domestic violence). Every weekend, people avoid their town and city centres for fear they will be attacked or intimidated by drunken youth.
>
> (Jack Straw, cited in Institute of Alcohol Studies 2005b: 1)

A study conducted for the Home Office in 1990 found that growth in beer consumption was the single most important factor in explaining crimes of violence against the person (Home Office 1990) while research also shows that a high proportion of victims of violent crime are drinking or under the influence of alcohol at the time of their assault, and a minimum of one in five people arrested by police test positive for alcohol (Bennett 2000). An all-party group of MPs investigating alcohol and crime was advised by the British Medical Association that alcohol is a factor in 60–70 per cent of homicides, 75 per cent of stabbings, 70 per cent of beatings and 50 per cent of fights and domestic assaults; the Police Superintendents' Association reported that alcohol is a factor in 50 per cent of all crimes committed; and the National Association of Probation Officers advised that 30 per cent of offenders on probation and 58 per cent of prisoners have severe alcohol problems which is a significant factor in their offence or pattern of offending (All-Party Group on Alcohol Misuse 1995).

Illegal drug use

Drug taking does not have as long an association with criminal behaviour as alcohol consumption. It was only at the beginning of the twentieth century that drugs were labelled as a major social problem and came to be regulated. Drugs are chemicals and once taken alter the chemical balance of the body and brain. This can affect behaviour but the way that it is altered varies according to the type and quantity of the drug taken (see Fishbein and Pease 1990; Pihl and Peterson 1993). The biological effects of cannabis and opiates such as heroin tend to reduce aggressive hostile tendencies, while cocaine and its derivative crack are more closely associated with violence. Interestingly, some see both alcohol and drug misuse as intrinsically wrong and thus in need of punishment; others see them as social and personal problems requiring understanding and treatment. The first solution has generally been applied in the case of (illegal) drugs, while the second has tended to be more acceptable in the case of (legal) alcohol.

In 2001/2, 15 per cent of men and 9 per cent of women aged 16 to 59 in England and Wales said that they had taken an illicit drug in the previous year. Among those aged 16 to 24, 35 per cent of males and 24 per cent of females said they had done so in the previous year. The most commonly used drug by young people was cannabis, which had been used by 33 per cent of young men and 22 per cent of young women during that time period. Ecstasy was the most commonly used class A drug, with higher use among the 16- to 24-year-olds than those aged 25 to 59. In 2001/2, 9 per cent of males and 4 per cent of females aged 16 to 24 had used ecstasy in the previous year. Since 1996 there has been an increase in the use of cocaine among young people, especially among males; in contrast, the use of amphetamines and LSD has declined (Institute of Alcohol Studies 2005a). Drug use has been found to be widespread among school pupils although there has been a decrease in prevalence since 2003. In that year 21 per cent of pupils admitted having taken a drug during the previous year; this figure had decreased to 18 per cent by 2004 (Department of Health 2005).

Breaking the link between drugs and other criminal behaviour has been a key feature of government anti-drug strategies since the mid-1990s (CDCU 1995; UKADCU 2000). Recent studies estimate the cost of drug offences to the criminal justice system as £1.2 billion (Brand and Price 2000) and the social costs of class A drugs have been estimated to be nearly £12 billion (Godfrey *et al.* 2002). Research on offender populations in the UK reveal that acquisitive crime (particularly shoplifting, burglary and fraud) are the primary means of funding drug consumption (Bennett 2000; Coid *et al.* 2000; Edmunds *et al.* 1999). The evidence points to users of heroin and cocaine (particularly crack) as the most likely to be prolific offenders (Bennett 2000; Stewart *et al.* 2000).

The NEW-ADAM research programme has found that those who report using heroin, crack or cocaine commit between five and ten times as many offences as offenders who do not report using drugs. Although users of heroin and cocaine/crack represent only a quarter of offenders, they are responsible for more than half (by value) of acquisitive crime (Bennett *et al.* 2001). Links between problematic drug use and crime are nevertheless complex. Edmunds *et al.* (1999) suggest that experimental drug use can pre-date contact with the criminal justice system and become problematic after extensive criminal activity. For those engaged in crime prior to drug use, their offending behaviour can increase sharply.

Socio-biological theories

Some of the studies reviewed above which propose that certain individuals have been born with a physiological condition which predisposes them to commit crime really do point to biological explanations of criminality, but this appears to be the case with only a tiny minority of offenders. Closer investigation of individual cases suggests that social and environmental background is at least equally as important. Evidence nevertheless suggests that in cases where the biology of the individual has been altered through the introduction of a foreign chemical agent – such as diet, alcohol and/or illegal drugs – behaviour can be substantially changed and involvement in criminal activity may well follow. In recent years, moreover, there has been a concerted attempt to rehabilitate biological explanations by incorporating social and environmental factors into a 'multi-factor' integrated theory approach which explains criminal behaviour (Vold *et al.* 1998). It is thus argued that the presence of certain biological predispositions – and the introduction of foreign chemical agents – may increase the likelihood, but not determine absolutely, that an individual will engage in criminal behaviour. These factors generate criminal behaviours when they interact with psychological and social factors.

Mednick and his colleagues (1977, 1987) propose that all individuals must learn to control natural urges that drive us toward anti-social and criminal behaviour. This bio-social theory acknowledges that the learning process takes place in the context of the family and during the course of interaction with peer groups, but proposes that punishment responses are, however, mediated by the autonomic nervous system. If the reaction is short-lived, the individual is said to have rewarded him or herself, and criminal behaviour is inhibited. A slow physiological recovery from punishment, nevertheless, does little to teach the individual to refrain from undesirable behaviour and it is proposed that offenders are those who experience slow autonomic nervous system responses to stimuli.

Jeffery (1977) argues that individuals are born with particular biological and psychological characteristics that not only may predispose them to, but also may actually cause certain forms of behaviour. This 'nature' is independent of the socialisation process that occurs within the social environment but it is recognised that there is a good deal of interaction between the physical environment and the feedback mechanisms that exist in human biochemical systems. Jeffery observes that it is poor people who are more likely to experience a poor quality diet and be exposed to pollutants with the resulting nutrients and chemicals transformed by the biochemical system into neurochemical compounds within the brain. Poverty thus leads to behavioural differences which occur through the interaction of individual and environment. This argument has been taken up and developed by key 'right realist' criminological theorists.

James Q. Wilson was a major influence on the development of the 'right realist' explanation of criminal behaviour that was so influential in the rehabilitation of the rational actor model of criminal behaviour we encountered in the previous chapter. It is in his work with Richard Herrnstein where he offers a more definitive account of the underlying causes of crime, synthesising both biological and environmental factors in an integrated criminological theory (Wilson and Herrnstein 1985); an amalgam of gender, age, intelligence, body type and personality factors which constitute the individual human being who is projected into a social world where they learn what kind of behaviour is rewarded in what circumstances.

Wilson and Herrnstein (1985) are heavily influenced by the psychological behaviourism of B.F. Skinner – which we will encounter in the next chapter – and propose that individuals learn to respond to situations in accordance with how their behaviour has been rewarded and punished on previous occasions. From this 'operant conditioning' perspective, it is proposed that the environment can be changed to produce the kind of behavioural response most wanted from an individual. Thus, in order to understand the propensity to commit crime it is important to understand the ways in which the environment might operate on individuals, whose constitutional make-up might be different, to produce this response. Within this general learning framework the influence of the family, the school and the wider community is located.

Central to this explanation of offending behaviour is the notion of conscience. Wilson and Herrnstein (1985: 125) support the conjecture made by Eysenck – again to be encountered in the next chapter – that 'conscience is a conditioned reflex' and propose that some people during childhood have so effectively internalised law-abiding behaviour that they could never be tempted to behave otherwise. For others, breaking the law might be dependent upon the particular circumstances of a specific situation, which suggests a less effective internalisation of such rules. For yet others, the failure to appreciate the likely consequences of their actions might lead them into criminal behaviour under any circumstances. In other words, the effectiveness of something termed 'the conscience' may vary in terms of the particular physiological constitution of the individual and the learning environment in which they find themselves.

These three different elements – constitutional factors, the presence and/or absence of positive and negative behavioural reinforcement, alongside the strength of the conscience – provide the framework in which Wilson and Herrnstein seek to explain crime, proposing that long-term trends in the crime statistics can be explained primarily by these factors. First, shifts in the age structure of the population will increase or decrease the proportion of young males in the population who are likely to be temperamentally aggressive and to have short-term horizons. Second, changes in the benefits and cost of crime will change the rate at which crimes occur. Third, broad social and cultural changes in the level and intensity of the investment made by society in terms of families, schools, churches and the mass media will affect the extent to which individuals at risk of becoming involved in offending behaviour are willing to postpone gratification and conform to rules.

Conclusions

This chapter has considered three general categories of biological explanations of youth offending. The first proposes that the young person is born with a physiological component of some kind that in some way predisposes them towards criminal behaviour. The second proposes that behaviour is heavily influenced by the introduction of external agents to the human body such as pollutants, poor diet, alcohol and drugs. The particular combination of individual biological predisposition and external agent is likely to lead to differential outcomes; thus while for some alcohol might fuel aggressive tendencies, others might become more passive than usual. A third category of socio-biological theories takes that argument a stage further and propose that biological predispositions are activated in very different ways in different environmental conditions, often dependent on the socialised upbringing of the young person. From this latter perspective the solution to the problem of young offending is to in some way change the environment of the young person, which is similar to the propositions of the cognitive behaviourist and sociological theories that we will encounter in the next two chapters.

Chapter 7

Psychological explanations of youth offending

Psychological explanations of offending behaviour direct our attention to the mind of the individual and it is here that we encounter notions of the 'criminal mind' or 'personality'. For purist advocates of the psychological variant of the predestined actor model – or psychological positivists – there are patterns of reasoning and behaviour that are specific to offenders and these remain constant regardless of their different social experiences. There are three broad categories of psychological theories of crimes and while the first two groupings, psychodynamic and behavioural learning theories, have firm roots in the predestined actor tradition, the third group, cognitive learning theories, reject much of the positivist tradition and, in their incorporation of notions of creative thinking and, thus, choice are, in many ways, more akin to the rational actor model of criminal behaviour. Each tradition, nevertheless, proposes that the personality is developed during the early formative childhood years of the individual.

Psychodynamic theories

Psychodynamic explanations of crime and criminal behaviour have their origins in the extremely influential work of Sigmund Freud (1856–1939) and his theories about how our personalities develop as an outcome of our intimate relationships – or lack of these – with our parents, and in particular, our mother. His assertion that sexuality is present from birth and has a subsequent course of development is the fundamental basis of psychoanalysis and one that has aroused a great deal of controversy. Freud had originally proposed that it was the experience of sexual abuse in childhood that is the basis of all neurosis, but he subsequently changed his mind: the abuse had not actually taken place but was merely fantasy. It is this notion of the repressed fantasy that is the core tenet of the psychoanalytic tradition.

Within the psychoanalytical model the human personality has three sets of interacting forces. First, there is the *id* or primitive biological drives. Second, there is the *superego* – or conscience – that operates in the unconsciousness but which is comprised of values internalised through the early interactions of the child, in particular those with their parents. Third, there is the *ego* or the conscious personality, which has the important task of balancing the demands of the id against the inhibitions imposed by the superego, as the child responds to external influences (Freud 1927).

Freud himself proposed two different explanations of offending behaviour, with the first viewing certain forms of criminal activity – for example arson, shoplifting and some sexual offences – as essentially reflecting a state of mental disturbance or illness. His theory of psychosexual development proposes a number of complex stages of psychic development that may easily be disrupted, leading to neuroses or severe difficulties in adults. Crucially, a disturbance at one or more of these stages in childhood can lead to criminal behaviour in later life. Of central importance to the psychosexual development of the child is the influence of the parents and the nature of the relationship it has with them. Significantly, many of these influences are unconscious, with neither the child or its parents aware of the impact they are having on each other. This is an important recognition, for, in a sense, it reduces the responsibility of the parents for producing children that become offenders.

Freud's second explanation of criminality proposes that offenders possess a 'weak conscience', the development of which is of fundamental importance in the upbringing of the child. A sense of morality is closely linked to guilt, and those possessing the greatest degree of unconscious 'guilt' are likely to be those with the strictest consciences and the most unlikely to engage in criminal behaviour. Guilt is something that results not from committing crimes, but rather from a deeply embedded feeling that develops in childhood, the outcome of the way in which the parents respond to the transgressions of the child. It is an explanation of criminal behaviour that has led to a proliferation of tests attempting to measure conscience or levels of guilt, with the belief that this would allow a prediction of whether the child would later become an offender.

The Freudian approach is firmly embedded in the predestined actor model of criminal behaviour: unconscious conflicts or tensions determine all actions; the purpose of the conscious (ego) is to resolve these tensions by finding ways of satisfying the basic inner urges by engaging in activities sanctioned by society, such as playing organised sport or involvement in drama or artistic activities. The subsequent Freudian tradition was concerned with elaborating the development of the ego more specifically.

Aichhorn (1925) argued that at birth a child is unaware of – and obviously unaffected by – the norms of society around it but has certain instinctive drives that demand satisfaction. The child is, at that time, in an 'asocial state' and the task is to bring it into a social state, but when the development process is ineffective he or she remains asocial. Thus, if the instinctive drives are not acted out they become suppressed and the child is in a state of 'latent delinquency'. Given outside provocative stimuli, this latent delinquency can, therefore, be translated into actual offending behaviour.

Aichhorn concluded that many of the offenders with whom he had worked had underdeveloped consciences and proposed that this was the outcome of the absence of an intimate attachment with their parents while children. The proposed solution was to rescue such children and place them in a happy environment where they could identify with adults in a way they had previously not experienced and, therefore, develop their superegos. Two further categories of offender were identified: first, there were those with fully developed consciences but who had clearly identified with parents who were themselves criminals; and second, there were those who had been allowed to do whatever they liked by overindulgent parents.

Healy and Bronner (1935) conducted a study of 105 pairs of brothers where one was a persistent offender and the other a non-offender and found that only 19 of the former and 30 of the latter had experienced good-quality family conditions, therefore suggesting that circumstances within a household may be favourable for one child but not the sibling. It was proposed that the latter had not made an emotional attachment to a 'good parent', hence impeding the development of a superego. The researchers also found that siblings exposed to similar unfavourable circumstances might react differently with one becoming an offender while others do not. From this perspective, offenders were considered to be more emotionally disturbed and needed to express their frustrated needs through deviant activities; non-offenders, on the other hand, channelled their frustrated needs into socially accepted activities.

Kate Friedlander (1947, 1949) argued that some children simply develop an anti-social behaviour or a faulty character that leave them prone to deviant behaviour; while Redl and Wineman (1951) similarly argued that some children develop a delinquent ego and a subsequent hostile attitude towards authority because they have not developed a good ego and superego.

John Bowlby (1952) influentially argued, in a study published by the United Nations, that offending behaviour takes place when a child has not enjoyed a close and continuous relationship with its mother during its formative years. He studied 44 juveniles convicted of stealing and referred to the child guidance clinic where he worked and he compared them with a control group of children – matched for age and intelligence – which had been referred but not in connection with offending behaviour. Problematically, no attempt was made to check for the presence of criminal elements in the control group, thus exposing the study to methodological criticism (Morgan 1975). Bowlby found that 17 of those with convictions for stealing had been separated from their mothers for extended periods before the age of five, in contrast to only two of the control group. Fourteen of the convicted group were found to be 'affectionless characters', persons deemed to have difficulty in forming close personal relationships, but none of the controls was thus labelled.

Maternal deprivation theory was to have a major and lasting influence on the training of social workers (Morgan 1975) while other researchers have sought to test it empirically. Their findings have tended to suggest that the separation of a child from its mother is not, in itself, significant in predicting criminal behaviour. Andry (1957) and Grygier (1969) both indicated a need to take account of the roles of both parents. Naess (1959, 1962) found offenders were no more likely to have been separated from their mothers than were non-offenders. Little (1965) found that 80 per cent of a sample of boys who had received custodial sentences had been separated from at least one parent for varying periods but found separations from the father more common. Wootton (1959, 1962) found no evidence that any effects of separation of the child from its mother will be irreversible. She accepts that a small proportion of offenders may be affected in this way but observes a lack of information about the extent of maternal deprivation among the non-offending population. Rutter (1981), in one of the most comprehensive examinations of the maternal deprivation thesis, concludes that the stability of the child/

mother relationship is more important than the absence of breaks and proposes that a small number of substitutes can carry out mothering functions, without adverse effect, provided that such care is of good quality. The crucial issue is considered to be the quality of child-rearing practices, which is considered in the following studies.

Glueck and Glueck (1950) found that the fathers of offenders generally provided lax and inconsistent discipline; the use of physical punishment by both parents was common and the giving of praise rare. Parents of non-offenders used physical punishment more sparingly and were more consistent in their use of discipline. McCord *et al.* (1959) agreed that the consistency of discipline is more important than the degree of strictness; while Bandura and Walters (1959) found that the fathers of aggressive boys are more likely to punish such behaviour in the home while approving of, and even encouraging, it outside.

Hoffman and Saltzstein (1967) identified and categorised three types of child-rearing techniques. First, there is power assertion, which involves the parental use of – or threats to use – physical punishment and/or the withdrawal of material privileges. Second, love withdrawal is where the parent withdraws – or threatens to withdraw – affection from the child, for example, by paying no attention to it. Third, induction entails letting the child know how its actions have affected the parent, thus encouraging a sympathetic or empathetic response. The first technique primarily relies on the instillation of fear, while the other two depend on the fostering of guilt feelings in the child.

Hoffman and Saltzstein offer five explanations for the association to be found between moral development and the use of childrearing techniques. First, an open display of anger and aggression by a parent when disciplining a child increases the dependence of the latter on external control, while dissolving both the anger of the former and the guilt of the latter more rapidly. Second, love withdrawal and induction, and the anxiety associated with them, have a longer-lasting effect so that the development of internal controls are more likely. Third, where love withdrawal is used, the punishment ends when the child confesses or makes reparation, and this is referred to as engaging in a corrective act; while, in the case of physical punishment, there is likely to be a lapse of time between it being carried out and the child performing a corrective act. Fourth, withholding love intensifies the resolve of the child to behave in an approved manner in order to retain love. Fifth, the use of induction is particularly effective in enabling the child to examine and correct the behaviour that has been disapproved of.

Hoffman and Saltzstein conclude that young people who have been raised through the use of love withdrawal or induction techniques develop greater internalised controls and are less likely to engage in offending behaviour. On the other hand, young people raised on the power assertion method depend on the threat of external punishment to control their behaviour and, therefore, will only remain controlled as long as that risk is present, certain and sufficiently intense. It is of course only internal controls that are likely to be ever-present.

A number of studies have gone beyond childrearing practices to assess the relevance of more general features of the family unit in the causation of criminal behaviour. Some of these have suggested that a 'broken home' – where one of the birth parents is not present – may be a factor in the development of offending behaviour. Glueck and Glueck (1950) found that 60 per cent of the offenders came from such a home, compared with only 34 per cent of their control group and in Britain, Burt (1945) and Mannheim (1948) had previously found that a high proportion of offenders came from such homes.

Others perceptively note that the 'broken home' is not a homogenous category and that a range of different factors need to be considered (Bowlby 1952; Mannheim 1948; Tappan 1960). Nye (1958) and Gibbens (1963) thus observed that offending behaviour is more likely to occur among children from intact but unhappy homes. West (1969) echoed the observations of Wootton (1959) about the difficulties of defining a broken home: his study with Farrington (1973) found that about twice as many offenders, compared with controls, came from homes broken by parental separation before the child was ten years old. Comparing children from a home broken by separation with those homes broken by the death of a parent, more children from the former were found to be offenders. Moreover, 20 per cent of the former group became recidivists, whereas none of those from the second group did.

Monahan (1957) suggested that broken homes were found far more among black than white offenders. Chilton and Markle (1972) later found that the rate of family breakdown is in general much higher in the case of black than white families and suggested that this may explain why it is that more black young offenders come from broken homes. Pitts (1986) claimed a link between criminality and homelessness and found that African Caribbean youths tend to become homeless more than their white counterparts.

Two more recent studies conducted in the UK have reported that broken homes and early separation predicted convictions up to age 33 where the separation occurred before age five (Kolvin et al. 1990) and predicted convictions and self-reported offending behaviour (Farrington 1992). Morash and Rucker (1989), nevertheless, found that although it was single-parent families who had children with the highest rates of deviancy, these were also the lowest-income families. Thus, the nature of the problem – broken home, parental supervision, low income – is unclear.

Behavioural learning theories

Behavioural learning theories assume at their most basic level that the behaviours we learn in our childhood formative years are caused, strengthened or weakened by external stimuli in our environment and are thus acquired as an automatic response to environmental stimulus without thought or reflection. They have their origins in the work of Ivan Petrovich Pavlov and B.F. Skinner. Pavlov famously studied the processes involved in very simple, automatic animal behaviours, for example, salivation in the presence of food, finding that responses that occur spontaneously in response to a natural (*unconditioned*) stimulus could be made to happen (*conditioned*) to a stimulus that was previously neutral, for example, a light. If you consistently turn the light on just before feeding the animal, then eventually the animal will salivate when the light comes on, even though no food is present. This conditioning can be undone and if you continue to present the light without the food, eventually the animal will stop salivating. To some extent the conditioning process is specific to the exact stimulus presented but it can also be generalised to other similar stimuli and, for behaviourists, the notion of differential conditioning is the key to understanding how learning works.

B.F. Skinner extended the behaviourist conditioning principle to active learning, where the animal has to do something in order to obtain a reward or avoid punishment. The same principle nevertheless applies: the occurrence of the desired behaviour is increased by positive reinforcement and eventually extinguished by non-reinforcement. Learned behaviours are much more resistant to extinction if the reinforcement has only occasionally been used during learning and the behaviour can be differentially conditioned so that it occurs in response to one stimulus and not another. In a sense all operant conditioning – as this is what this type of learning is called – is differential conditioning, where the animal learns to produce certain behaviours and not others, because only these receive reinforcement.

Operant conditioning – sometimes referred to as instrumental conditioning – is thus a method of learning that occurs through rewards and punishments that become associated with that behaviour. Through operant conditioning, an association is made by the individual child or young person between a particular behaviour and the consequences that arise from their involvement and there are many examples to be observed throughout the social world. Thus, children complete homework to earn a reward from a parent or teacher, or employees finish projects so as to receive praise or promotions. In these examples, the promise or possibility of rewards causes a qualitative increase in behaviour, but operant conditioning can also be used to reduce less desirable activities. For example, a child may be told that they will have privileges withdrawn if they misbehave or talk in class and this it is this potential for punishment that may lead to a decrease in disruptive behaviour.

Hans Eysenck sought to build a general theory of criminal behaviour based on the psychological concept of conditioning although it is not easy to compartmentalise. Eysenck was a behaviourist who considered learned behaviours to be of great significance but primarily considered personality differences to be a product of our individual genetic constitution, and he is predominantly interested in temperament. He thus argues from the biological predestined actor perspective that individuals are genetically endowed with certain learning abilities but these are conditioned by stimuli in the environment. At the same time, he accepts the rational actor model premise that crime can be a natural and rational choice activity where individuals maximise pleasure and minimise pain. Eysenck essentially proposes that people learn the rules and norms of society through the development of a conscience which they acquire through learning the outcomes of what happens when you take part in certain activities in other words, good behaviour is rewarded and bad behaviour is punished.

Eysenck describes three dimensions of personality – *extroversion* (E), *neuroticism* (N) and *psychoticism* (P) – and each takes the form of a continuum that runs from high to low, with scores obtained by the administration of a personality questionnaire. Each of these personality dimensions has distinct characteristics, thus someone with a high E score is outgoing and sociable, optimistic and impulsive; a high N person is anxious, moody and highly sensitive, while those with low scores on these continuums present the very opposite of these traits.

Eysenck (1977) argues that various combinations of different personality dimensions within an individual affects their ability to learn not to offend, and consequently the level of offending in which they engage. Thus, someone with a high E and a high N score, a neurotic extrovert, will not condition well; a low E and N score, a stable introvert, is on the other hand, the most effectively conditioned. Stable extroverts and neurotic introverts come somewhere between the two extremes.

Various researchers subsequently sought to test Eysenck's theory. Little (1963) compared the scores for convicted young offenders on the extroversion and neuroticism dimensions and found that neither appeared to be related to repeat offending. Hoghughi and Forrest (1970) compared scores for neuroticism and extroversion between a sample of convicted youths and a control group with no convictions and found that the former rated higher on the neuroticism scale but were less extroverted than their controls. This is a finding that could nevertheless be explained by the possibility that it is the experience of incarceration itself that could make a young person neurotic. Hans and Sybil Eysenck (1970) tested incarcerated young offenders on all three personality dimensions and followed up this research on their release, finding that two-thirds had been reconvicted and all of these scored significantly higher in relation to extroversion than the others. Allsopp and Feldman (1975) conducted a self-report study and found a significant and positive association between scores for E, N and P levels of anti-social behaviour among girls between 11 and 15 years of age, with the strongest association found in relation to psychoticism. A study of schoolboys conducted the following year reached similar conclusions (Allsopp and Feldman 1976). The association between psychoticism and criminal behaviour has been the subject of very little research, although Smith and Smith (1977) and McEwan (1983) found a positive relationship between psychoticism and repeat offending. The work of Allsopp and Feldman (1975, 1976) and McGurk and McDougall (1981) does, nevertheless, suggest that combinations or clusters of scores for the three dimensions are more important than scores for individual dimensions.

There seems to be considerable uncertainty and ambiguity about the validity and veracity of Eysenck's theory. Farrington (1994) does suggest an identified link between offending and impulsiveness but could find no significant links with personality and hence no evidence of the existence of a 'criminal personality'.

Cognitive learning theories

We have seen that both psychodynamic and behavioural learning theories have clear foundations in the predestined actor model of criminal behaviour but later more sophisticated variants of those traditions became more readily accepting of rational actor model notions of, albeit limited, choice. They nevertheless both remained committed to the central notion of psychological positivism which proposes that there are patterns of reasoning and behaviour specific to offenders that remain constant regardless of their different social experiences. The third psychological tradition – cognitive or social learning theories – have their foundations in a fundamental critique of the predestined actor model and explain human behaviour in terms of a three-way, dynamic reciprocity in which personal factors, environmental influences and behaviour continually interact.

The behavioural learning theorists emphasised the role of environmental stimuli and overt behavioural response, but significantly failed to explain why it is that people attempt to organise, make sense of and often alter the information they learn. Thus, there emerged a growing recognition that mental events – or cognition – could no longer be ignored (Kendler 1985). Cognitive psychologists controversially proposed that by observing the responses made by individuals to different stimuli it is possible to draw inferences about the nature of the internal cognitive processes that produce those responses.

Many of the ideas and assumptions of cognitivism have their origins in the work of the Gestalt psychologists of Germany, Edward Tolman of the USA and Jean Piaget of Switzerland. Gestalt psychologists had emphasised the importance of organisational processes in perception, learning and problem-solving and proposed that individuals were predisposed to organise information in particular ways (Henle 1985). Tolman (1959) had been a prominent learning theorist, at the time of the behavioural movement, but subsequently developed a distinctively cognitive perspective including internal mental phenomena in his perspective of how learning occurs. Piaget (1977) constructed a highly influential model of learning founded on the idea that the developing child builds cognitive structures – mental 'maps', schema or networked concepts – for understanding and responding to physical experiences in their environment. Piaget further asserted that the cognitive structure of a child increases in sophistication with development, moving from a few innate reflexes such as crying and sucking to highly complex mental activities.

B.F. Skinner (1981) had argued, from an operant conditioning perspective, that the person must actively respond if they are to learn, and cognitive behaviourists share that view but nevertheless emphasise mental rather than physical activity. This social learning theory emphasises that behaviour may be reinforced not only through actual rewards and punishments, but also through expectations that are learned by watching what happens to other people. Thus, ultimately the person will make a choice as to what they will learn and how.

An early proponent of the notion that crime is simply a normal learned behaviour was Gabriel Tarde (1843–1904), who argued that criminals are primarily normal people who by accident of birth are brought up in an atmosphere in which they learn crime as a way of life. His 'laws of imitation' were essentially a cognitive theory in which the individual was said to learn ideas through the association with other ideas; and behaviour was said to follow from those ideas, people simply imitate and copy one another in proportion to how much contact they have with each another. These three 'laws of imitation': the law of close contact; the law of imitation of superiors by inferiors; and the law of insertion, sought to describe and explain why people become involved in criminal behaviour (Tarde 1969). First, the law of close contact proposes that individuals in close intimate contact with one another imitate the behaviour of each other. Thus, if a child or young person is regularly in the company of people involved in deviant or criminal behaviour they are more likely to imitate the behaviour of these individuals than they would others with whom they had little association. In this way direct contact with criminal behaviour is said to produce more criminality. Second, the law of imitation of superiors by inferiors proposes that youngsters imitate older individuals, and that crime among young, poor or lower-class people is really their attempt to imitate wealthy, older, high-status people. Certainly, young people, 'hanging out' on the street tend to take their cues and be heavily influenced by older children and young people as we shall see later in this book. Third, the law of insertion proposes that new activities and behaviours are superimposed on old ones and subsequently either reinforce or discourage previous customs. This law refers to the power said to be inherent in newness or novelty where new fashions are said to replace old 'customs'. Thus, for example, illicit drug taking may become popular among a group of young people who had previously favoured alcohol. This group may, nevertheless, find a combination of both substances to be even more pleasurable than when used on their own and this could lead to an increase in both drug and alcohol use. The replacement of the knife by the gun as a weapon of choice among young people has, on the other hand, been cited as an example of where a new criminal custom replaces an older one.

The work of Gabriel Tarde has had a considerable impact on the study of deviance and social control. Social psychologists have proposed that patterns of illicit drug use can have their origins in the observation of parental drug use which begins to have a damaging effect on children as young as two years old. This has been found to be particularly problematic when children imitate the behaviour of parents with drug-related personality problems. Wills *et al.* (1996) found that children whose parents use illicit drugs are more likely to have persistent drug-use problems than the children of non-users, because one is more exposed intimately to the activity than the other. Children and young people nevertheless respond to peer group influences more readily than adults because of the crucial role these relationships play in identity formation. Their greater desire for acceptance and approval from their peers makes them more susceptible to peer influences as they adjust their behaviour and attitudes to conform to those of their contemporaries. Significantly, young people 'commit crimes, as they live their lives, in groups' (Morse 1997a: 108) and this important concept of deviant subcultural groups is discussed in more detail in the following chapter. More indirectly, the desire of children and young people for peer approval could affect the choices that they make, without any direct coercion. Morse (1997b) observes that peers may provide models for behaviour that adolescents believe will assist them in accomplishing their own ends.

Gabriel Tarde also heavily influenced Edwin H. Sutherland, whose later differential association theory has had an understandably significant impact on criminological explanation. Sutherland first used the term 'differential association' to explain interaction patterns, by which offenders were restricted in their physical and social contacts to association with like-minded others, and later proposed that crime is a learned activity much like any other. He argued that it is the frequency and consistency of contacts with patterns of criminality that determine the chance that a person will participate in systematic criminal behaviour (Sutherland 1939). The basic cause of such behaviour is the existence of different cultural groups, with different normative structures, within the same society that have produced a situation of *differential social organisation*.

Sutherland later revised his theory to argue that criminal behaviour occurs when individuals acquire sufficient sentiments in favour of criminality to outweigh their association with non-criminal tendencies. Those associations or contacts that have the greatest impact are those that are frequent, early in point of origin or the most intense. It was not necessary to explain why a person has particular associations because this involved a complex of social interactions and relationships, but he maintained that it was the existence of differential social organisation that exposed people to varied associational ties. Differential association, therefore, remains in contrast to other psychological explanations, in that it retains a dominant sociological argument that the primary groups to which people belong exert the strongest influence on them.

Burgess and Akers (1968) later revised the principles of differential association in the language of operant conditioning and proposed that criminal behaviour can be learned both in non-social situations that are reinforcing and through social interaction in which the behaviour of other persons helps to reinforce that behaviour. Akers (1985) later revised the theory further and focused on four central concepts. First, differential association is considered the most important and refers to the patterns of interactions with others that are the source of social learning and which can be either favourable or unfavourable to offending behaviour. Moreover, the indirect influence of more distant reference groups such as the media is now also recognised and we might want to consider here the contemporary issue of Internet access which can bring like-minded people together from all around the world (Hopkins Burke and Pollock 2004). Second, definitions reflect the meanings that a person applies to their own behaviour, for example, the wider peer group might not define recreational drug use as deviant. Third, differential reinforcement refers to the actual or anticipated consequences of a particular behaviour. Thus, it is proposed that children and young people will do things that they think will result in rewards and avoid activities that they think will result in punishment. Fourth, imitation involves observing what others do but whether a decision is made to imitate that behaviour will be dependent on the characteristics of the person being observed, the actual behaviour the person engages in and the observed consequences of that behaviour for others. If the observed young person – or persons – appears to be 'cool', is engaged in deviant or criminal activities that likewise appear to be 'cool', rewarding and/or pleasurable, it is likely that the behaviour will be imitated.

Akers *et al.* (1979) propose that the learning of criminal behaviour takes place through a specific sequence of events. It starts with the differential association of the individual with others who have favourable definitions of criminal behaviour and they provide a model to be imitated and which is socially reinforced. Thus, primarily differential association, definitions, imitation and social reinforcements explain the initial participation of the individual child or young person in criminal behaviour. After the individual has commenced offending behaviour, differential reinforcements determine whether the person will continue with that behaviour. Akers (1992) argues that the social learning process explains the link between the social structural conditions we will encounter in the following chapter and the behaviour of individuals.

The emergence of learning theories has led to the development of a range of behaviour modification treatment strategies introduced with the intention of changing behaviour. As the above theorists had proposed that behaviour is related both to the setting in which the offence takes place and the consequences of involvement in such activities, strategies were developed to modify both the environment in which the offence took place and the outcomes of the behaviour. Bringing about change through modification of the environment is called stimulus control and is a standard technique in behaviour modification (Martin and Pear 1992). It is most apparent in situational crime prevention where the intention is to reduce offending by either reducing the opportunity to commit an offence or increasing the chances of detection (Hopkins Burke 2005).

Similarly, there is a range of established methods that seek to modify the consequences that follow a given behaviour and such techniques are widely used not just with convicted offenders, but in most mainstream schools as a means of controlling children. This approach has encouraged books on positive parenting, where 'praise is much more potent than criticism or punishment'. Strategies that focus explicitly on overt behaviour are often termed behaviour therapy, although the basic underpinning theory is the same as that which informs behaviour modification. By the 1970s the notion of skills training in the health services was developed and quickly became widespread in the form of assertion, life and social skills training, the latter becoming widely used with a range of offenders (Hollin 1990a).

A number of particular techniques have become associated with more recent cognitive-behavioural practice, including self-instructional training, 'thought stopping', emotional control training and problem-solving training (Sheldon 1995). The rationale under-pinning this approach is that by bringing about change of internal – psychological and/or physiological – states and processes, this covert change will, in turn, mediate change at an overt behavioural level. Changes in overt behaviour will then elicit new patterns of reinforcement from the environment and so maintain behaviour change. These cognitive-behavioural methods have been widely used with young offenders (Hollin 1990b) where social skills training, training in problem-solving and moral reasoning techniques have been popular and have been shown to have some success in reducing offending (McGuire 2000) and provide the rationale for many contemporary youth justice interventions with young offenders and which we will encounter in the third part of this book.

Conclusions

Psychological explanations of crime and criminal behaviour have firm foundations in the predestined actor model of criminal behaviour and it is the implication of both psychodynamic and behaviourist learning traditions that there is such a thing as the criminal mind or personality and that this in some way determines the actions of the individual. The causes are dysfunctional, abnormal emotional adjustment or deviant personality traits formed in early socialisation and childhood development and as a result of these factors the individual is destined to become a criminal. The only way to avoid that destiny is to identify the predisposing condition and provide some form of psychiatric intervention that will in some way ameliorate or preferably remove those factors and enable the individual to become a normal law-abiding citizen.

The more recent cognitive learning approach involves a retreat from the purist predestined actor model approach. First, there is recognition of the links between the psychology of the individual and important predisposing influences or stimuli available in the social environment, but the behavioural learning theorists accept that point. It is the second recognition that is the important one. Offenders now have some degree of choice and they can, therefore, choose whether or not to imitate the behaviours of others. There may be a substantial range of factors influencing their decision and these may suggest to the individual that in particular circumstances – when the opportunity arises – criminal behaviour is a rational choice to make. Thus, we can see here the links between recent cognitive learning theories and contemporary variants of the rational actor model. In short, the active criminal can in favourable circumstances choose to cease offending or alternatively an individual living in circumstances where criminal behaviour is the norm can choose not to take that course of action in the first place. From this perspective, crime is not inevitably destiny.

Chapter 8

Sociological explanations of youth offending

We saw in the previous two chapters that both the biological and psychological variants of the predestined actor model of criminal behaviour locate the primary impulse for criminal behaviour in the individual, whether it is a biological predisposition or criminal personality. We nevertheless found that in both cases the influence of environmental factors is highly significant. Thus, an individual may well have a certain physiological tendencies but these are only likely to be activated in a deviant or criminal fashion when particular environmental conditions are present; moreover, altered biological states, whether these are the product of poor diet, alcohol or drug use, are very likely to be the outcome of social influence. Personalities – whether they be 'criminal' or otherwise – are clearly the creation of social or environmental circumstances and are highly dependent on the nature of the socialisation experiences of the young person, the quantity and quality of parenting and the peer groups encountered in the geographical location in which the young person lives. The sociological variant of the predestined actor model which is considered in this chapter rejects individualist explanations of criminality and examines the environmental factors that are seen as significant in the creation of crime and criminal behaviour. It is a tradition which is very much informed by the increasingly influential social theory of Emile Durkheim and his concerns with the social problems created by rapid social change (see Hopkins Burke 2005).

The social disorganisation thesis

Emile Durkheim and the division of labour in society

Durkheim (1933, originally 1893) argued that earlier forms of pre-modern society were characterised by high levels of mechanical solidarity, and on the other hand, more developed industrial modern societies could be differentiated by an advanced stage of 'organic' solidarity. The former were epitomised by the conformity of the group where there is a likeness and a similarity between individuals who have very much the same experiences of life, attitudes and beliefs which bind them together as close-knit, like-minded communities with shared values but where, conversely, the ability of an individual to develop a sense of personal identity or uniqueness is severely restricted. Thus, such pre-industrial societies had very intense and rigid collective consciences where members held very precise shared ideas of what is right and wrong. There were, nevertheless, individuals who transgressed against the norms of the group and in these cases the law was used as a means to maintain that uniformity. Moreover, repressive and summary punishments were used against individuals and minority groups that transgressed against the collective conscience of the majority. This punishment of dissenters served a useful functional purpose by emphasising their inferiority while at the same time encouraging commitment to the majority viewpoint. Thus, in this sense crime is a normal feature of societies with high levels of mechanical solidarity. Punishment performs a necessary function by reinforcing the moral consensus – or worldview – of the group and any reduction in behaviour defined as criminal would as a necessity lead to other previously non-criminal activities becoming criminalised. Durkheim, takes this argument further and claims that a society with no crime would be abnormal. The imposition of rigorous controls that make crime impossible would seriously restrict the potential for social progress. Individuals who challenge the boundaries of the social consensus are, in fact, functional rebels who are necessary for the healthy development of society (Taylor *et al.* 1973).

Durkheim argues that with greater industrialisation societies develop greater levels of organic solidarity with a more developed division of labour and (sometimes very) different groups that are, nevertheless, dependent on each other. Social solidarity is now less dependent on the maintenance of uniformity between individuals, however, and more on the management of the diverse functions of different groups. A certain degree of uniformity, nevertheless, remains essential or else social cohesion would be impossible. Significantly, for Durkheim, the division of labour is a progressive phenomenon; its emergence does not mean the inevitable collapse of morality, but the manifestation of a new content for the collective conscience. In pre-modern societies dominated by mechanical solidarity the emphasis is on the obligation of the individual to society but with modern organic formations, the focus is increasingly on the obligation of society to the individual. Now to give the maximum possible encouragement to individual rights does not mean that altruism – that is, self-sacrifice for others – will disappear; on the contrary, moral individualism is not unregulated self-interest but the imposition of a set of reciprocal obligations that bring together individuals together into social solidarity (Durkheim 1933, originally 1893). Here lies the essential originality of Durkheim's interpretation of the division of labour.

Adam Smith, the founder of free-market economics, had argued that the specialisation of economic exchange is simply an effect of the growth of wealth and the free play of economic self-interest, but, for Durkheim, the real significance of the division of labour lies in its moral role, for it is a source of restraint which is placed upon otherwise unbridled self-interest and as a result provides the basis of a cohesive society. Durkheim had considered the cohesion of nineteenth-century *laissez-faire* society, with its wholly unregulated markets, its arbitrary inequalities, and its restrictions on social mobility and its 'class' wars, as a dangerous condition. Such imperfect social regulation leads to a variety of different social problems, he argued, including crime.

Durkheim provides a three-fold typology of deviants. The first typology is the biological deviant who is explained by the genetic or psychological malfunctioning we encountered in the previous two chapters, and these can be present in a normal division of labour. The other two typologies are linked to the nature and condition of the social system and are present in an abnormal or forced division of labour. The second typology, the functional rebel, is therefore a 'normal' person who is simply reacting to a pathological society, rebelling against the existing, inappropriate and unfair division of labour and indicating the existence of strains in the social system. For Durkheim, such a person expresses the true 'spontaneous' or 'normal' division of labour as opposed to the artificial 'forced' or 'pathological' one currently in operation (Taylor *et al.* 1973). The third typology, skewed deviants, is those who have been improperly socialised into a disorganised pathological society and are the usual focus of the student of deviance and criminal behaviour.

Durkheim presented two central arguments to explain the growth of crime and criminal behaviour in modern industrial societies with a pathological division of labour. First, such societies encourage a state of unbridled 'egoism' – the notion that individuals should pursue their own rational self-interest without reference to the collective interest of society – and that this is contrary to the maintenance of social solidarity and conformity to the law. Second, the likelihood of inefficient regulation is greater at a time of rapid modernisation, because new forms of control have not evolved sufficiently to replace the older and now less appropriate means of maintaining solidarity. In such a period, society is in a state of normlessness or 'anomie'; a condition characterised by a breakdown in norms and common understandings.

Durkheim notably claimed that without external controls human beings have unlimited needs and it is, therefore, appropriate for society to indicate the extent of acceptable rewards for their endeavours. This all works reasonably well in times of social stability, he argues, but at times of economic upheaval, society is unable to control the aspirations of individuals. Thus, during an economic depression, people are forced to lower their sights, a situation which some will find intolerable and yet when there is an improvement in economic conditions social equilibrium will break down, with uncontrollable aspirations released. Both situations can lead to increased criminality, the first through need, the second through greed. This social disorganisation thesis was later developed by the American structuralist sociologists based at the University of Chicago.

American structuralism

The Chicago School sociologist Ernest Burgess (1928) produced an influential model for understanding the social foundations of crime in complex industrial societies, arguing that as modern cities expand in size, their development is patterned socially and they grow radially in a series of concentric zones or rings. Burgess observed that commercial enterprises were located in the central business district and the most expensive residential areas were in the outer suburbs, away from the bustle of the city centre and the homes of the poor but it was the 'zone in transition' – containing rows of deteriorating tenements and often built in the shadow of ageing factories – that was the centre of academic attention. The outward expansion of the business district led to the constant displacement of residents, and as the least desirable living area, the zone was the focus for the influx of waves of immigrants who were too poor to reside elsewhere. Burgess observed that these social patterns weakened family and communal ties and resulted in 'social disorganisation' and criminal behaviour.

Clifford Shaw and Henry McKay (1972, originally 1931) found that crime levels were highest in the slum neighbourhoods of the zone of transition regardless of which racial or ethnic group resided there and significantly, as these groups moved to other zones, their offending rates correspondingly decreased. It was this observation that led the researchers to conclude that it was the nature of the neighbourhoods – not the nature of the individuals who lived within them – that regulated involvement in crime.

Shaw and McKay emphasised the importance of neighbourhood organisation in allowing or preventing offending behaviour by children and young people. They noted that in more affluent communities, parents fulfilled the needs of their offspring and carefully supervised their activities. In the zone of transition, families and other conventional institutions were strained, if not destroyed, by rapid urban growth, migration and poverty. Left to their own devices, young people in this zone were not subject to the social constraints placed on their contemporaries in the more affluent areas, and were more likely to seek excitement and friends in the streets of the city.

Shaw and McKay concluded that disorganised neighbourhoods help produce and sustain 'criminal traditions' that compete with conventional values and can be 'transmitted down through successive generations of boys, much the same way that language and other social forms are transmitted' (Shaw and McKay 1972: 174). Thus, young people growing up in socially disorganised inner-city slum areas characterised by the existence of a value system that condones criminal behaviour could readily learn these values in their daily interactions with older adolescents.

Shaw and McKay fundamentally argued that offending by children and young people can only be understood by reference to the social context in which young people live. In turn, this context itself is a product of major societal transformations brought about by rapid urbanisation and massive population shifts. Young people born and brought up in the socially disorganised zone of transition are particularly vulnerable to the temptations of crime, as conventional institutions disintegrate around them, they are given little supervision and are free to roam the streets where they are likely to become the next generation of carriers of the criminal tradition in the area.

In short, the US variant of social disorganisation theory called for efforts to reorganise communities with treatment programmes that attempt to reverse the criminal learning of offenders. From this perspective, it is argued that young offenders should be placed in settings where they will receive pro-social reinforcement, for example, through the use of positive peer counselling.

Robert Merton and anomie theory

Durkheim had proposed that human needs or aspirations are 'natural' in an organic society, that is, in the sense that they are socially constructed by reference to other individuals and groups and then a ceiling is placed upon material aspirations by a benign and neutral state. His US successor, Robert Merton, in contrast, argued that needs are usually socially learned, while – and this is the central component of his argument – there are social structural limitations imposed on access to the means to achieve these goals. Merton (1938) distinguished between *cultural goals,* that is, those material possessions, symbols of status, accomplishment and esteem that established norms and values encourage us to aspire to, and are, therefore, socially learned; and *institutionalised means,* that is, the distribution of opportunities to achieve these goals in socially acceptable ways. He observes that it is possible to overemphasise either the goals or the means and the outcome of this situation is social strains, or 'anomie'.

Deviant, especially criminal, behaviour results when cultural goals are accepted, for example, and people would generally like to be materially successful, but where access to the means to achieve that goal is limited by the position of individuals in the social structure. Merton outlined five possible reactions – or adaptations – that can occur when people are not in a position to legitimately attain internalised social goals. First, *conformity* is a largely self-explanatory adaptation whereby people tend to accept both the cultural goals of society and the means of achieving them, even if they find their social ascent to be limited, they still tend not to 'deviate'. Second, *retreatism* is the least common adaptation being those who reject both the dominant social goals and the means of obtaining them and are, therefore, a category of social 'drop-outs'. Third, *ritualism* is where a person adheres to rules for their own sake and takes pleasure and pride in ultra-conformity. Fourth, *rebellious* people are those who not merely reject the dominant norms but also wish to change the existing social system and its goals. Finally, the *innovator* – the usual focus for the student of criminal behaviour – is keen to achieve the standard goals of society, wealth, fame or admiration, but, probably due to blocked opportunities to obtain these by socially approved means, embarks on novel, or innovative, routes.

Many 'innovative' routes exist in complex organic societies, so much so that some innovators may be seen to overlap with 'conformists', for example, the sports, arts and entertainment industries frequently attract, develop and absorb 'innovators', celebrating their novelty in contrast to the conformist or ritualist, and thus providing opportunities for those whose circumstances may frustrate their social ascent through conventionally prescribed and approved routes. In short, the innovator may be seen to overemphasise the goals of achievement over the means. Thus, conventionally regarded success may be achieved by any means that seem appropriate to the innovator, who strives to overcome barriers by adopting any available strategies for attaining their objective and this includes, appreciably, involvement in criminal behaviour. Merton's thesis has attracted criticisms[1] but has remained extremely influential and this is readily apparent in the discussion of deviant subcultures below.

Deviant subculture theories

Deviant subcultural criminological explanations emerged in the USA during the 1940s and 1950s and although there are different variations, all share a common perception that certain social groups have values and attitudes that enable or encourage them to become involved in offending behaviour. Young people come together and engage in activities which may or may not be deviant or criminal because these appear to be 'cool' and the individual can gain 'respect' from their peers by becoming involved.

Albert Cohen (1955) influentially argued that youth offending was prevalent among lower-class males and that the most common variant was the juvenile gang and, moreover, these delinquent subcultures were said to have values in opposition to those of the dominant culture. Emerging in the slums of some of the largest cities in the USA, subcultures were said to have their foundations in class differentials, parental aspirations and school standards. Cohen observes that the family position in the social structure determines the nature of the problems the child will face later in life. They will experience status frustration and strain and adapt into either a 'corner boy', 'college boy', or a 'delinquent boy'. Corner boys were observed to lead a conventional lifestyle and make the most of the situation in which they found themselves, spending most of their time with peers from whom they could receive status and support in group activities. There were few of these boys, nevertheless, and their chances of obtaining material success were limited because their academic and social limitations prevented them from achieving middle-class standards. Delinquent boys, on the other hand, come together to define status with their offending behaviour serving no real purpose, often discarding or destroying what they have stolen, they are a simply a short-term hedonistic subculture. Cohen observes that offending tends to be random and directed at people and property; they often act on impulse, often without any consideration or thought for the future but nevertheless remain loyal to each another and allow no one to control their behaviour. Stealing, in the gang context, serves as a form of achieving peer status within the group, there is no other motive. It is simply 'cool'.

Cohen's work has received both praise and criticism but it certainly provides some answers to questions that had remained unresolved by the earlier anomie theories, and his notion of status deprivation has been usefully adopted and adapted by subsequent researchers. Significantly, he fails to explain why it is that some members of delinquent subcultures eventually become law-abiding even when their social class position is fixed.

Miller (1958) rejected the notion that youth offending has its foundations in working-class opposition to middle-class values and argued that working-class morality has emerged as a response to living in the brutalised conditions of the slums and it was this that generates offending behaviour. He uses the concept of focal concerns – and not values – to describe important aspects of being involved in this working-class subculture. First, there is a concern over trouble: both getting into trouble and staying out of it are very important daily preoccupations which can mean obtaining respect from one's peers or ending up in prison. Second, toughness represents a further commitment to breaking the law and being a problem to others, with machismo and daring emphasised. Third, smartness is the ability to gain some advantage by outsmarting or conning others, with prestige and respect often the reward for those demonstrating such skills. Fourth, excitement is living on the edge and doing dangerous things for 'the buzz' and which are 'cool'. Fifth, fate is of crucial concern to the lower class, with many believing their lives are subject to forces outside of their control. Sixth, autonomy signifies being independent, not relying on others and a rejection of authority. Miller's theory has attracted considerable support but others have noted that he fails to explain why many – if not most – lower-class people actually conform to societal norms.

Cloward and Ohlin (1960) combine strain, differential association and social disorganisation perspectives in their differential opportunity theory and propose that delinquent subcultures flourish among the lower classes, but take different forms, with the means to achieve illegitimate success no more equally distributed than those for legitimate success. They propose the existence of three different types of deviant subculture and argue that the capacity for each to flourish is dependent on the locality in which they develop and the availability of deviant opportunities. First, criminal gangs emerge in those areas where conventional as well as non-conventional values of behaviour are integrated by a close connection of illegitimate and legitimate businesses. It is a type of gang substantially more stable than the following two where older criminals serve as role models, teach the necessary criminal skills and provide available opportunities and a career structure for the younger generation. Second, the conflict or violent gang is a non-stable and non-integrated grouping which exists where there is an absence of a stable criminal organisation and the members of which seek a reputation and respect for toughness and destructive violence. Third, the retreatist gang is equally unsuccessful in the pursuit of illegitimate as legitimate opportunities and is seen to be a double failure, retreating into a world of sex, drugs and alcohol.

Spergel (1964) identified an 'anomie gap' between aspirations, expected occupations and income, finding that the extent of this differed significantly between offenders, non-offenders and different subcultures. He thus rejected Cloward and Ohlin's subculture categories and replaced them with his own three-part typology: first, a racket subculture which is said to develop in areas where organised adult criminality is already in existence and highly visible; second, a theft subculture, involving offences such as burglary, shoplifting, taking and driving away cars, would develop where a criminal subculture was already in existence but not very well established; and third, conflict subcultures, involving gang fighting and the pursuit of 'reputation' where there is limited or no access to either criminal or conventional activities. Drug misuse was found to be common to all subcultures as part of the transition from adolescent delinquent activity to either conventional or fully developed criminal activity among older adolescents and young adults.

These early US deviant subcultural theories have been widely accused of being overly determinist, with offenders seen to be not only different from non-offenders but in some way committed to an alternative 'ethical' code making involvement compulsory. While it is extremely likely that some young people are so strongly socialised into the mores of a particular worldview – or mechanical solidarity – through membership of a particular ethnic group, the upbringing of their parents and the reinforcing influences of neighbourhood groups or gangs, that they do not challenge this heritage in any way, it also likely that many others have less consistent socialisation experiences and have a far more tangential relationship to such deviant behaviour, although they may be at considerable risk of being drawn into a far deeper involvement.

The most comprehensive critique of the highly determinist early deviant subculture tradition is provided by Sykes and Matza (1957), who observe that their criminological predecessors simply failed to explain why it is that most young offenders 'grow out' of their criminality. Their drift theory proposes that juveniles sense a moral obligation to be bound by the law and if that bond remains in place they will remain law-abiding most of the time. It is when that bond is not in place that the young person will drift between involvement in legitimate and illegitimate activities. Most young offenders actually hold values, beliefs and attitudes very similar to those of law-abiding citizens and, indeed, they actually recognise an obligation to be bound by the law, and this being the case the issue remains as to how it is that these young males can justify their involvement in criminality. The answer proposed is that they learn 'techniques' which enable them to 'neutralise' their law-abiding values and attitudes temporarily and thus drift back and forth between legitimate and illegitimate behaviours. Sykes and Matza observe that at times – and this might well be most of the time – such young people participate in conventional activities but nevertheless shun such involvements while engaging in offending behaviour. In such situations the young offender disregards the controlling influences of rules and values and utilises techniques of neutralisation to 'weaken' the hold society has over them. In other words, these techniques act as defence mechanisms that release the young person from the constraints associated with the moral order.

Matza (1964) simply rejects the notion that young offenders maintain a set of values independent from the dominant culture; they actually do appreciate the culturally held goals and expectations of the middle-class but feel that the pursuit of such behavior would be frowned upon by their peers and not considered to be 'cool'. Moreover, such beliefs remain almost unconscious – or 'subterranean' – because delinquents fear expressing these to their peers. It is when the young person reaches a situation where they can admit this appreciation to a close friend that both will simply grow out of offending. Of course some never do this and it is these young people who invariably develop adult criminal careers.

Early British deviant subcultural studies tended to follow the lead of the US theories discussed above. Mays (1954) argued that in some areas, the residents share a number of attitudes and ways of behaving that predispose them to criminality and these attitudes have existed for years and are passed on to newcomers. He found working-class culture to be intentionally criminal; it is just a different socialisation, which, at times, happens to be contrary to the legal rules. Criminal behaviour, in particular adolescent criminal behaviour, is not therefore, a conscious rebellion against middle-class values but arises from an alternative subculture that has been adopted over the years in a random sort of way.

Morris (1957) argued that social deviancy is common among the working classes and that it is the actual characteristics of that class that create the criminality. Forms of anti-social behaviour exist throughout society but the way in which it is expressed differs. Criminal behaviour is largely a working-class expression. The family controls middle-class socialisation, it is very ordered and almost all activities are centred on the home and the family; in contrast, the socialisation of the working-class child tends to be divided between family, peer group and street acquaintances, with the latter likely to have a less ordered and regulated upbringing. The peer group is a much stronger influence from a much earlier age among the working classes and they encounter controls only after they commit a crime and when they are processed by the criminal justice system. The whole ethos of the working class, according to Morris, is oriented towards anti-social and criminal, rather than 'conventional', behaviour.

Downes (1966) conducted a study among young offenders in the East End of London and found that a considerable amount of offending took place but this mostly happened in street-corner groups, rather than organised gangs. Status frustration did not occur to a significant degree among these young males; instead, their typical response to lack of success at school or work was one of 'dissociation', a process of opting out rather than reaction formation. There was an emphasis on leisure activities, not on school or work, with a dominant interest in commercial forms of entertainment rather than youth clubs with their middle-class orientation. Access to leisure pursuits was significantly restricted by a lack of money and youngsters would take part in offending to find excitement and a 'buzz'. Peter Wilmott (1966) also conducted a study of teenagers in the East End of London and reached much the same conclusions as

Miller in the USA, finding that adolescent offending behaviour was simply part of a general lower working-class subculture. Teenagers became involved in petty crime simply for the fun and 'togetherness' of the shared activity experience which again is simply 'cool'.

Parker (1974) conducted a survey of unskilled adolescents in an area of Liverpool with a high rate of youth offending and found a pattern of loosely knit peer groups with criminality a central activity. Young males shared common problems such as unemployment, while leisure opportunities were limited and consequently, some of their number had developed a temporary solution in the form of stealing car radios. The community in which they lived largely condoned this behaviour as long as the victims were from outside the area.

Pryce (1979) studied African-Caribbean youngsters in the St Paul's area of Bristol and found that their parents had arrived in the UK during the 1950s with high aspirations but had been relegated to a cheap labour force and both generations were subject to racism and discrimination which contributed to a pattern of 'endless pressure'. There appeared two types of anomic adaptation to this pressure: one was to be stable, conformist and law-abiding, the other was to adopt an expressive, disreputable rebellious attitude. Younger African-Caribbeans were significantly more likely to adopt the second response.

These earlier British deviant subculture studies are extremely important because they draw our attention to specific historical factors, in particular the level of economic activity, and to the importance of a structural class analysis in helping to explain subcultural youth offending (Hopkins Burke and Sunley 1996, 1998). They also demonstrate that different groups within the working class had identified distinct problems in terms of negative status and had developed their own solutions to their perceived problems.

Studies of deviant youth subcultures conducted in the USA since the late 1960s have predominantly focused on issues of violence, ethnicity and poverty. Wolfgang and Ferracuti (1967) identified a 'subculture of violence' where there was an expectation that the receipt of a trivial insult should be met with violence and the failure to respond in this way was greeted with social censure from the peer group. Curtis (1975) adapted this theory to explain violence among US blacks, arguing that the maintenance of a manly image was essential and individuals who were unable to resolve conflicts verbally were more likely to resort to violence in order to assert their masculinity. Behaviour was seen to be partly a response to social conditions and partly the outcome of the ideas and values absorbed from the subculture of violence.

Recent US research has proposed that poverty is unequivocally the root cause of gangs and the violence they produce. Miller (1958) had argued that lower-class delinquency was a normal response to socio-cultural demands. In his later writings he essentially adopts a 'culture of poverty' view to explain the self-perpetuation of gang life, a view that emphasises the adaptational aspects of the gang to changing socio-economic circumstances (Miller 1990). The most popular recent theory to explain criminal behaviour among poor young people in inner-city USA is, nevertheless, William Julius Wilson's (1987) 'underclass theory' where he argues that groups in socially isolated neighbourhoods have 'few legitimate employment opportunities; while inadequate job information networks and poor schools not only give rise to weak labour force attachment but also raise the likelihood that people will turn to illegal or deviant activities for income' (Wilson 1991: 462).

Wilson has been accused of failing to address the issues of gang formation and explain the development of specific types of gang problems (Hagedorn 1992) but nevertheless, a number of observers assume a close correlation between gangs, gang violence and the development of a socially excluded underclass (Krisberg 1974; Anderson 1990; Taylor 1990). Poverty is central to the underclass thesis and various writers recognise that the absence of economic resources leads to compensatory efforts to achieve some form of economic and successful social adjustment (Williams 1989; Moore 1991; Hopkins Burke 1999a). It is in this context that Spergel (1995: 149) argues that 'a sub-culture arises out of efforts of people to solve social, economic, psychological, developmental, and even political problems', an argument to which we will return later in this chapter.

The concept of deviant subculture was subsequently revised and revitalised by radical neo-Marxist sociologists and criminologists based at the Birmingham Centre for Contemporary Cultural Studies in the UK during the 1970s (see Brake 1985; P. Cohen 1972; S. Cohen 1973; Hebdige 1976, 1979). These researchers observed that youth subcultures arise at particular historical 'moments' as cultural solutions to the same structural economic problems created by rapid social change identified earlier by Durkheim – and Merton in a rather different way – as an anomic condition. The central concern of these studies was to locate the historical and environmental context in which particular youth subcultures arose and the details of 'style' adopted. The focus was on two broad areas: mainstream youth and delinquency and expressive or spectacular youth subcultures.

The two major studies of mainstream youth subcultures are those of Willis (1977) and Corrigan (1979) and both were concerned with the transition from school to work among urban lower working-class adolescent boys. Their 'problem' was found to be an alien or irrelevant education system followed by the prospect of a boring and dead-end job (or, nowadays, training and the benefits queue, see Hopkins Burke 1999) and the 'solution' was a 'culture of resistance' manifested in truancy and petty offending. Spectacular youth subcultures – such as Teddy Boys, Mods, Skinheads and Punks – involve the adoption, by young people of both sexes of a distinctive style of dress and way of using material artefacts combined, usually, with distinctive lifestyles, behaviour patterns and musical preferences. Both variants of subculture invariably involve a contemporary manifestation of parent culture values that have been adapted to the changed socio-economic circumstances in which the group finds itself.

The Birmingham studies represented an important development of the earlier deviant subcultural tradition – which had recognised that deviance often occurs in response to economic or status deprivation – and identified that particular subcultures or status groups have arisen as a response to the economic problems encountered by particular groups. Hopkins Burke and Sunley (1996, 1998), nevertheless, observe that these studies presume a linear development of history where different subcultures arise, coalesce, fade and are replaced as economic circumstances change; for example, the Mods were a product of the upwardly mobile working-classes during the optimistic 1960s (Hebdige 1976; 1979; Brake 1980), whereas the Punks were a product of the 'dole-queue' despondency of the late 1970s (Hebdige 1979; Brake 1980, 1985).

Hopkins Burke and Sunley (1996, 1998) subsequently observed the coexistence of a number of different subcultures and propose these to be an outcome of a fragmented society where different groups of young people have coalesced to create solutions to their specific socio-economic problems. Central to this account is the possibility of choice. The simultaneous existence of different subcultures enables some young people to choose the solution to their problem from the various subcultures available, although that choice will be crucially and significantly constrained by structural factors.

The early deviant subcultural studies – and indeed the work of the Birmingham School – tended to suggest that young people had limited choices, if any, between the subculture available, at a particular time and in their geographical location, and a life of conventionality. This more contemporary – or postmodernist – interpretation of youth subcultures enables us to recognise that individuals, and different groups of young people, not all members of the traditional working class, but in existence concurrently at the same historical moment, have had very different experiences of the radical economic change that has engulfed British society since the late 1970s.

Social control theories

Social control theories are long established, with strong foundations in both the rational actor and predestined actor models of criminal behaviour, and they are fundamentally founded in a conception of human nature which proposes that there are no natural limits on elementary human needs and desires. People will always want and seek further economic reward and it is not therefore necessary to seek motives for engaging in criminal activity. Human beings are born free to break the law and will only refrain from doing so under particular circumstances, and it is these fundamental rational actor model assumptions that provide the foundations of the later social control theories.

Criminological theories under whatever guise usually view conformity to be the natural state of humanity; in other words, criminal behaviour is simply abnormal and it is this orthodox way of thinking about crime that social control theory seeks to challenge. Thus, the central question asked is not the usual, 'why do some people commit crimes?' but rather, 'why do most of us conform?' The unifying factor in the different versions of control theory is the assumption that crime and deviance are only to be expected when social and personal controls are in some way inadequate and fail to restrain the individual from criminal involvement.

Early control theories attached much importance to psychological factors. Reiss (1951) distinguished between the effects of 'personal' and 'social' controls, proposing that the former arise when individuals internalise the norms and rules of non-deviant primary groups to such an extent that they become their own; the latter are founded in the ability of external social groups or institutions to make rules or norms effective. Conformity involves simple acquiescence and does not require the internalisation of rules and norms within the value system of the individual. Reiss proposed that personal controls are far more important in preventing deviance than external social controls.

Nye (1958) sought to locate and identify the factors that encourage conformity in adolescents and focused his attention on the family, which, because of the affectional bonds established between members, were considered to be the most important mechanism of social control. He identified four modes of social control generated by the family. First, direct control is imposed through external forces such as parents, teachers and the police using direct restraint and punishment. Second, individuals themselves in the absence of external regulation exercise internalised control. Third, indirect control is dependent upon the degree of affection that an individual has for conventional significant others. Fourth, control through alternative means of needs satisfaction works by reducing the temptation for individuals to resort to illegitimate means of needs satisfaction. Though independent of each other, these four modes of control were considered mutually reinforcing and to work more effectively together.

Reckless (1967) later sought to explain why it is that despite the various 'push' and 'pull' factors that may tempt individuals into criminal behaviour, most people resist these pressures and remain law-abiding citizens. He argued that a combination of control factors, both internal and external to the individual, serve as insulators or 'containments' but he, nevertheless, attached much more importance to internal factors, arguing that these tend to control the individual irrespective of the extent of external environment change and he identified four key components. First, individuals with a strong and favourable self-concept are better insulated against those 'push' and 'pull' factors that encourage involvement in criminal activity. Second, goal orientation is the extent to which the individual has a clear direction in life oriented towards the achievement of legitimate goals such as educational and occupational success. Third, frustration tolerance is where contemporary society – with its emphasis on individualism and immediate gratification – might generate considerable frustration. Fourth, norm retention is the extent to which individuals accept, internalise and are committed to conventional laws, norms, values and rules and the institutions that represent and uphold these.

Reckless (1967: 476) described the process by which norm retention is undermined, thus making deviance more possible, as one of norm erosion and involves 'alienation from, emancipation from, withdrawal of legitimacy from and neutralisation of formerly internalised ethics, morals, laws and values'. This idea of individuals being able to neutralise formerly internalised norms and values to facilitate deviant or offending behaviour were, of course, a prominent element in the drift theory of David Matza encountered above.

Travis Hirschi (1969) made the most influential contribution to later social control theory and observed that at their simplest level all such theories share the basic assumption that offending behaviour occurs when the bond of an individual to legitimate society is weak or broken, and he identified four elements of this social bond. First, attachment refers to the capacity of individuals to form effective relationships with other people and institutions: in the case of children and young people, with their parents, peers and school. Second, commitment refers to the social investments made by the individual to conventional activities that could be put at risk by engaging in deviant behaviour. Third, involvement refers to the simple reality that a person may be too busy doing conventional things to find time to engage in deviant activities. Fourth, beliefs are a set of impressions and convictions that are in need of constant reinforcement and which are closely connected to the pattern and strength of attachments an individual has with other people and institutions. These four variables, though independent, are also highly interrelated and, it is argued, help to prevent law-breaking activities in most people.

Subsequent research has tended to find that the aspects of the social bond most consistently related to offending behaviour are those of the family and the school (Thomas and Hyman 1978; Thompson *et al.* 1984) and there is substantial evidence that juveniles with strong attachments to their family are less likely to engage in offending behaviour. The evidence on the association between attachment and commitment to the school, particularly poor school performance, not liking school and low educational and occupational aspirations and delinquency, is even stronger (Hopkins Burke 2005).

Hirschi's original formulation of control theory did not escape criticism and he himself acknowledged that it overestimated the significance of involvement in conventional activities and under-estimated the importance of offending friends, and these problems appear to have emanated from the assumption of a natural motivation towards offending behaviour (Box 1981; Downes and Rock 1998). Other critics noted that the theory cannot account for the specific form or content of deviant behaviour; there is thus a failure to consider the underlying structural and historical context in which criminal behaviour takes place and while it clearly considers primary deviance among adolescents, habitual 'secondary deviance' appears to be outside its conceptual remit. Other researchers subsequently sought a solution to these identified defects by integrating control theory with other theoretical perspectives.

Elliot *et al.* (1979) developed a model that sought to expand and synthesise anomie theories, social learning and social control perspectives, and their starting point is the assumption that individuals have different early socialisation experiences which lead to variable degrees of commitment to the conventional social order and these initial social bonds can then be reinforced by positive experiences at school and in the wider community. The structural dimension is most explicit with their analysis of the factors that serve to loosen social bonds such as limited or blocked opportunities, which include economic recession and unemployment.

Stephen Box (1981, 1987) was to integrate control theory with a labelling/conflict perspective and argue that differential policing practices, and institutional biases at different stages of the criminal justice system, all operate in favour of the most advantaged sections of society and very much to the detriment of its less favoured citizens. This is not simply a product of discriminatory decision-making criteria made on the basis of the individual characteristics of the suspect, however, for such outcomes can be a response to structural social problems of which the individual is merely a symbol. Stigma, disadvantage and a sense of injustice engendered by the consequential criminalisation process, particularly when it is perceived as discriminatory, provide further impetus towards criminal behaviour (Box 1981).

Box (1987) later uses his version of social control theory to help us understand how the impact of economic recession – such as that experienced in Britain during the 1980s – could lead to an increase in criminal activity. First, by further reducing legitimate opportunities and increasing relative deprivation, recession produces more 'strain' and, therefore, more individuals with a motive to deviate, particularly among the economically disadvantaged. In such cases, the commitment of the individual to society is undermined because their access to conventional modes of activity has been seriously reduced. Second, by undermining the family and conventional employment prospects, the ability and motivation of an individual to develop an attachment to other human beings, who might introduce a controlling influence in his or her life, is substantially reduced.

John Braithwaite's (1989) theory of 'predatory' crime – that is, crimes involving the victimisation of one party by another – builds upon and integrates elements of control, labelling, strain and subcultural theory and proposes that the way to reduce crime is to have a commitment to 'reintegrative' forms of shaming. Braithwaite makes a crucial distinction between the negative shaming identified by the labelling theorists that we shall encounter below, and which leads to stigmatising and the outcasting of the individual, and that which is reintegrative and ends disapproval with rituals of forgiveness. The latter approach is seen to control crime while the former merely pushes offenders toward criminal subcultures which become increasingly attractive to the stigmatised because they can provide emotional and social support.

Braithwaite observes that participation in these groups can also supply criminal role models, knowledge on how to offend and techniques of 'neutralisation' that taken together can make the choice to engage in crime more attractive, likely and, indeed, rational. Therefore, a high level of stigmatisation in a society is a key factor in stimulating the formation of criminal subcultures. Braithwaite claims that individuals are more susceptible to positive reintegrative shaming when they are enmeshed in multiple relationships of interdependency and it is thus communitarian societies that shame most effectively. It is such societies or cultures – constituted of dense networks of individual interdependencies characterised by mutual help and trust – rather than individualistic societies, that are more capable of delivering the required more potent shaming that is reintegrative. This is a crucial observation and the contemporary philosophy of communitarianism, which has been so influential with New Labour in the UK and the development of the contemporary youth justice system, is discussed in the third part of this book.

Both Box and Braithwaite have sought to rescue the social control theory perspective from its emphasis on the individual, or more accurately family culpability, that had made it so popular with conservative governments both in the UK and the USA since the 1980s. Box has clearly located his radical reformulation of social control theory within the victimised actor model (Box 1981, 1987) but it is the notion of 'reintegrative shaming' developed by Braithwaite that has been influential with New Labour.

Gottfredson and Hirschi (1990) combine rational actor model notions of crime with a predestined actor model theory of criminality in order to produce an inevitably flawed 'general theory of crime' which ambitiously seeks to explain all criminality. Crime is defined as acts of force or fraud undertaken in the pursuit of self-interest, and the authors propose that the vast bulk of criminal acts are trivial and mundane affairs that result in little gain and require little in the way of effort, planning, preparation or skill, and their 'versatility construct' considers crime to be essentially interchangeable. The characteristics of ordinary criminal events, it is argued, are simply inconsistent with notions of specialisation or the 'criminal career'. Since the likelihood of criminal behaviour is also closely linked to the availability of opportunity, the characteristics of situations and the personal properties of individuals will jointly affect the use of force or fraud in the pursuit of self-interest. This central concept of their explanation of criminality – low self-control – is not confined to criminal acts, it is also implicated in many 'analogous' acts, such as promiscuity, alcohol use and smoking where such behaviour is portrayed as the impulsive actions of disorganised individuals seeking quick gratification.

Gottfredson and Hirschi turn to the predestined actor model in order to account for variations in self-control among individuals, and argue that the main cause is 'ineffective parenting'. They propose that failure to instil self-control early in life cannot easily be remedied later, any more than effective control, once established, can be later undone. According to this 'stability postulate', levels of self-control will remain stable throughout the life course and, therefore, by asserting that crime is essentially interchangeable while the propensity to become involved in criminality remains stable throughout the life course, the theory has no need to provide separate explanations for different types of crime, nor for primary or persistent secondary deviation.

Problematically though, even if the proposition that low self-control is a causal factor in some, or even most types of crime is accepted, it is questionable whether we can accept a straightforward association between low self-control and ineffective parenting. Although the literature discussed elsewhere in this book does suggest a relationship between parenting and offending behaviour, this is compromised and complicated when structural factors are considered. For example, while her study of socially deprived families in Birmingham did find that parental supervision was an important factor in determining adolescent offending behaviour, Harriet Wilson (1980: 233–4) warned against the misinterpretation of her findings, arguing that it is the position of the most disadvantaged groups in society, and not the individual, which is in need of significant improvement.

Hirschi (1995) has more recently and influentially argued that policies designed to deter (the rational actor model) or rehabilitate (the predestined actor model) will continue to have little success in reducing criminal behaviour, proposing that effective state policies are those that support and enhance socialisation within the family by improving the quality of childrearing practices with the focus on the form, size and stability of the family unit. Thus, there should always be two parents for every child, no more than three children in a family and the relationships between parents and children strong and durable. Furthermore, it is not young teenage mothers who are a problem that causes offending behaviour in children; it is having a mother without a father. Therefore, effective policies are those that focus not on preventing teenage pregnancies, but on maintaining the involvement of the father in the life of the child. Hirschi proposes that these policy reforms will strengthen family bonds, increase socialisation and create greater self-control in the child that will make it unlikely that they will become involved in criminality.

Victimised actor model theories

The victimised actor model of criminal behaviour is a more recent criminological tradition that proposes – with increasingly radical variants – that the criminal is in some way the victim of an unjust and unequal society; thus, it is the behaviour and activities of the poor and powerless in society that are targeted and criminalised, while the sometimes dubious activities of the rich and powerful are simply ignored, or not even defined as criminal. Table 8.1 summarises the main points of the victimised actor model of criminal behaviour.

Labelling theories

Labelling – or social reaction – theories are the first to be considered and these have unequivocal foundations in the victimised actor model. They were considered a radical new form of criminological explanation during the late 1960s and early 1970s, focusing on social processes, including reactions and counteractions, and came to consider how 'labels' are developed, negotiated, exchanged and applied to people (see Wilkins 1963; Cohen 1972). It is the central proposition of labelling theories that in the case of all social behaviours, it is

Table 8.1 The victimised actor model of criminal behaviour

- The criminal is in some way the victim of an unjust and unequal society.
- The behaviour and activities of the poor and powerless sections of society are targeted and criminalised.
- The dubious activities of the rich and powerful are ignored or not even defined as criminal.
- Neither punishment nor treatment of offenders is proposed but a radical restructuring of society to eradicate or least significantly reduce unequal power relations.

---

the reactions of other people, or an audience, that is the important variable in the ongoing process of action. For example, crashes on the Stock Exchange produce panic as a reaction, and this panic leads to more selling, which amplifies the original panic. Social reaction theorists propose that the same occurs in the case of youth offending. Thus, for example, the influential deviant subculture theorist Albert Cohen (1955), who we encountered above, had emphasised the negative and malicious characteristics of young offender activities and how these engender a strong societal reaction which can lead to young offenders being categorised as abnormal and, therefore, helps the authorities denounce them as unacceptable. The outcome of this reaction formation is the denial of legitimate opportunities for young people labelled as deviant and this in itself encourages them to revert to illegitimate opportunities and thus the cycle is perpetrated.

Societal reaction is, therefore, a significant component in explaining youth offending. Stan Cohen (1972) had instigated a significant interest in the activities of prominent agents of social reaction – especially those in the media – and devised the now almost household term 'moral panic'. His account of how the media amplified the initially rather innocuous mod and rocker 'riots' that occurred at Clacton at Easter 1964 are now well known to students of deviancy and the main points of his account are clear: the media stereotyped and polarised the contending groups (not only mods and rockers, but young people in general and the police) and increased the sensitivity of the participants, therefore, encouraging further delinquent behaviour. This is a famous analysis, but still rather a speculative one which ends with an important note of caution that we still do not know very much about the effects of labels on individuals, although there are reasons to believe that these are complex.

Social reactions have been studied at the micro level and this brings us to the classic work of Howard Becker (1963), who argues that since social groups create rules, they also create deviants or outsiders; in other words, if you have no rules, you have no deviancy. Deviancy is consequently not about the quality of the act itself, but of the social process of recognition and rule enforcement and our attention is directed to the rule-makers and enforcers – the 'moral entrepreneurs' – as much as to deviants. Morality is therefore an enterprise, not just a simple natural social process and our attention is directed to the values of those who have the power to label. This involves a critique of those values because these can no longer be seen as natural or neutral and in this sense, the approach takes the side of the disadvantaged (Becker 1967). The work of Becker is the usual source of radical variants of labelling theory and this work implies there is no need to explain deviance in the first place, that it is simply a very common social activity, a normal one, which only becomes abnormal when it is to so labelled by an outside audience. The application of the label thus confirms the initial diagnosis and becomes a self-fulfilling prophecy launching young people on a deviant career from which they will have increasing difficulty leaving.

Conflict and radical theories

Conflict and radical theories have developed the labelling and social reaction thesis further and sought to explain crime and criminal behaviour in terms of the unequal nature of the socio-political structure of society. Conflict theorists take a pluralist stance and propose that society consists of numerous groups all involved in struggle to promote their interests while the radical variants are invariably informed by various interpretations of Marxist social and economic theory. Despite these differences in emphasis both groups have a common concern with the social struggle for power and authority. There subsequently developed among young radicals in the UK during the early 1970s a concern to restore some dignity to the deviant person and restore meaning to their deviant actions, to regard them as knowing people responding rationally, albeit sometimes rebelliously, to their circumstances. The classic text in this tradition is Taylor *et al. The New Criminology* (1973) which, while drawing heavily on labelling theory, argued that the power to criminalise, make laws and prosecute offenders, or particular groups that are perceived as offenders, is a function of the state.

There are at the current time two variants of the radical criminological tradition: one version, 'left realism', is considered below; the other, critical criminology, is the only version with unequivocal foundations in the victimised actor model. Critical criminologists define criminality in terms of the concept of oppression and observe that some groups in society – the working class, women and ethnic minority groups – are the most likely to suffer oppressive social relations based upon class division, sexism and racism. Criminal behaviour among such groups is seen to be the rational outcome of the interaction between the marginalisation or exclusion from access to mainstream institutions and that of criminalisation by the state authorities. The latter involves a process in which the law, agencies of social control and the media associate crime with particular groups who are subsequently identified and targeted as a threat. Scraton and

Chadwick (1996) argue that this process is used to divert attention from economic and social conditions, particularly at times of acute economic change that could provide the impetus for serious political unrest. Criminalisation can, therefore, be used to justify harsher social control measures that are often taken against economically and politically marginalised groups who have few means of resisting these initiatives.

I have previously used the term 'the schizophrenia of crime' to refer to the apparently contradictory duality of attitude to criminal behaviour that is a significant characteristic of contemporary post-industrial society (Hopkins Burke 2005, 2007). Thus, on the one hand, there is a widespread populist public demand for a rigorous intervention against criminality that has made the 'war against crime' a major political issue and has seen the major political parties seeking to outbid each other for electoral gain with a consequential major expansion in situational crime-prevention strategies epitomised by the ubiquitous existence of closed-circuit television cameras (Hopkins Burke 2004b), a whole raft of crime control legislation that has placed increasing restrictions on our civil liberties and human rights (Hopkins Burke 2004c), and the introduction of rigorous 'zero-tolerance-style' policing interventions (see Hopkins Burke 1998; 2002, 2004a). On the other hand, criminality is observed to be widespread to the virtual point of universality, with many people having committed criminal offences at some stage in their life – not least when they were children and young people – with a great many continuing to do so. There is therefore a considerable moral ambiguity about crime and criminal behaviour in contemporary society which sends out confused measures to many young people, not least because of the widely advertised pleasure of criminality and doing crime which clearly conveys a widely received message that doing crime is 'cool' (Hopkins Burke 2007).

Cultural criminologists have examined the pleasures to be enjoyed from engaging in deviant and criminal activities (Katz 1988; Presdee 2000) and identify the long-established tradition of 'carnival' functions as a playful and pleasurable resistance to authority where those normally excluded from the exercise of power celebrate their anger at this exclusion. Presdee (2000) argues that the outcome of living in a world dominated by scientific rationality and social control has been the fragmentation of organised carnival with its fragments distributed far and wide in acts of transgression and crime and thus, from this perspective, many pleasurable activities such as rave culture, drug taking, body modification, binge-drinking, Internet use, joy riding, and

153

sado-masochist activities contain many elements of the carnivalesque and crime; while the much reported and discussed deviant activity of the past 30 years, football hooliganism, can be conceptualised in this context (Hopkins Burke 2005). From this perspective crime is simply normal, non-pathological and enjoyable.

Left realism

Left realism as a criminological perspective recognises the almost universal pleasures and attractions of involvement in criminality but at the same time accepts that these activities have victims which include – particularly in the case of young offenders – many of the perpetrators themselves, for whom a life of criminality and involvement with the criminal justice system is not going to be a happy one.

Left realism has it origins in the writings of a group of British criminologists, some of whom had been in the forefront of the radical criminology of the 1970s, which emerged in response to four closely interconnected factors. First, there was a reaction to what they perceived to be 'left idealism' (see Young 1994), the extreme positions that their previous associates in the radical/critical criminological tradition had now developed into the critical criminology above. Second, there was a response to the ever-increasing criminal victimisation that was so readily apparent and where poor people were overwhelmingly the victims. Nevertheless, it seems extremely unlikely, that these writers and researchers would have so readily discovered this new reality but for the important impetus provided by the other two factors (Hopkins Burke 2001, 2005). Thus, third, there was the crucial rise to prominence and power of the populist conservatives or the 'new right' and, fourth, the rediscovery by right realist criminologists of the rational actor model of crime and criminal behaviour that was discussed in Chapter 5.

This group of criminologists on the left of the political spectrum – such as Jock Young, John Lea and Roger Matthews – became increasingly worried during the 1980s that the debate on crime control had been successfully appropriated by the political right. The critical criminologists, by denying that working-class crime was a real problem and concentrating instead on 'crimes of the powerful' and the politics of oppression, were ignoring the plight of working-class victims of predatory crime. Moreover, successive electoral defeats of the British Labour Party convinced them that they had allowed the political high ground to be captured by the new populist conservatives with the rediscovered rational actor model gaining increasing favour with the Home Office. Lea and Young (1984) thus observed the need for a 'radical realist' response to the populist conservatives: one which recognised the impact of crime but which at the same time, addressed the context in which it occurred.

For left realists, crime, then, is a real problem that must be addressed. Lea and Young deal with the argument that corporate crime is more important: yes, 'crimes of the powerful' do exist and are to be condemned, but the effects of corporate crime are generally widespread, while those of direct-contact crime are concentrated. Corporate crime may indeed cause financial loss and even death and danger, but the real problem for those living in high-crime areas is posed by predatory offenders in their midst. Left realism thus takes into account the immediate fears that people have and seeks to deal with them.

From a left realist perspective, crime is a real problem for ordinary people that must be taken seriously, and central to their crime control strategy is the proposition that crime requires a comprehensive solution: there must be a 'balance of intervention' against both crime and the causes of crime. For the British New Labour government unquestionably influenced by this criminological discourse, it is an approach to crime and criminal behaviour summarised and popularised by the oft-quoted sound bite of Prime Minister Tony Blair when Shadow Home Secretary, 'tough on crime, tough on the causes of crime'. The first part of that equation proposes that offenders should accept and take responsibility for their actions and is in theoretical accordance with the prescriptions of the rational actor model; the second part proposes a tough stance on the causes of crime by targeting both those individual and structural factors which, in some way, encourage criminality and is thus in accordance with not only the predestined actor model but also – and most appropriately for a socialist political party, however much they might like to disguise that fact – rooted most firmly in the victimised actor model. The theoretical justification for that governmental approach – and it is one that sets it apart from its political opponents and predecessors in government – is offered by the following realist examination of the creation of an apparently criminal 'underclass'.

An analysis of a socially excluded underclass – whose members are overrepresented among the ranks of convicted offenders – when conducted from a left realist perspective requires that we consider theoretical inputs from each of the three models of criminal behaviour.

The structural model of the underclass – incorporating accounts by Dahrendorf (1985), Field (1989), Jordan (1996) and from the USA, William Julius Wilson (1987, 1991) discussed above – is usually associated with the political 'left' and has its theoretical foundations firmly located in both the conflict, radical and critical variants of the victimised actor tradition and the sociological predestined actor model tradition. Primarily various forms of social exclusion, poverty, material deprivation and patterns of inequality are emphasised and it is recognised that entry into and membership of this class are explained by the inadequacy of state-provided welfare services, changes in the labour market and exclusion from full citizenship. The behaviourist or culturalist model, on the other hand – incorporating accounts from James Q. Wilson and Herrnstein (1985) Murray (1990, 1994) and Herrnstein and Murray (1995) – is usually associated with the new political 'right' or populist conservatives and has its theoretical foundations in the rational actor model and the biological variant of the predestined actor model. This model of the underclass came to prominence during the 1980s following the rise in the number of long-term unemployed, the fast-expanding lone parent population, increased welfare dependency and rising crime and disorder and it is argued, from this perspective, that the provision of state welfare erodes individual responsibility by giving people incentives not to work and provide for themselves and their family. Moreover, it is argued that the 'controls' and social bonds that stop individuals and communities from behaving badly, such as stable family backgrounds and in particular positive male role models do not exist for many members of this underclass. Left to their own devices without the controls and rewards of the labour market but provided with basic support by the welfare system, young people are free to develop with other like-minded others a deviant invariably criminal subcultural solution to their socially excluded existence.

Research evidence has shown that non-participation in the labour market fails to contribute, in any simple way, to the creation of a distinctive subculture (Westergaard 1995; Marshall *et al.* 1996; Levitas 1996; Crowther 1998) and people can remain unemployed for many years, surviving on a very limited income while remaining law-abiding citizens. On the other hand, it is important to recognise that there has been a real problem of crime and anti-social behaviour inflicted on some invariably poor working-class communities by gangs of socially excluded, usually young males living in their midst (Campbell 1993; Jordan 1996).

I have proposed elsewhere that a left realist analysis requires the development of a process model of the underclass that both locates the structural preconditions for the emergence of this social grouping while at the same time examining the nature of their behavioural response to their found predicament (Hopkins Burke 1999, 2005) and it is an analysis that provides a theoretical justification for a balanced intervention in their lives. The structural preconditions for the emergence of an underclass were undoubtedly the collapse of the unwritten post-war social contract between governments and the unskilled working class in advanced industrial societies which had been fundamentally founded on the provision of full employment and the safety net of a relatively generous welfare state. With the major economic restructuring that occurred during the late 1970s and throughout the 1980s, non-skilled young people, in particular young males, entering into the labour market became increasingly over-represented among the ranks of the unemployed and at the same time, changes to social security entitlement in 1988 – instigated by the populist conservatives with the conscious intention of eradicating welfare dependency – had meant that 16- and 17-year-olds lost their automatic right to benefits while 18- to 24-year-olds saw a dramatic reduction in the amount of money they could claim. Caroline Adams from the charity Action for Children estimated that this was a contributory reason why 75,000 16- to 17-year-olds at the time had no source of income whatsoever (Hopkins Burke 1998c). In short, the collapse of the economic basis of their existence provides the structural element of a process model of the creation of an underclass (Hopkins Burke 2000).

The behavioural response of this group has its origins in changes to familial living arrangements encouraged by the aforementioned economic upheaval. The ideal type of nuclear family of industrial modernity (Parsons 1951) had been based on a division of labour and interdependency between men and women that had made considerable sense with the former invariably the main breadwinner and the latter the provider of home conditions to support the man and nurture and socialise the next generation. It was a rational arrangement because there were very few – if any – realistic alternatives available to either man or woman but in changed socio-economic circumstances it was a form of social arrangement that was to become less of a rational choice for potential participants. Feminists have observed that, stripped of their role as the breadwinner, 'workless' men now had little to offer women and their children other than the erratic affection, violence and child abuse that had often been present in working-class families (Campbell 1993). Moreover, in a situation where the modernist state was quite understandably prepared to place women and children at the head of the queue for welfare benefits and 'social' housing provision, the former had relinquished their economic dependency on men to become dependent upon an increasingly inadequate welfare state (Field 1989).

Many young men were now stripped of the informal controls of waged employment and family responsibilities that had previously restrained their wilder excesses and which had brought them back into the fold of conforming non-offending by their early 20s. Unskilled and poorly educated, they were now completely superfluous to the long-term requirements of post-industrial society. Unable to obtain legitimate employment opportunities and appearing as unattractive propositions to young women as partners and fathers for their children, many of these young men found themselves 'frozen in a state of persistent adolescence' (Pitts 1996: 260). Moreover, these restricted life chances had significant implications for their involvement in criminal behaviour because the evidence suggests that growing out of crime is simply part of growing up (Rutherford 1992). Pitts (1996: 262) observes that 'stripped of legitimate access to adulthood these young men were trapped in a limbo world somewhere between childhood and adulthood long after the developmental tasks' of adolescence had been completed. Now into their second – or even third – generation of what is a workless underclass in some geographical localities, this widely ostracised grouping has become stereotyped as inherently criminogenic and drug-ridden, with images that are frequently racialised (see Rose 1999; Parenti 2000; Bauman 1998, 2000).

In conclusion, it is important to recognise that the left realist perspective has been extremely influential with the New Labour government elected in 1997. There was a readily identified need for a balanced intervention that tackles both offending behaviour and the social and environmental conditions that support and encourage that behaviour but the outcome would be an attempt to reintegrate back into included society the socially excluded 'underclass' identified above, as part of a major government project – or 'big idea' – that this author has termed 'reintegrative tutelage' and which was introduced in Chapter 4 and which is discussed more fully in the third part of this book. Pitts (2001), nevertheless, observes in this context that while New Labour accounts of the origins of the socially excluded underclass have tended towards the structural with the logical outcome being a challenge to social inequalities and the provision of legitimate life chances for young people, their actual proposed solutions have instead tended to tackle the behavioural/culturalist facets of teenage pregnancy, bad behaviour and welfare dependency. The following part of this book discusses the rise of New Labour, the creation and the working of the contemporary youth justice system in the context of these debates about social exclusion.

Note

1 See Hopkins Burke (2005) for a full discussion.

Part III

The Contemporary Youth Justice System and its Critics

Chapter 9

New Labour and the new youth justice

In the first part of this book we encountered the history of the juvenile justice system from its origins and formation through to the election of a New Labour government in 1997. This third part considers the contemporary youth justice system established in the aftermath of that electoral success. It is, moreover, a significant change in terminology because the new government sought to signify a clear break with what was perceived as the failings of the previous system and had decided to start again from 'year zero' (Warner 1999). This chapter considers the origins of the new system and commences with the emergence of New Labour as an electoral force during the mid-1990s and its commitment to the philosophy of communitarianism.

New Labour and communitarianism

The Labour Party has since its formation in the early twentieth century been the principal left-wing political party of the UK. At the time of writing it is the party of government. Labour won a landslide 179-seat majority in the 1997 general election under the leadership of Tony Blair but this was its first electoral success for nearly a quarter of century and the first time since 1970 that it had exceeded 40 per cent of the popular vote. Its large majority in the House of Commons was slightly reduced to 167 in the 2001 general election and more substantially to 66 in 2005.

The Labour Party has its origins in the trade union movement and socialist political parties of the late nineteenth century and continues to call itself a party of democratic socialism. 'New Labour' is an alternative 'brand name' for the party and one which originated in 1994 as part of the ongoing rightwards shift to the centre of the British political spectrum started under the previous leadership of Neil Kinnock (Labour Party 2006). The term 'Old Labour', nevertheless, continues to be used by commentators to describe the older, more left-wing members of the party, or those with strong trade union connections. The name New Labour originates from a conference slogan first used by the party in 1994 and which was later seen in a draft manifesto published by the party two years later called *New Labour, New Life For Britain* (Labour Party 1996). The term was intended as part of an acknowledged new 'branding' of the party in the eyes of the electorate and coincided with the rewriting of Clause IV of the party constitution and its rejection of its traditional socialist roots epitomised by its commitment to the common ownership of the means of production (Labour Party 2006).

Tony Blair, Gordon Brown, Peter Mandelson and Alastair Campbell are most commonly cited as the creators and architects of New Labour and were among the most prominent advocates of the right-wing shift in European social democracy during the 1990s that came to be known as the Third Way (see Giddens 1998). The use of 'new' echoes slogans widely used in US politics over the years and associated with the Democratic Party, such as *New Deal* (Roosevelt), *New Frontier* (Kennedy), *New Covenant* (Clinton). What brings together the New Democratic politics introduced by Bill Clinton in the USA and those of New Labour in the UK into a new 'third way' entity is the influential philosophy of communitarianism.

Communitarianism emerged in the USA during the 1980s as a response to what its advocates considered to be the limitations of liberal theory and practice but significantly, diverse strands in social, political and moral thought, arising from very different locations on the political spectrum – such as Marxism (Ross 2003) and traditional 'one-nation' conservatism (Scruton 2001) – can be identified within the body of communitarian thought. Its dominant themes are that the individual rights vigorously promoted by traditional liberals need to be balanced with social responsibilities, and moreover, autonomous individual selves do not exist in isolation but are shaped by the values and culture of communities. Communitarians, therefore, propose that unless we redress the balance toward the pole of community our society will continue to become normless, self-centred and driven by special interests and power seeking.

The critique of the one-sided emphasis on individual civil or human rights promoted by liberalism is, therefore, the key defining characteristic of communitarianism. Rights, it is argued, have tended to be asserted without a corresponding sense of how they can be achieved, or for that matter, exactly who will pay for them. 'Rights talk' is thus seen to corrupt political discourse by obstructing genuine discussion and is employed without a corresponding sense of responsibilities (see Emanuel 1991; Glendon 1991; Etzioni 1993 1995).[1]

Communitarians argue that the one-sided emphasis on rights in liberalism is related to its conception of the individual as a 'disembodied self', uprooted from cultural meanings, community attachments, and the life stories that constitute the full identities of real human beings. Dominant liberal theories of justice, as well as much of economic and political theory, presume such a self (see Etzioni 1991). Communitarians shift the balance, arguing that the 'I' is constituted through the 'We' in a dynamic tension. Significantly, this is not an argument for the traditional community with high levels of mechanical solidarity, repressive dominance of the majority or the patriarchal family although some on the conservative fringes do take up that position.[2] Mainstream communitarians are, in fact, critical of community institutions that are authoritarian and restrictive and that cannot bear scrutiny within a larger framework of human rights and equal opportunities. They, therefore, accept the (post)modern condition that we are located in a complex web of pluralistic communities – or organic solidarity – with genuine value conflicts within them and within selves.

Etzioni *et al.* (1991) outline the basic framework of communitarianism, urging that we start with the family and its central role in socialisation and, moreover, they argue that employers should provide maximum support for parents through the creation of work time initiatives such as the provision of crèche facilities and warn against avoidable parental relationship breakdowns in order to put the interests of children first. Communitarians, consequently, demand a revival of moral education in schools at all levels, including the values of tolerance, peaceful resolution of conflict, the superiority of democratic government, hard work and saving. They also propose that government services should be devolved to an appropriate level, with the pursuit of new kinds of public–private partnerships, and the development of national and local service programmes.

Communitarians in the USA consider themselves to be a major social movement similar to that of the progressive movement in the early twentieth century.[3] Their ideas have been very influential and were to filter into the Clinton administration during the 1990s and beyond. In a pamphlet written shortly after he became prime minister of the UK, Tony Blair (1998: 4) demonstrated his communitarian or 'third way' credentials:

> We all depend on collective goods for our independence; and all our lives are enriched – or impoverished – by the communities to which we belong ... A key challenge of progressive politics is to use the state as an enabling force, protecting effective communities and voluntary organisations and encouraging their growth to tackle new needs, in partnership as appropriate.

The most familiar and resonant of the 'abstract slogans' used by Blair in the promotion of the importance of community has been the idea that rights entail responsibilities, and this is taken from the work of Etzioni (1993). In contrast to the traditional liberal idea that members of a society may be simply entitled to unconditional benefits or services, it is proposed that the responsibility to care for each individual should be seen as lying, first and foremost, with the individual themselves. For Blair and his sociological guru Anthony Giddens (1998), community is invoked very deliberately as residing in civil society: in lived social relations, and in 'commonsense' notions of our civic obligations. The 'third way' is presented as avoiding what its proponents see as the full-on atomistic egotistical individualism entailed by the Thatcherite maxim that 'there is no such thing as society', and on the other hand, the traditional social-democratic recourse to a strong state as the tool by which to realise the aims of social justice, most notably that of economic equality. For Blair, 'the grievous 20th century error of the fundamentalist Left was the belief that the state could replace civil society and thereby advance freedom' (Blair 1998: 4). The state has a role to play, he readily accepts, but as a facilitator, rather than a guarantor, of a flourishing community life.

Dissenters have, however, noted that the implementation of the New Labour agenda has seemed, in fact, to take rather a different course. Its character appears rather more authoritarian – and thus, centred more on the usage of the state apparatus to deliver particular outcomes – than is suggested by the rhetorical appeal to the relatively autonomous powers of civil society to deliver progress by itself (see Driver and Martell 1997; Jordan 1998; Clinics 2001). New Labour neo-communitarian credentials can be clearly identified in the

Crime and Disorder Act 1998 and the subsequent establishment of the contemporary youth justice system which is epitomised by the central state control of youth offending teams by a dictatorial Youth Justice Board.

It was argued at the end of Chapter 4 that this distinctive New Labour approach to youth justice can be conceptualised as part of a wider government strategic initiative introduced with the intention of seeking to reintegrate those sections of the population that have become increasingly socially and economically excluded during the past 20 years. We will now consider that neo-communitarian reintegrative tutelage project further.

New Labour and reintegrative tutelage

Two major criminological theoretical influences on New Labour youth justice policy have been left realism and reintegrative shaming, and these were introduced briefly earlier in this book. We have seen that left realism significantly has its origins in the election of the populist conservatives in 1979 and the subsequent response of a group of radical criminologists on the political left who had become worried that the debate on crime control had been lost to the political right. These 'new realists' argued for an approach to crime that recognised both the reality and impact of crime – not least on poor people who were significantly overrepresented among the ranks of its victims – but which also addressed the socio-economic context in which it occurred (Lea and Young 1984). Inasmuch as the 'right realists' – who had provided at least a partial intellectual justification for the new conservative criminal justice perspective – had focused their efforts on targeting the offender in traditional rational actor fashion, 'left realists' with their intellectual foundations in both the predestined and victimised actor traditions emphasised the need for a 'balance of intervention'.

Left realism can be summarised briefly for our purposes here: first, there is recognition of the necessity and desirability of offenders taking responsibility for their actions (rational actor model) and second, it is acknowledged that account must be taken of the circumstances in which the crime took place (predestined actor model). It is an approach that became popularised by the oft-quoted soundbite of Tony Blair – made when he was Shadow Home Secretary in 1994 – 'tough on crime, tough on the causes of crime'.

The second – and less obvious – theoretical contribution to New Labour youth justice policy and a significant criminological contribution to the notion of reintegrative tutelage is provided by the Australian criminologist John Braithwaite (1989), who has developed a theory of 'predatory' crime – crimes involving the victimisation of one party by another – where he argues that the key to crime control is a cultural commitment to shaming in ways that he describes as 'reintegrative'. For our purposes here it will be sufficient to say that Braithwaite offers a radical reinterpretation and reworking of the labelling theory tradition that we encountered in the second part of this book. In brief, labelling theories propose that no behaviour is inherently deviant or criminal but only comes to be considered as such when others confer this label upon the act. Central to this perspective is the notion that being found out and stigmatised, as a consequence of rule-breaking conduct, may cause an individual to become committed to further deviance, often as part of a deviant subculture (Lemert 1951; Becker 1963). Braithwaite argues that Western industrial societies have a long established tradition of negative shaming where young offenders become social outcasts and turn to others sharing their plight for succour and support with the inevitable outcome being the creation of a virtual criminal underclass living outside of the respectable society from which they find themselves excluded.

Braithwaite has turned our attention to another tradition among the aboriginal tribes of Australasia and the industrial society of Japan – or at least the low-crime Japan of the 1980s – where shaming is used in a far more positive fashion. Thus, the notion of reintegrative shaming involves a closely linked two-part strategy for intervening in the life of the offender. First, the offending activities of the individual are shamed, with punishment administered where this is felt appropriate, and this will usually involve some form of reparation to the victim. Second, and this is the crucial element, rituals of reintegration are undertaken where the individual is welcomed back into an inclusive society that values their role and person.

The active involvement of victims of crime in the youth justice process is a key element of the contemporary youth justice system. Actions to achieve these aims are usually called restorative justice and seek to balance the concerns of the victim and the community with the need to reintegrate the young person into society. They also seek to assist the recovery of the victim and enable all parties with a stake in the justice process to participate in it (Marshall 1998) and these have been shown to be effective in reducing re-offending by young people (Sherman and Strang 1997; Nugent *et al.* 1999; Street 2000), especially by violent young people (Strang 2000), and provide greater satisfaction for victims (Wynne and Brown 1998; Umbreit and Roberts 1996; Strang 2001). Compliance with reparation has been found to be generally higher in restorative schemes than through the courts (Marshall 1999).

We have seen previously in this book that it is the purpose of restorative justice to bring together victims, offenders and communities to decide on a response to a particular crime. The intention is to put the needs of the victim at the centre of the criminal justice system and to find positive solutions to crime by encouraging offenders to take responsibility for their actions. Victims may thus request a restorative justice approach to make an offender realise how the crime has affected their life, find out information to help put the crime behind them for example, why it was the offender targeted them, and to openly forgive the offender.

Whereas 'traditional justice' is about punishing offenders for committing offences against the state, restorative justice, on the other hand, is about offenders making amends directly to the people, organisations and the communities they have harmed. The New Labour government supports restorative justice because it gives victims a greater voice in the criminal justice system, allows victims to receive an explanation and more meaningful reparation from offenders, makes offenders accountable by allowing them to take responsibility for their actions and it is intended to build community confidence that offenders are making amends for their wrongdoing.

Perpetrators and victims are brought into contact through, first, direct mediation, where victim, offender, facilitator and possibly supporters for each party meet face to face; second, indirect mediation, where victim and offender communicate through letters passed on by a facilitator; or third, conferencing, which involves supporters for both parties and members of the wider community, and is thus similar to direct mediation, except the process focuses on the family as a support structure for the offender. It is this latter approach that is found to be particularly useful when working with young offenders. There are, however, prominent concerns about the efficacy of restorative justice in practice and we return to this theme later in this book.

It was observed in the first of this book that is this notion of reintegration into the community that enables us to explain the approach to youth justice favoured by the Labour government elected in 1997 and which enables us to distinguish its policies from those of its populist conservative predecessors. It is a distinctive approach that is part of a wider set of government strategies that have sought to reintegrate those sections of the population that have become increasingly socially and economically excluded during the past 30 years.

New Labour youth justice policies can, therefore, be located in the context of a range of other initiatives introduced to tackle the causes of crime and criminality among young people identified in the second part of the book and help to reintegrate the economically and socially excluded into inclusive society.

First, measures were introduced to support families, including assistance for single parents to get off benefits and return to work, to help prevent marriage and family breakdown and to deal with such breakdown, if it was to occur, with the least possible damage to any children.

Second, policies were introduced to help children achieve at school, including: good-quality nursery education for all four-year-olds (and progressively for three-year-olds too); higher school standards, with a particular focus on literacy and numeracy skills in primary schools; steps to tackle truancy and prevent exclusions; the provision of study support out of school hours; and better links between schools and business to help young people make the transition to adult working life.

Third, the provision of opportunities for jobs, training and leisure, through the New Start strategy aimed at re-engaging in education or training youngsters up to 17 who have dropped out of the system; through the welfare-to-work New Deal for unemployed 18–24-year-olds; and through the creation of positive leisure opportunities, including those which involve young people themselves in preventing crime.

Fourth, action to tackle drug misuse with new initiatives in the criminal justice system, innovative projects showing what schools and the wider community can do and through the work of the new UK Anti-Drugs Co-ordinator in putting forward a new strategy aimed at young people (Hopkins Burke 1999 2005).

New Labour neo-communitarianism youth justice only makes sense, however, in the context of other socio-political developments that have occurred during the past two decades. It is to these issues that we now turn our attention and we will start with the concept of the risk society.

The risk society

For most of the twentieth century crime control was dominated by the 'treatment model' prescribed by the predestined actor model of criminal behaviour which we encountered in the second part of this book. This model proposes that criminality is at least partly determined by factors either internal to the individual (physiological or psychological) or by external environmental influences (sociological) and was closely aligned to the powerful and benevolent modernist state which was obliged to intervene in the lives of individual offenders and seek to diagnose and cure their criminal behaviour (Hopkins Burke 2001, 2005). It was the apparent failure of that interventionist modernist project epitomised by chronically high and seemingly ever-increasing crime rates and the corresponding failure of criminal justice intervention which led to new modes of governance.

The outcome has been a new contemporary governmental style organised around economic forms of reasoning which has been reflected criminologically in those contemporary rational actor theories which view crime simply as a matter of opportunity and participation which requires no special predisposition or abnormality. Consequently, there has been a shift in policies from those directed at the individual offender to those directed at 'criminogenic situations' which include – to quote Garland (1999: 19), a major proponent of this viewpoint – 'unsupervised car parks, town squares late at night, deserted neighbourhoods, poorly lit streets, shopping malls, football games, bus stops, subway stations and so on'.

Feeley and Simon (1994) have influentially argued that these changes in styles of governance should be understood as part of a paradigm shift in the criminal process from the 'old penology' with its central concern of identifying the individual criminal for the purpose of ascribing guilt and blame, and the imposition of punishment and treatment; to the to the 'new penology' and concerns with developing techniques for identifying, classifying and managing groups, who are then catalogued in terms of levels of dangerousness based not on individualised suspicion, but on the probability that an individual may be an offender. Feeley and Simon observe that justice is, therefore, becoming 'actuarial', its interventions increasingly based on risk assessment, rather than on the identification of specific criminal behaviour. We are, therefore, it is argued, witnessing an increase in, and the legal sanction of, such actuarial practices as preventive detention, offender profiling and mass surveillance (Norris and Armstrong 1999).

The past 20 years have witnessed an ever-increasing use of surveillance technologies designed to regulate groups as a part of a strategy of managing danger. Strategies include the ubiquitous city-centre surveillance systems referred to above, testing employees for the use of drugs (Gilliom 1993) and the introduction of the blanket DNA testing of entire communities (Nelken and Andrews 1999). The introduction of these new technologies often tends to be justified in terms of their ability to monitor 'risk' groups who pose a serious threat to society; however, once introduced, the concept of dangerousness is broadened to include a much wider range of offenders and suspects (see Pratt 1989).

For some – following the influential Ulric Beck (1992) – these trends are indicative of a broader transition in structural formation from an industrial society towards a risk society. Now, this concept is not intended to imply any increase in the levels of risk in society but rather a social formation which is organised in order to respond to risks. As Anthony Giddens observes, 'it is a society increasingly preoccupied with the future (and also with safety), which generates the notion of risk' (Giddens 1999: 3). Beck (1992: 21) himself defines risk in such a social formation as 'a systematic way of dealing with hazards and insecurities induced and introduced by modernisation itself'.

Human beings have always been subjected to certain levels of risk but modern societies are exposed to a particular type that is the outcome of the modernisation process and this has led to changes in the nature of social organisation. Thus, there are risks such as natural disasters that have always had negative effects on human populations but these are produced by non-human forces; modern risks, in contrast, are the product of human activity. Giddens (1999) refers to these two different categories as external and manufactured risks. Risk society is predominantly concerned with the latter.

Because manufactured risks are the product of human agents there is the potential to assess the level of risk that is being or about to be produced. The outcome is that risks have transformed the very process of modernisation. Thus, with the introduction of human-caused disasters such as Chernobyl (in the Ukraine)[4] and the Love Canal crisis (in New York City)[5] public faith in the modernist project has declined, leaving only variable trust in industry, government and experts (Giddens 1990). The increased critique of modern industrial practices has resulted in a state of reflexive modernisation with widespread consideration given to issues of sustainability and the precautionary principle that focuses on preventative measures to reduce risk levels. Contemporary debates about global warming and the future of the planet should be seen in the context of debates about the risk society.

Social relations have changed significantly with the introduction of manufactured risks and reflexive modernisation, with risks, much like wealth, distributed unevenly in a population and this, differentially, influences the quality of life. People will nevertheless occupy social risk positions that they achieve through aversion strategies, which differs from wealth positions which are gained through accumulation. Beck (1992) proposes that widespread risks contain a 'boomerang effect' in that individual producers of risk will at the same time be exposed to them, which suggests, for example, that wealthy individuals whose capital is largely responsible for creating pollution will suffer when, for example, contaminants seep into the water supply. This argument might appear to be oversimplified, as wealthy people may have the ability to mitigate risk more easily but the argument, nevertheless, is that the distribution of the risk originates from knowledge as opposed to wealth.

Ericson and Haggerty (1997) accordingly argue that in the sphere of criminal justice we are witnessing a transformation of legal forms and policing strategies that reflect the transition to a risk society. Policing has become increasingly proactive rather than reactive and, given that risk assessment is probabilistic rather than determinist, it requires the assignment of individuals and events to classificatory schemes which provide differentiated assessment of risk and calls for management strategies. Offenders are now classified as 'prolific' rather than merely opportunistic and having been designated as such, the individual becomes a candidate for targeting by more intensive forms of surveillance. The emphasis on risk makes everyone a legitimate target for surveillance and – as Norris and Armstrong (1999: 25) pithily observe – 'everyone is assumed guilty until the risk profile assumes otherwise'.

Significantly, many of the programmes of practical action which flow from strategies of 'risk management' are increasingly addressed not by central state agencies such as the police, but to quote Garland (1996: 451), 'beyond the state apparatus, to the organisations, institutions and individuals in civil society' (see also O'Malley 1992; Fyfe 1995). Thus, following the demise of the interventionist welfare state that had been the cornerstone of high modernity (Hopkins Burke 1999), there was to be an emphasis on individuals managing their own risk and this was to find converts from all parts of the political spectrum (Barry et al. 1996).

Pat O'Malley (1992) observes, therefore, the emergence of a new form of 'prudentialism' where insurance against future risks becomes a private obligation of the active citizen. Responsibilisation strategies are also designed to offload the responsibility for risk management from central government on to the local state and non-state agencies, hence the increasing emphasis on public/private partnerships, inter-agency co-operation, intergovernmental forums and the rapid growth of non-elected government agencies. The composition of such networks allows the state to 'govern at a distance' – to utilise the norms and control strategies of those formerly autonomous institutions identified by Foucault (1971, 1976) – while leaving, to quote Garland (1996: 454), 'the centralised state machine more powerful than before, with an extended capacity for action and influence'.

This author has previously directed our attention not just to the increasing pervasiveness of policing in its various disguises in society but also significantly to our own contribution in the legitimisation of this state of affairs (Hopkins Burke 2004) and this neo-Foucauldian left-realist variation on the carceral surveillance society, which was outlined in Chapter 2, proposes that in a complex, fragmented, dangerous risk society it is we the general public – regardless of class location, gender or ethnic origin – that have a material interest in the development of that surveillance matrix.

Developments in the contemporary youth justice system reflect these wider societal trends. Social policy, thus, focuses on children 'at risk' and the management of that risk pervades every sphere of activity within the system. The commencement of intervention itself is regulated through a detailed assessment of risk through the Asset profile form, which contains a scoring system that predicts the likelihood of offending and will determine the level of intervention and surveillance the young person will experience (Youth Justice Board 2002). Moreover, the widespread introduction of mechanisms for risk management coupled with the emphasis on interventions to change individual behaviour are a significant contrast to previous approaches such as the emphasis on system management and diversion in the late 1980s and early 1990s, or earlier approaches such as intermediate treatment that characterised the previous orthodoxy of the treatment model.

Most critics of the risk analysis criminal justice model of intervention observe this to be indicative of a contemporary social policy which focuses on the shortcomings of the individual while ignoring significant structural factors such as poverty and unemployment (Goldson and Muncie 2006). It is, moreover, argued that this preoccupation with risk has displaced welfare considerations and 'need' and provides an overly confident sense of being able to successfully tackle something as significantly complex as the offending behaviour of young people (Smith 2006).

Three further closely linked influences on the development of the contemporary youth justice system can be identified: the new public management, quality assurance and the audit society, and these all have their origins in the widespread notion that previously the public sector had been poorly managed and was at the time a bottomless conduit of resources while lacking any proper accountability to the public for how this was spent. With the rise of the populist conservatism we encountered in Chapter 4, that state of affairs was to be increasingly challenged in the UK.

The new public management, quality assurance and the audit society

It could be argued that the most important development in the public sector during the past 30 years has been the increasing encroachment of the new public management (NPM), which has involved the transfer of business and market principles and management techniques from the private into the public sector. NPM is founded on a neo-liberal understanding of the state and economy epitomised by the regimes of Margaret Thatcher in the UK ('Thatcherism') and Ronald Reagan in the USA ('Reaganomics') where the goal has been a slimmed-down, minimal state, in which any public activity is significantly reduced and, if undertaken at all, exercised according to business principles of efficiency. NPM is based on the understanding that all human behaviour is motivated by self-interest and, specifically, profit maximisation and is popularly denoted by concepts such as project management, flat hierarchies, customer orientation, abolition of the career civil service, depoliticisation, total quality management, and the contracting-out of services, all in the name of market-oriented efficiency (Manning 2005). Cost-effective, efficient private-sector style management techniques have become increasingly fashionable in the UK and are closely linked to notions of the audit society.

Complex and differentiated contemporary economies require large numbers of managers whose economic function is essentially the co-ordination of the activities of specialised workers but the nature of managerialism appears to vary between countries according to the dominant disciplinary background of managers. Charlton (1999) observes that in Germany engineers form the most dominant school of managers and, therefore, engineering concepts dominate managerial ideologies. In the UK the dominant style of managerialism is derived from accountancy because managerial consultancy is dominated by the big accountancy firms and consequently audit-derived concepts and technologies dominate managerialism. The concepts of 'accountability' and 'quality' are, therefore, representative of UK managerial discourse.

The current managerial use of 'quality' was developed and adapted to the needs of managerialism during the last two decades of the twentieth century and what has emerged is a generic, audit-based version of quality control usually termed 'quality assurance' (QA) and this has transformed 'quality' into an abstract requirement for a particular kind of regulatory system. Quality assurance now refers to auditable systems, not guaranteed excellence, while the current era has been described as the audit society because corporate life is increasingly dominated by these accountancy-derived concepts and technologies (Power 1997, 1998). Accountability is – as its name implies – one of these concepts and the desirability of 'increased accountability' has become ubiquitous in political, managerial and even journalistic discourse.

Charlton (1999) observes that accountability is, therefore, assumed in common discourse to be an intrinsically desirable goal. Nobody has ever argued that one can have 'too much' accountability and the demand is always for more. Accountability in its technical sense has, however, almost the opposite meaning to those democratic, egalitarian, radical and 'empowering' values that are associated with the term in general usage. Charlton thus argues that the drive for increased accountability operates as merely an excuse to justify further managerial control with behaviour becoming labelled as unaccountable (hence unacceptable) simply because it is not subject to managerial control, and this is taken (by managers and politicians who wish to control this behaviour) to imply a need to introduce audit systems. Audit systems can be established to advance the interests of those who have introduced them with autonomy re-packaged as irresponsibility while the subordination of employees and hierarchical control mechanisms is reiterated in terms of 'increased accountability'.

Charlton (2001) observes, moreover, that quality assurance (QA) is a technical managerial term for that type of auditing which is concentrated upon systems and processes rather than outcomes. It is built on the assumption that any properly constituted organisation should be based around a system of auditing systems and processes. In other words, with the introduction of QA only those activities and systems which are transparent to auditing – and thus amenable to comprehensive and self-consistent documentation – are considered to be appropriate. It is the existence of such documentation that renders all significant organisational activities visible to external gaze.

Since the rise of the 'audit society' and the dominance of managerial discourse over practice, for an organisation to be 'opaque' to auditing, to include significant activities that are not documented, is regarded as intrinsically deficient and probably dishonest (Power 1997). Yet, although transparency has become a term of approval among managers and politicians, it is merely a technical term that refers to auditability and, therefore, does not carry any necessary implications of responsibility to the public, or of excellent or desirable practice, especially when auditing is implemented and evaluated by government officials.

The conflation of 'transparency' with probity has arisen because modern managers equate a properly constituted organisation with a fully auditable organisation and this equation is endorsed because, in the accountancy-dominated world of UK managerialism, managers exert control by means of auditing. Transparent organisations are auditable, and auditable organisations are manageable and vice versa. By its concentrations upon systems and procedures, QA provides a mechanism for quantifying almost any aspect of organisational performance that can be given an operational definition – 'quality', 'excellence', 'equity', 'access' or whatever the current terminology happens to be. Any aspects of measured organisational performance may be attached to these terms with no more justification than plausibility, then these can be quantified 'objectively' and judged against pre-established 'performance' criteria. The magic of QA is that what was unmeasurable has been rendered measurable – so long as one does not inquire too carefully into what words like 'quality' actually mean in operational terms.

Stephenson *et al.* (2007) observe, in this context, that confidence in the traditional authority of independent professionals wielding invariably unaccountable discretionary power has declined in the public sector and this has been replaced with a dependency on audit and inspection systems. This transformation is nowhere more apparent than in the contemporary youth justice system, where the term 'practitioner' has become the orthodox terminology rather than the previously widely used term 'professional'. The challenge to professionalism by the new public management has, however, not escaped criticism from those who consider these changes in emphasis to reflect a dehumanisation of youth justice with the sole purpose of delivering a cost-effective 'product' (Muncie 2004), the 'zombification of youth justice professionals' (Pitts 2001a) and the replacement of the principled 'systems management of the 1980s with a technocratic management with no principles or independent rationale' (Smith 2003: 3). Stephenson *et al.* (2007) respond to these criticisms with the observation that unsupervised professional autonomy may obscure vested interests, problematic perspectives and indeed incompetence. There is, moreover, no necessary conflict between the observation of the rights of children and a managerialist and audit culture. The quality assurance framework for measuring the effectiveness of the contemporary youth justice system, whereby practitioners audit their own performance within a framework of evidence-based practice, is introduced below. We will first consider the impact of the independent public-sector auditing body on the development of that system.

The Audit Commission and the youth justice system

The Audit Commission is an independent body responsible for ensuring that public money is used economically, efficiently and effectively. Its current strategic plan presents five strategic objectives which clearly delineate its central role in the public sector audit society:

- to raise standards of financial management and financial reporting in the public sector;
- to challenge public bodies to deliver better value for money;
- to encourage continual improvement in public services so they meet the changing needs of diverse communities and provide fair access for all;
- to promote high standards of governance and accountability;
- to stimulate significant improvement in the quality of data and the use of information by decision-makers. (Audit Commission 2006)

The Audit Commission (1996) report *Misspent Youth: Young People and Crime* influentially examined – and was highly critical of – what it perceived to be an expensive and inefficient juvenile justice system in place at the time.

First, it found that crime committed by young people was a significant problem that had impacted, in particular, on some poor disadvantaged neighbourhoods. Of known offenders, 26 per cent were found to be aged under 18, 40 per cent of offences were concentrated in 10 per cent of geographical areas and the total cost of crime committed by young offenders in terms of public services was £1 billion per annum.

Second, it was proposed that resources could have been better used. The youth court process took four months, on average, from arrest to sentence; the whole process cost around £2,500 for each young person sentenced; half the proceedings commenced were discontinued, dismissed or ended in a discharge; the many different agencies involved did not always agree on the main objectives to be achieved; and the monitoring of reoffending after the imposition of sentences was rare.

Third, proposals were made for improving the youth justice process in the short term. Thus, it was proposed that the court process should be accelerated and the time from arrest to sentence monitored; persistent offenders on community sentences should and could be more intensively supervised; 'caution plus' programmes, compensating victims and addressing offending behaviour were identified as alternatives to the court process; and it was observed that the impact on reoffending of different interventions needed to be monitored regularly.

Fourth, it was recognised that prevention is better than cure and offending by young people at the greatest risk of involvement could be reduced by targeting, piloting and evaluation, with assistance to be given with parenting skills; structured education for under-5s introduced; support given for teachers dealing with badly behaved pupils; and the provision of positive leisure opportunities.

Fifth, it was proposed that all agencies involved should work together more effectively. All services for children and young people should share information and target areas at the greatest risk, while local residents in those areas should be consulted.

Sixth, it was proposed that central government could provide important assistance. Local authorities should be given a duty to lead in developing multi-agency work, the resources released from court processes could fund local services that reduce offending and all agencies should contribute to monitoring and evaluating preventive programmes.

In summary, the Audit Commission (1996) identified a need for a more effective youth justice system that prevented and reduced youth offending and provided considerably more value for money than the system in place at the time. Central to the new cost-effective, efficient system would be the concept of evidence-based practice.

Effective and evidence-based practice, the human services and youth justice

Stephenson *et al.* (2007) observe that the general public might reasonably assume that the actions of practitioners in the human services are determined largely by the most up-to-date research findings. Yet they observe that this has often not been the case and studies across most disciplines indicate a variety of reasons why many practitioners only make a relatively limited use of research findings in their day-to-day decision-making. It is noted that more significant influences on practice are knowledge gained during primary training, prejudice and opinion, the outcomes of previous cases, fads and fashions and the advice of senior and not-so-senior colleagues who 'have seen it all' (Trinder and Reynolds 2000). Three possible explanations are offered for why this has been case. First, much of the available research is said to lack methodologies rigorous enough or appropriately consistent to be applied with any degree of confidence. Second, the excessive volume of available research, irrespective of its methodological merits, can often overwhelm practitioners. Third, many practitioners simply lack the appraisal skills to assess the methodologies employed and the overall quality of research. Thus, in the arena of social work, the human services and youth justice, interventions were for a long time based upon practice wisdom and intuition rather than proven research.

Evidence-based practice has emerged during the past decade as a contemporary approach to work in the human services and allows the articulation of a proven basis for interventions and assessments by encouraging practitioners to continuously and consistently challenge their practice and support accountability aspects of such work. This approach enables workers to employ practice interventions that have more informed outcomes, engage clients more effectively in the decision-making process and develop greater professional and personal authority.

The concept of evidence-based practice should, therefore, be seen as a response to concerns that professional practice is not always based on the 'best evidence' or is minimally informed by research knowledge (Carew 1979; Osmond and Darlington 2000; Rosen 1994). As such, it is proposed that it can assist practitioners to identify, call upon and utilise the 'best' research in their daily practice. Moreover, while it discourages guess-work, intuition, unsystematic thinking, uncritical and unreflective practice and heightens the likelihood of critically aware, informed, independent and systematic practitioners who are continually updating and expanding their knowledge bases, it is an approach that seeks to combine the expertise and experience of practitioners with the current 'best' evidence on practice topics and issues. Professional judgement is, therefore, not devalued or substituted but is extended and empowered by external sources of evidence (MacDonald 1998) and this, it is argued, can lead to practices with clients that are helpful, effective and informed (Osmond and Darlington 2000).

Wilcox (2003) observes, however, that an evidence-based approach does not necessarily imply an evidence-led one, as there are other influences and constraints on policy-makers and these include public opinion, the Treasury, European and international law and interest groups. Moreover, some propose that policy should actually be led by values and not research evidence and, indeed, it has been observed that the latter is more likely to influence policy if the findings are relatively uncontroversial, the implied changes fall within the existing capabilities and resources of the programme, or the policy is in crisis and no other options are available (Nutley *et al.* 2000). In short, evidence-based practice does not mean that all research is taken into account when developing a policy or stratagem, but merely that the evidence which is selected is compatible with the worldview of the government or organisation. Goldson and Muncie (2006) observe that this selective use of evidence by policy-makers has led to a gap between research findings and policy formation and practice development and, moreover, this situation can be compounded by a lack of methodological rigour of some evaluations (Bottoms 2005).

Evidence-based practice in criminal justice has been closely linked with the 'what works' agenda, which has its origins in the title of the influential article written by Robert Martinson (1974) and introduced earlier in this book, which had concluded that, on the basis of then existing research, there was no clear pattern to indicate the effectiveness of any particular method of treatment. The conclusion was contested and Martinson acknowledged that the poor design quality of many research programmes might preclude the detection of any positive outcome but even so, it is only in recent years that a consensus has developed among some academics that some approaches to working with young people who offend appear to be capable of having an impact on preventing offending.

Stephenson *et al.* (2007) observe that in order for services to address the question of 'what works?' and reflect this in their day-to-day practice, they require access to sound critical knowledge and information about the impact of current policies and practice, an evidence-led approach to planning provision and an allied training strategy. These issues apply in youth justice services, in particular the need for specialist training for practitioners and managers in identifying 'what works?' The effective practice agenda challenges everyone involved in the contemporary youth justice system to make its provision and outcomes more transparent and to establish the role of knowledge in the application of youth justice policies. There are, however, significant criticisms of the application of the 'what works' approach to the system, with Bateman and Pitts (2005) arguing that – regardless of claims to the value-free, objective application of rigorous research findings to youth justice interventions – the reality is a distortion and selectivity of research findings, the deskilling and wasting of practitioner creativity and justifications that simply fail to reduce offending behaviour.

The increasing emphasis placed on 'value for money', 'effectiveness' and best value by successive governments influenced by the new public management and audit society agenda has, however, clearly encouraged youth justice agencies to focus far more clearly on the evidence of effectiveness in these services. Meta-analysis, a statistical tool which facilitates the aggregation of results from different studies, has also been used since the mid-1980s to review a large number of research programmes which, in combination, has confirmed a positive overall effect. Clear trends have been detected concerning the components of programmes with higher or lower levels of effectiveness in reducing offending. The term 'what works?', therefore, refers to that body of research knowledge and the principles deriving from it. Meta-analysis reviews do not suggest that there is any single, outstanding approach that is by itself guaranteed to work as a means of reducing reoffending but these studies have, nevertheless, helped recover confidence in official circles that there is promising evidence of social interventions which can have a direct and positive effect on people who offend and on their behaviour (see, for example, Lipsey 1992; Lipsey and Wilson 1998; Trotter 1999; McGuire 2000; Andrew *et al.* 2001). Criticisms of meta-analysis tend to fall into two categories. Thus, some observe that meta-analysis obscures important qualitative information by 'averaging' simple numerical representations across studies, while others argue that research is best reviewed by a reflective expert (Kulik and Kulik 1989).

The Youth Justice Board (YJB), which has overseen the development and introduction of the contemporary youth justice system, has identified effective practice as a key element in developing and improving youth justice services and is committed to identifying and promoting such practice throughout the system to ensure that work with young people is as effective as possible and based on best practice and research evidence. It has, therefore, introduced the *Key Elements of Effective Practice* (KEEPs) documents, which describe the features of effective services and support the identification of staff learning and development needs. The KEEPs also provide the foundations of a simple quality assurance system that has been implemented in all youth justice services. These describe effective practice as currently defined and are informed by the latest research, national standards and existing legislation. As new research becomes available or as legislation or national standards change, the YJB revises and reissues the documents to reflect changes in the youth justice system.

The work of the contemporary youth justice system and its commitment to effective practice is examined in Chapter 11. The following chapter discusses the introduction of that system and the concerns of academics and practitioners at the outset and in the aftermath of its establishment.

Notes

1 Communitarians nevertheless promote the preservation of traditional liberal rights and their extension in non-democratic regimes or those that practice discrimination, but propose that these rights need to be located in a more balanced framework.

2 See Hughes (1998) for an overview of the different variants of communitarianism.

3 Progressivism was the reform movement that ran from the late nineteenth century through the first decades of the twentieth century, during which leading intellectuals and social reformers in the USA sought to address the economic, political and cultural questions that had arisen in the context of the rapid changes brought with the Industrial Revolution and the growth of modern capitalism in America. The progressives believed that these changes marked the end of the old order and required the creation of a new order appropriate for the new industrial age.

4 The Chernobyl disaster was an accident at the Chernobyl Nuclear Power Plant on 26 April 1986, consisting of an explosion at the plant and subsequent radioactive contamination of the surrounding geographic area (see: Davidson 2006).

5 Love Canal is a neighbourhood in Niagara Falls, New York, the site of the worst environmental disaster involving chemical wastes in the history of the USA (see: Mazur 1998).

Chapter 10

The contemporary youth justice system

In the last chapter we considered the origins and foundations of the contemporary youth justice system with the emergence of New Labour as an electoral force and its commitment to the philosophy of communitarianism, the notion of reintegrative tutelage (and its constituent criminological perspectives of left realism, reintegrative shaming and restorative justice), the risk society, the new public management, quality assurance and the audit society, the Audit Commission and its influential critique of the then juvenile justice system, and effective and evidence-based practice. This chapter examines the parameters of the contemporary youth justice system and the concerns of academics and other commentators at the outset and in the aftermath of its establishment.

The Youth Justice Board and youth offending teams

The Youth Justice Board (YJB) for England and Wales was established by the Crime and Disorder Act 1998 (CDA 1998) and is a non-departmental public body, sponsored by the Home Office which supervises the operation of youth offending teams (YOTs) and the contemporary youth justice system as a whole.[1] The CDA 1998 placed a statutory duty on the YJB and all those working in the contemporary youth justice system to give primary consideration to the principal aim of preventing offending by children and young people and this was to be achieved through six key objectives: (1) the swift administration of justice; (2) ensuring that young people face up to the consequences of their offending; (3) ensuring that the risk factors associated with offending are addressed in any intervention; (4) ensuring that punishment is proportionate to the seriousness and frequency of offending; (5) encouraging reparation by young offenders to their victims; and (6) reinforcing parental responsibility.

The CDA 1998 significantly introduced new structures at local and national level to provide the framework of an institutional youth offending response. Youth offending teams brought together staff and wider resources from the police, social services, the Probation Service, education and health, in the delivery of youth justice services, with the scope to involve others, including the voluntary sector in a multi-agency response.[2]

Jones (2001) observes an openly acknowledged New Labour YJB policy of suppressing all youth justice knowledge and practice prior to the introduction of the new system but, at the same time, observes a widespread challenge to this 'year zero' thesis from academics and practitioners. Goldson (1999) was thus concerned from the outset that youth justice practitioners with extensive prior experience and expertise in working with offending children and young people had been disillusioned and alienated by the speed of change and called for a return to first principles, citing the substitution of 'offending' for 'justice' in the title of the new practitioner teams which, he argued, symbolised a move whereupon those in trouble were to be considered primarily 'offenders' rather than 'children' as under the previous juvenile justice regime (Goldson 2000a). Walsh (1999) noted in this context that the new contemporary youth justice system appeared to be more concerned with the maintenance of social order than with the welfare of the child; Goldson (2000b) perceived 'crude' policy formulations invariably 'underpinned by condemnatory rhetoric'; and Campbell (1999) accused the government of considering children to be 'an unruly constituency' to be patrolled, policed and trained, which – as the evidence presented in this book shows – is absolutely nothing new and has been the case since the beginnings of industrial modernity and the social construction of notions of childhood, adolescence and delinquency. Hogg (1999) observed the CDA 1998 to be simply 'the latest step to enforce social cohesion by coercion' and a major challenge to the principles of the Children Act 1989 which had prioritised the welfare of the child.[3]

Muncie (1999b: 59) noted that under the new regime misbehaviour and crime were now synonymous and that 'a logic of prevention' and 'risk management' was being used to justify any number of repressive and retrograde strategies for intervening in the lives of young people in trouble. He perceives this to be part of 'the dehumanisation of the youth crime issue' at the expense of cost-effective management performance indicators and observes a contemporary 'institutionalised intolerance' (Muncie 1999c). Diduck (1999) noted that 'the rhetoric of morality trips off the tongues of both the New Right and the New Labour communitarianism'.

Concerns about the limited resources estimated by the government to implement the new system were expressed by various commentators who at the same time acknowledged that these were rather optimistically dependent on savings to be made elsewhere in the system (Padfield 1998; Cavadino 1997). Newburn (1998) raised similar concerns about the need for appropriate levels of funding for YOTs.

Others identified potentially significant problems with the whole notion of multi-agency working in the context of the new youth justice system. Goldson (2000a) proposed that the distancing of the management and accountability of YOTs from social services children and family teams would lead to the welfare needs of children being undermined and replaced by a focus on their offending. Muncie (1999b) expressed disquiet, in this context, about the likelihood of maintaining equity of power and influence between the different agencies; Jackson (1999: 142) identified 'little acknowledgement of differing agency policies, practices, philosophies and priorities'; while, Harvey (2000: 141) added that 'different social agencies have different histories, agendas and responsibilities – reflected in very different cultures and discourses'. Progressive developments in the contemporary youth justice system have nevertheless been subsequently identified which can be attributed to close and committed inter-agency working (Smith 2007).

Pickford (2000b: 10–11) noted that the new system brought with it the inevitability of net-widening and, therefore, 'even greater State intervention in, and control of, the lives of marginalised communities lacking social or economic power' and argued that YOT practitioners 'represent occupations which have a tendency to categorise any anti-social behaviour as troublesome and as requiring a more punitive approach'. Smith (2007: 208) subsequently observed the accuracy of the net-widening prediction noting pertinently that:

> As they move into the criminal sphere, more young people are being formally processed (rather than receiving informal sanction); they are being drawn into the justice system

younger, for more relatively minor offences; and they are experiencing formal and recordable disposals earlier in their offending careers. The loss of the option to administer second and subsequent cautions following the 1998 legislation almost certainly ensures quicker progression to court, where the option of a Conditional Discharge is effectively removed, and more demanding and intrusive programmes are imposed at an earlier stage, effectively compressing the sentence tariff. At the same time, the opportunities for non-compliance, failure and breach action are inevitably increased.

Radical new measures

The Crime and Disorder Act 1998 had introduced radical new measures with the intention of transforming the youth justice system. Thus, a new system of reprimands and a final warning scheme were introduced to replace the police cautioning of young offenders. Reprimands could now be given to first-time offenders for minor offences but any subsequent offending – and this includes minor offences – would result in either a final warning or a charge. Muncie (1999b) expressed concern at the outset that young people were being consistently set up to fail, and Justice (2000) observed the lack of explicit legal assistance to be made available to children who could acquire a criminal record at an early stage of their lives. Bell (1999: 202) noted that as 'the police are particularly poor judges of the quality of their own evidence', many young people were 'likely to accept a Final Warning (and the consequent criminal record) in cases where the evidence did not merit it' while the police would assume 'the role of investigator, prosecutor, judge and jury'. Butler and Drakeford (1997: 218) found incomprehensible the replacement of a cautioning system which they – and many practitioners – considered to have been 'the one demonstrable success of youth justice in the United Kingdom since the war'.[4] The Youth Justice Board (2002) subsequently acknowledged an increase from 52 per cent to 70 per cent in the use of final warning programmes during the period 2000 to 2001/2 despite significant evidence that questioned their value (Hine and Celnick 2001).

The final warning would inevitably initiate an immediate referral – via a referral order – to a local YOT which would then assess the young person and – unless considered inappropriate – prepare a rehabilitation, or 'change', programme designed to tackle the reasons for the offending behaviour in order to prevent any repeat episodes. This process of risk assessment was also to involve contacting the victim to assess whether victim/offender mediation (restorative justice) or some form of reparation to the victim or community would be appropriate. Wonnacott (1999: 287) nevertheless argued that the idea of the 'contract' – between the young person and the YOT – which underpins the notion of the referral order is a deception, because it is based on a fundamental imbalance of power and concludes that 'a contract agreed under compulsion is not a contract at all'. Ball (2000) argued that these orders would fail to achieve the desired twin objectives of restorative justice and the reduction of youth offending and, moreover, could well result in disproportionate sentencing for minor, first offenders, and more severe punishment of those who are unable to keep to their 'contract'.

Wedd (2000) argued that the referral order puts the reflexive practitioner into potential conflict with their client and that the likely outcome would be an institutionalised bullying and unfairness, arguing that 'being invited to agree to a contract in a room full of adults may make the youngster feel under unfair pressure', and urged solicitors to arrange to be outside the panel hearing and for the young offender to seek legal advice if in doubt about the proceedings (see also Ashford and Chard 2000). Goldson (2000b) suggested that the referral order could well be incompatible with international treaties, standards and rules for youth justice; while Crawford and Newburn (2003) later observed that the principle of 'voluntarism' has thus now been eradicated from all stages of the youth justice process and that the failure to comply – or the commission of further offences – would put young people on the fast track to a 'persistent young offender' designation, therefore qualifying them for even more intrusive forms of constraint and surveillance, regardless of the gravity of their actions.

The CDA 1998 introduced reparation orders, which require offenders to make specified reparation to their victim, if he or she consents, or to the community at large. Reparation might involve writing a letter of apology, apologising to the victim in person, cleaning graffiti or repairing criminal damage for which the offender has been responsible. The purpose is to help young offenders understand and face up to the consequences of their actions, and offer some practical recompense to victims. The reparation must, however, be commensurate with the seriousness of the offence for which the order is being given, but may not exceed a total of 24 hours in aggregate. The YOT, meanwhile, is responsible for co-ordinating arrangements for the provision of reports to the courts and communicating with the victim to ascertain whether reparation is appropriate.[5]

There have, again, been significant concerns about the implementation of reparation orders in practice. Dignan (2000), reporting on the evaluation of pilot projects, raised concerns about the inconsistency between the time necessary to engage sensitively with victims and the pressure to accelerate young offenders through the youth justice process. The same author – although a keen advocate of reparation and generally favourable to the orders – was concerned that they would become 'simply another way of punishing offenders', within the broader context of New Labour 'toughness' rhetoric, arguing that this would undermine their potential, as would the failure to seek consent of the offender, the absence of standards and safeguards for the restorative justice processes, and the 'hidden agenda' of punitiveness lying behind police support for the Orders (Dignan 1999). Akester (2000) argued that referral orders were likely to be undermined by the way that they are conceived in the CDA 1998 which is totally contradictory to the informality and flexibility that has been shown to work elsewhere; while Justice (2000) raised concerns that the procedures indicate the letter, but not the spirit, of co-operation. Bell (1999: 209) noted that Reparation Orders might well comprise a form of 'junior community service' which is contrary to child employment and health and safety laws, while Haines (2000) observed that the emphasis on the restorative principle removes the focus from the best interest of the child and transfers it to the victims. Walklate (1998: 220), meanwhile, argued that the orders have been based on overambitious claims for restorative justice by its advocates.

Morris and Gelsthorpe (2000), drawing on their significant experience in researching and monitoring the application of restorative justice in the Antipodes, also viewed the reparation order as being 'at odds with restorative values', observing that the family group conferences in that constituency were used for medium to serious offences or with persistent offenders. They observe that the British examples typically cited to support the reparation order – such as the Thames Valley Police project (Young and Goold 1999) – are located merely on the margins of the criminal justice system, deal with low-level incidents of criminality, and are often an alternative to 'no further action' or 'warnings'. Wasik (1999) argued, moreover, that the orders fail to adequately address the complex issue of who really is the victim. Thus, if the parents of the offender are distressed by the offence, then they could be entitled to reparation. The legislation could clearly be interpreted in this way but, on the other hand, these very same parents can also be punished by a parenting order (see below).

The CDA 1998 introduced child safety orders, whereby a Family Proceedings Court can subject a child under the age of ten to an order if they commit an act which might have been conceived as an offence if they were over ten (the age of criminal responsibility), and child curfew schemes, to keep children in this age group off the streets. Both Fionda (1999: 45) and NAPO (1998) observe that these orders and schemes abandon the minimum age of criminal responsibility via 'the back door' and effectively 'reduce the age of criminal responsibility to zero'.[6] Idriss (2001) proposed that curfew schemes are generally unworkable and in some cases members of the public have been put at risk. Piper (1999: 406) observes that the child safety order is essentially a supervision order (with requirements) but notes that it has none of the safeguards built into its use which govern other supervision orders, whether through welfare or criminal routes (see also Hayes and Williams 1999).

The rule of *doli incapax*, which had presumed that a child under 14 does not know the difference between right and wrong, was to be 'modernised' by the CDA 1998.[7] Cavadino has been one of the major critics of the significant abolition of the rebuttable presumption that a child is *doli incapax* and is, therefore, incapable of understanding that certain behaviour is seriously wrong and the implications for them of becoming involved in such criminality. He observes that the existence of the presumption had previously made 'lawyers, magistrates and judges stop and think about the degree of responsibility of each individual child' aged 10–13 years (Cavadino 1997a: 4; Cavadino 1997b: 164). Ashford (1998) proposed that abolition would have 'dire consequences' for children, giving them criminal records from the age of ten; Fionda (1999) accused the government of 'a dangerous blindness to the incapacities of childhood'; while Haydon and Scraton (2000: 429) argued that the government had simply polarised 'serious wrong and simple naughtiness, without acknowledging the terrain that lies between'.

Some of the most concerted criticisms of any part of the CDA 1998 have been in relation to the Anti-Social Behaviour Order (ASBO), which is a civil order designed to respond to alleged anti-social behaviour but with the power of imprisonment on breach (Ashworth *et al.* 1998). The minimum length of an ASBO is for two years and anyone from the age of ten can become subject of an order if their behaviour is deemed to be anti-social. The actual content 'consists of prohibitions ... [these] can range from prohibiting an individual from entering a specified area to a more general statement prohibiting them from acting in an anti-social manner in the local authority area' (Campbell 2002: 3).

Critics have argued that the ASBO gives power to local officials to criminalise conduct in a way which is in total contradiction to other strategies to reduce social exclusion and it has 'inappropriately low' standards of proof, can be made without the defendant being heard, and can prohibit conduct which is wholly legal. The ASBO was, moreover, originally introduced with the main aim of placing restrictions on the anti-social behaviour of adults but that situation was to change and 'children have seemingly become the main focus of concern relating to anti social behaviour in our communities' (Howard League for Penal Reform 2005). Squires and Stephens (2005: 25) observe that 'much of the government's actions on anti social behaviour have been driven precisely by a concern to address such perceptions about young people slipping "out of control"'.

Hopkins Burke and Morrill (2002, 2004) observe that the ASBO is a significant communitarian initiative introduced with the intention of protecting the rights of citizens whose lives have been blighted by others who behave in anti-social ways in their communities, but conclude that the balance may well have shifted too much in favour of 'communities' at the expense of individual liberties and human rights. Due-process values have been sacrificed in the increased pursuit of crime control outcomes with, in particular, a worrying potential to absorb further – in a widening net – a whole group of relatively non-problematic young people who, left pretty much to themselves, it is argued, could probably grow out of their anti-social activities and become respectable members of society. The situation does not appear to have improved since, with the excessive length and blanket coverage of some orders rendering them both extremely difficult to enforce and liable to the claim that they are simply irrational reactive responses to problems which could have been dealt with in another way (Smith 2007). Fletcher (2005), for example, alerts us to the case of a 15-year-old boy with Aspergers syndrome[8] who was made the subject of an ASBO with the condition that he did not stare over the neighbour's fence, which was a feature of his behaviour.

Many criticisms of the ASBO have their origins in the complexities found in defining the term 'anti-social behaviour' itself, with Burney (2005: 2) stating that the term 'has no clear identity'. The Home Office (2004) nevertheless define anti-social behaviour as 'acting in a manner that caused or was likely to cause harassment, alarm or distress to one or more persons not of the same household (as the defendant)' and the following examples are cited: nuisance neighbours, rowdy and nuisance behaviour, yobbish behaviour and intimidating groups taking over public spaces and vandalism, graffiti and fly-posting. However, these are only a small selection of the behaviours and acts that are covered within the parameters of the guidance although it is clear from just this small selection that the scope of this term is far reaching.

Even the legislation addressing anti-social behaviour fails to provide further clarity, which creates inevitable difficulties in deciding what behaviours should be targeted as unacceptable and where usually acceptable behaviour becomes classified as anti-social. Squires (2006: 226) observes that 'there are potentially no limits to which can be construed as "antisocial behaviour"'. On the other hand, the Home Affairs Committee sees the openness of the phrase positively, concluding 'that this "flexibility" was more a positive feature than a negative one' (Thomas 2005: 6). This interpretation, it is argued, allows the community itself to decide what forms of unacceptable behaviour are having a negative impact upon them rather than having to abide by government guidelines prescribing what acts are to be considered within the parameters of anti-social behaviour.

The Youth Court and its disposals

The Youth Court was given new sentencing and remand powers by the CDA 1998 and the Youth Justice and Criminal Evidence Act 1999. Young people aged between the ages of 10 and 17 inclusive are now mainly dealt with in the youth courts by specially trained magistrates and no person is allowed to be present unless authorised by the court.[9] Exceptions to this regulation are members and officers of the court, parties to the case (normally including parents/guardians), their legal representatives, witnesses and bona fide representatives of the media. Proceedings can be reported in the press but the young person may not generally be identified. A child or young person will, in general, be tried in the youth court unless any of the following apply: he or she is charged with homicide (e.g. murder or manslaughter), when they are sent to the Crown Court for trial; he or she is aged 14 or over and is charged with a 'grave crime' (an offence for which an adult could be imprisoned for at least 14 years), indecent assault or dangerous driving. These cases are sent to the Crown Court if the magistrates conclude that if convicted, the appropriate sentence would be more than they have the power to give; or he or she is charged jointly with another person aged 18 or more, when both should be dealt with in the Crown Court. Young people aged under 17 who are charged and not released on bail will usually be remanded to local authority accommodation. Conditions such as a curfew can be imposed on the child and the authority.

Courts have the power to order a secure remand direct to local authority accommodation. This provision is available for females aged 12 to 16 and males aged 12 to 14 where the child is charged with or convicted of a violent or sexual offence, or an offence where an adult could be sentenced to 14 years or more imprisonment. This provision is also available for the same age groups if there is a recent history of absconding while remanded to local authority accommodation and if the young person is charged or convicted of an imprisonable offence committed while remanded. Additionally, the court must be of the opinion that only a remand to secure accommodation would be adequate to protect the public. In the case of boys aged 15 and 16, secure remands will generally be to prison service accommodation. In exceptional cases where the boy is deemed vulnerable, the remand may be made to secure local authority accommodation.

Detention and training orders (DTOs) were introduced and came into effect on 1 April 2000 and are the new main custodial sentence for juveniles; they replace the secure training order for 12- to 14-year-olds and detention in a young offender institution for 15- to 17-year-olds. A DTO is a two-part sentence which combines a period in custody with a period spent under supervision in the community. Subject to provisions for early or late release, half the term of the order is spent in custody and half under supervision in the community. The emphasis is on clear sentence planning to ensure that time in custody is spent constructively and this is followed up by effective supervision, support on release and, significantly, positive reintroduction to the community. This disposal is available for 12- to 17-year-olds for any imprisonable offence sufficiently serious to justify custody under section 1 of the Criminal Justice Act 1991. Moreover, if the child or young person is aged 12 to 14 the court must be of the opinion that he or she is a persistent offender. The DTO is available to the youth court and the Crown Court. The court can impose an order of between four and 24 months provided it does not exceed the maximum term that could be imposed on an adult offender by the Crown Court. Anyone found guilty of murder committed when under the age of 18 must be sentenced to 'detention during Her Majesty's pleasure'. A person aged under 18 convicted of an offence other than murder for which a life sentence may be passed on an adult may be sentenced to 'detention for life'.[10]

A range of non-custodial sentences have been introduced and consolidated. Where the youth court considers it to be appropriate, young offenders may be given absolute and conditional discharges as is the case for adults. Young offenders aged 16 and over may receive a probation order, a community service order, or a combination order in the same way as adults. Young offenders aged 10 to 17 may also be fined and in certain cases their parent or guardian can be ordered to pay.

Supervision orders can be given to any young offender and can last between three months and three years. These require that the young person is supervised by a probation officer, the local authority or a member of the YOT. They are required to meet with their supervisor at regular intervals and can be required to undertake what are known as 'specified activities' to help them address their offending behaviour. The CDA allows an element of reparation to be attached to the order and this works in the same way as the reparation order discussed above.

The aim of the attendance centre order is that the offender should be 'given, under supervision, appropriate occupation and instruction' and it may be given to any offender aged between 10 and 20. For those 18 or over the maximum period of the order is 36 hours, but in the case of those aged under 18 the order must be for 12 hours unless there are exceptional circumstances, when it may be reduced or increased. The order requires the young person to attend a local centre for a maximum of three hours per day where they usually receive instruction on social skills and physical training. Action plan orders (APOs) are designed to provide a short but intensive and individually tailored response to offending behaviour, so that the causes of that offending as well as the offending itself can be addressed. This may include making reparation to the victim if this is considered appropriate and the victim consents. Certain requirements are placed on the young offender, who is supervised by a caseworker, and the orders must last for three months in total. Holdaway *et al.* (2001) were nevertheless critical of the approach they observed in some areas which they attributed to staff with prior youth offending experience under the previous juvenile justice regime bringing 'old ways of working' with them and turning APOs into 'mini-supervision orders'. The models of intervention observed could, therefore, be characterised as essentially 'correctional' although others have observed a strong welfare element including family support, assistance with accommodation or addressing issues arising from school exclusion (Smith 2007).

Parental bind-overs were introduced for where it is judged that parents or guardians have not exercised proper care and control over the child or young person. These require the former to exercise proper care and control over the young person or be liable for the sum specified which may not exceed £1,000. In the case of young persons under 16, courts must give reasons for not binding over parents or guardians. Parental bind-overs are discretionary for courts in the case of 16- and 17-year-olds and the period of the bind-over may not exceed three years or until the young person reaches the age of 18.

Parenting orders can be given to the parents/carers of young people who offend, play truant from school, or who have received a Child Safety Order, Anti-Social Behaviour Order, or Sexual Offences Prevention Order. These do not result in the parent/carer getting a criminal record and the recipient will normally be required to attend counselling or guidance sessions for a period of up to three months. They may also have conditions imposed on them such as attending meetings with teachers at their child's school, ensuring their child does not visit a particular place unsupervised or is at home at particular times. These conditions can last for a period up to 12 months and a parent/carer can be prosecuted for failing to keep the requirements of the order.

Several commentators have argued that the imposition of parenting orders would inevitably increase tension between parents and children and could lead to more parents requesting the local authority to accommodate their children (Childright 1998; Cavadino 1997a; Hogg 1999; Drakeford and McCarthy 2000); while Hogg (1999) observes that the imposition of financial penalties on families that are dependent on state support would render them less functional. Padfield (1998) claimed there was no evidence that parenting orders would work; while Hogg (2000) expressed surprise at the lack of research into the nine years' experience of parental bind-overs introduced in 1988. Gelsthorpe and Morris (1999) were particularly concerned about an inherent assumption of 'wilful neglect' on the part of parents and the apparent belief that the latter will respond to coercion rather than advice and assistance; Goldson (1999b) observed the orders to be 'fundamentally at odds' with all other child welfare principles,[11] while Bell (1999: 199) remarked that for parents, read 'women', as the imposition of such orders would almost certainly be gendered. Gelsthorpe (1999) thus noted that the 'war on crime' has simply become a 'war on parents' and believes that 'the stigmatisation and potential resentment' felt by parents could exacerbate rather than alleviate difficulties. Smith (2007) subsequently observes that parents are to be persuaded – or when that fails coerced – into ensuring conformity among their children. Pitts (2000: 10) had previously suggested that the contemporary youth justice system reflects this kind of agenda and targets both young people and their parents:

> The new professional practices in the form of cognitive-behavioural treatment, reparation and mediation and mentoring all strive to make good these defects in their behaviour, beliefs and attitudes of young offenders and their parents, and to instill in them a new, disciplined, capacity for self-regulation.

Monaghan (2000: 154) predicted a significant increase in remands to care and custody with the introduction of the contemporary youth justice system and was concerned that a failure to develop confidence in the Young Offender Panel would lead to more punitive disposals, in 'a sentencing arena with more snakes and fewer ladders' (see also Ball 1998: 423). The subsequent conviction statistics are, nevertheless, ambiguous. Thus, while overall crime levels seem to have been falling, those proceeded against and found guilty were steadily increasing in number by 2004 (Home Office 2005). Conversely, the number of young people – aged 10 to 17 being proceeded against for more serious (indictable) offences was declining sharply from their peak in 2001. The proportion of young people being processed – cautioned or found guilty – was also falling (1,671 per 100,000 population compared with 1,962 per thousand in 1998). This suggests a decline in the rate at which young people were being processed and subsequently sentenced for more serious offences (Smith 2007). Bateman (2006), nevertheless, observes a significant readiness to instigate formal interventions at the lower end of the scale, which has been reflected in a persistently high use of custody, identifying a 55 per cent increase in custodial disposals during the period 1992 to 2003, which is far higher than anywhere else in Europe. Smith (2007) observes that the evidence suggests that reforms progressively implemented from 2000 onwards have had little effect on the use of custody: in March 2000, there were 2,650 young people in secure facilities, and by March 2006, this figure was 2,785 although there was some fluctuation in the intervening years.

Both Bateman (2005) and Goldson (2006) observe a political need for senior government figures to 'appear' tough on crime and, therefore, the persistent reliance on a comparatively high use of custody. This, nevertheless, appears to be contrary to the principal objective of the contemporary youth justice system which is to prevent offending by young people. In the following chapter we will examine evidence-based effective practice in that system and consider how it does seek to achieve the principal aim of significantly reducing criminality by children and young people.

Notes

1 The Youth Justice Board consists of between 10 and 12 members appointed by the Secretary of State, including people who have extensive recent experience of the youth justice system.
2 Youth offending teams were established and came into being from 1 April 2000.
3 See also Gelsthorpe and Morris (1999), Stern (1998) and Sclater and Piper (2000).
4 See also Reid (1997).
5 A reparation order cannot be combined with a custodial sentence, or with a community service order, a combination order, a supervision order or an action plan order.
6 See also the Family Policy Studies Centre (1998), Walsh (1999), Hayes and Williams (1999).
7 The *doli incapax* rule has previously presumed that a child less than ten years old cannot be held legally responsible for their actions and so cannot be convicted for committing a criminal offence. The age was seven at common law, raised by the Children and Young Persons Act 1933 to eight and by the Children and Young Persons Act 1963 to ten and this remains the age of criminal responsibility in England and Wales.
8 Asperger's disorder is a milder variant of autistic disorder. Both Asperger's disorder and autistic disorder are in fact subgroups of a larger diagnostic category termed either autistic spectrum disorders (mostly in European countries) or pervasive developmental disorders (PDD) in the USA. Affected individuals are characterised by social isolation and eccentric behaviour in childhood. There are impairments in two-sided social interaction and non-verbal communication.
9 The Criminal Justice Act 1991 s.70 had previously established the youth court as a successor to the juvenile court and this had dealt with offenders up to and including those aged 16.
10 Since the Criminal Justice and Court Services Act 2000 became law, all convicted defendants aged 18 or over at the time of conviction are sentenced as adults.
11 See also Newburn (1998).

Chapter 11

Effective youth justice in practice

We have seen how the contemporary youth justice system was designed and implemented via the Crime and Disorder Act 1998 by a New Labour government with a commitment to communitarianism. Moreover, we have seen how this present-day system can be located in the context of other significant socio-political developments of the past three decades. First, there is the notion of the risk society and the recognition of a need to identify, eradicate but essentially manage criminological risks. Thus, the contemporary youth justice system is very much founded on the assessment and management of individuals and their risk of offending. Second, there is the influence of the new public-sector management, quality assurance and the audit society which are all part of an agenda to promote management competence, quality of service delivery and value for money in the public services. Thus, the Audit Commission report *Misspent Youth* (1996) was influentially critical of a youth justice system it perceived as expensive, inefficient and failing to reduce youth offending, recommending in its place a more rigorously managed and evaluated multi-disciplinary youth justice system using the latest research to inform a practice effective in challenging and reducing youth offending.

This chapter considers the work of the contemporary youth justice system in practice. We have seen that the system implemented and overseen by the Youth Justice Board through the medium of local youth offending teams (YOTs) is very much founded on the notion of effective evidence-based practice. We saw in the previous chapter that the notions of evidence-based policy and practice and their application to criminal justice have received fairly extensive criticism and it has been argued that a wide range of policy initiatives appear to either ignore some of the research and evaluation evidence while those strategies that are instigated seem to be based on carefully selected findings that are complementary to the dominant government worldview. Stephenson *et al.* (2007: xvi) both acknowledge and challenge these criticisms, observing that the YJB takes a far less dogmatic perspective than other areas in the criminal justice system with far more opportunity given for the development of a workforce that reflects critically upon the research evidence and uses it 'creatively to come up with solutions to demanding policy initiatives within the constantly challenging, uncertain, and often frustrating world of youth justice'. We here examine the role and significance of the identified key areas of effective practice – and the evidence on which they are based – in a multi-agency youth justice system with the central aim of reducing youth offending.

Risk and effective practice in the youth justice system

The identification and management of risk is, as we have seen, central to the contemporary youth justice system and the research considered in the opening chapter of this book supports the notion that young people who have one or more risk factors present in their lives are far more likely to be involved in criminal behaviour. The contemporary youth justice system is very much influenced by the work of Utting and Vennard (2000), who summarise four categories of risk factors identified in the research literature. First, they identify family factors which involve low income, poor parental supervision, harsh or erratic discipline, physical abuse, parental conflict, having a parent with a criminal record, and having parents or carers whose attitudes condone or even support anti-social or criminal behaviour. Second, there are educational factors which entail low educational achievement, aggressive and disruptive behaviour (including bullying), a lack of commitment to school (including truancy), and attending a disorganised school with poor academic standards and a lack of classroom discipline. Third, there are community factors which involve the ready availability and acceptability of illegal drugs, growing up in a disadvantaged area with a high population turnover, community disorganisation and neglect, and a lack of attachment and commitment to the neighbourhood among residents. Fourth, there are individual/peer factors which are hyperactivity and impulsivity, rebelliousness, alienation and lack of social commitment to law-abiding society, attitudes that condone law-breaking, early involvement in offending behaviour and having friends involved in crime and/or whose attitudes condone law-breaking. Critics observe the absence of important structural factors such as unemployment and poverty which, although included in the research literature, are not cited (see Pitts 2003b) but it is also reasonable to contend that each of the apparently individualised risk factors is in some way linked to social class location and the absence of legitimate access to the appropriate life chances.

Utting and Vennard (2000) also identify three categories of protective factors which the research literature suggests help defend a young person against the pressure to become involved in criminal behaviour and these are very much based on the relatively recent variants of social control theories established by Travis Hirschi (1969) and which we encountered in the second part of this book. First, there are social bonding factors where children enjoy strong bonds of affection with law-abiding parents, family members and other significant people in their lives. Second, there are healthy beliefs and clear standards where families, schools and behavioural norms in the wider community guide children away from crime, drugs and other anti-social behaviour. Third, there are opportunities, skills and recognition where children have available legitimate and satisfying opportunities within their families, schools, peer groups and communities to make a positive contribution, when they have the cognitive and social skills to take advantage of those opportunities, and when their contribution receives praise and encouragement.

The contemporary youth justice system thus seeks to eradicate – or often more realistically reduce – those significant risk factors identified by research in the life of the young person while, at the same time, encouraging and strengthening those factors considered to offer protection against involvement in criminal behaviour.

Youth justice effective practice

In the rest of this chapter we shall consider how different key elements of the Youth Justice Board effective practice agenda contribute to the implementation of the contemporary youth justice system. These key areas of effective practice that are considered here are not mutually exclusive but are closely interconnected and form part of a system for identifying and responding to youth offending. We shall look at these areas of intervention in the following categories: assessment of risk and intervention planning; risk and protective factors; and implementing intervention. It should be noted that the sub-division of these areas of intervention into these categories is simply a matter of social scientific convenience that helps us to understand the contribution of each in the contemporary youth justice system. These areas could be legitimately categorised in other ways – and perhaps in a different chronological order – and Stephenson *et al.* (2007) do this in their far more detailed discussion of effective practice in the contemporary youth justice system, to which the student is referred.

Assessment of risk and intervention planning

Assessment, planning and supervision

Assessment, planning and supervision are considered to be essential elements of practice with young people at all stages of the contemporary youth justice system because they guide and shape all subsequent work that is conducted. Good practice in these areas is identified as being essential for ensuring that: first, all work conducted in YOTs and the secure estate contributes to the aim of reducing offending; second, young people receive a good-quality service that is relevant to their needs; and, third, there is available evidence to show the effectiveness of work that has been conducted. These three core tasks are closely linked activities that inform planning and which need to be periodically revised. It is recognised that young people present a complex and constantly changing mix of attitudes, circumstances, problems and positive factors and it is thus considered essential to regularly review progress and revise planned interventions. The increasing range of the latter now on offer by a variety of service providers is seen to present both an opportunity and a challenge and differences in the intensity, length, structure and aims of each one means that careful decisions need to be made about the allocation of young people to interventions that are suitable for them. Effective assessment, planning and supervision are, therefore, considered essential to an effective youth justice intervention.

Fundamental to the ability of young people to effectively participate in the process of assessment, planning and supervision and other aspects of the contemporary youth justice system is recognised to be the nature of their individual learning style and this is likely to be influenced by factors such as age, maturity, levels of literacy or educational achievement. It is, therefore, essential that the methods and materials used in all interventions are appropriate to the stage of development of the young person.

Building self-esteem has been identified as an important part of the learning process (Andrews 1995; Strachan and Tallant 1997), while Gardner (1993) refers to 'multiple intelligences' to describe the different ways in which people think and solve problems. These include, for example, 'verbal and linguistic' abilities (understanding and expressing ideas through language), 'bodily-kinaesthetic' skills (gaining knowledge through feedback from physical activity) and 'visual-spatial' intelligence (learning directly through images and thinking intuitively without the use of language). It is, therefore, proposed that learning experiences should be designed with these differences in mind (Chapman 2000) while assessment should also take into account the diverse family, ethnic and cultural backgrounds of young people.

The assessment of risk and need then provides the foundations of planning and supervising interventions (Chapman and Howe 1998; Coulshed and Orme 1998) and the Youth Justice Board itself (2001b) identifies three reasons why good quality assessment in youth justice is essential. First, it provides a key contribution to effective practice and helping to prevent offending by young people. Second, it is crucial in helping to meet the needs of young people who offend and ensuring that interventions are appropriate to the particular circumstances of each young person. Third, it is in the interests of public protection and the wider community by identifying young people likely to reoffend or cause serious harm to others.

On the other hand, there have been significant criticisms of the assessment of risk and planning in the contemporary youth justice system. Two evaluations of the Asset risk assessment tool used in YOTs discovered that it had a predictive accuracy of 67 per cent (Baker *et al.* 2002; Baker *et al.* 2005) and various other critics have been concerned at its low predictive value (Annison 2005; Smith 2006). Others have questioned the fundamental validity of the actuarial approach to assessment. First, it has been argued that it identifies risks associated with the young person without necessarily addressing their needs. Second, young people are said to be stereotyped and demonised, which consequently facilitates a culture of control. Third, it avoids traditional criminal justice concerns for justice, fairness and due process in the interests of removing potential risks. Fourth, it simply promotes an oversimplified technical fix to the complex and ambiguous reality that is offending behaviour by young people (see Haines and Drakeford 1998; Muncie 2000; Pitts 2001a; Smith 2006).

Final warnings

Final warnings were – as we saw in the previous chapter – introduced to replace the use of police cautions for young people with the intention of tackling offending behaviour at the earliest stage and endeavouring to divert young people away from further criminality. Research suggests the benefits of efficient and appropriate risk and needs assessment at the intake point in the youth justice process (Mears and Kelly 1998) but it is observed that there should be a regular review of intervention content against original intent to make sure it stays true to its original aim.

Research indicates, as we have seen in this book, that it is not unusual for young people to commit minor offences. While the majority of young people who are apprehended by the agents of the contemporary youth justice system will commit one offence and no more, a minority will, nevertheless, go on to engage in more serious anti-social behaviour (Farrington 1995, 1996; Jessor and Jessor 1997). For the majority of first-time offenders, the impact of being apprehended will be enough, it is argued, to prevent further offending and, therefore, no further input is required from the youth justice system. If they reoffend, however, then they can be assessed to see whether they are likely to commit further offences and also be given help and support to try to stop them reoffending, in the form of structured interventions.

The CDA 1998 states that a reprimand should be given for a first offence, with a final warning given for the second offence, and this should normally be accompanied by some form of intervention. However, research indicates that – and our knowledge of labelling theories supports this supposition – early entry into the youth justice system can lead to increased offending. It is, therefore, essential that the degree of the final warning intervention is commensurate with the degree of risk presented by the young person and, moreover, practitioners are required to ensure strategies are in place to graduate interventions incrementally to make sure they are appropriate in each instance (Dunkel 1996; Hallet and Hazel 1998).

Strategies of gradual intervention can be observed throughout the criminal justice process (Feest 1990) and can include first, at entry stage, reprimand and/or mediation; second, at processing stage, final warning, unconditional and conditional discharges; third, at the remand stage, bail supervision; fourth, at conviction stage, reparation, restorative interventions, referral order/young offender panels, sentence deferment; fifth, at the threshold of custody, Intensive Supervision and Surveillance Programme (ISSP) or other intensive interventions.

Graduated interventions should be seen as filters: at each stage of the criminal justice process, different groups may be filtered from an initial cohort of alleged offenders; the precise nature of these filtering systems and their eligibility criteria differ between youth justice systems (Dunkel 1996; Hallet and Hazel 1998; Neubacher *et al.* 1999). Thus, in this context, the European Commission has urged member states to develop graduated interventions for young people, with the emphasis on education and social reintegration (Dunkel 1996) and the case for these with first- and second-time less serious offenders is strong. In England and Wales, 80 per cent of those cautioned for a first-time offence did not return to the notice of the police within two years; however, the rate of reoffending increases as subsequent cautions are given (Rutter *et al.* 1998). Effective intervention at this early stage is, therefore, considered to be vital. Moreover, successful early intervention does not merely have benefits for the individual young person; the cost saving to society – in terms of public perception of crime and the financial gain – is considerable (Cohen 1998).

Risk and protective factors

We have identified throughout this book risk factors linked to offending by young people and these were summarised above by Utting and Vennard (2000), albeit without the explicit inclusion of significant structural factors such as poverty and unemployment previously identified in the research literature. It is, nevertheless, proposed here that these apparently invisible factors are implicitly taken into account as the following discussion clearly shows. The key areas of effective practice for identifying and responding to these risk and protective factors in the contemporary youth justice system are parenting; education, training and employment; substance misuse; and mental health.

Parenting

The research evidence shows that children who are subject to harsh, neglectful or inconsistent parenting are at a significantly increased risk of involvement in offending when they reach the age of adolescence. Furthermore, adverse family factors have a marked effect on the development of children and potential future problems include prenatal and perinatal factors, poor supervision and discipline, and family conflict (see Hopkins Burke 2005). McCord (1982) found offending to be common in men raised in broken homes without affectionate mothers but also in families experiencing conflict where parents stayed together. Studies conducted in both the UK and North America show that children are more likely to become offenders if a parent or older sibling has been involved in crime (Farrington 1995).

Living in impoverished family circumstances is also a recognised predictor of criminogenic tendencies. The Cambridge Longitudinal Study identified an increased risk of self-reported offending (Farrington 1992a, 1992b) and found that boys who came from low-income families were twice as likely to have a criminal record at age 18 than those whose families were adequate or comfortable. It was also found that around 55 per cent of boys observed to be poorly supervised at eight years of age had been convicted of offences by the age of 32, compared with a third of the overall sample, while conflict between two parents was also shown to carry an increased risk of later delinquency for boys. Loeber and Stouthamer-Loeber (1986) found four interrelated parenting factors – neglect, family conflict, deviant behaviour and attitudes on the part of parents, and disrupted family life – to be linked to behavioural problems and delinquency. On the other hand, it has been shown that parental involvement in the form of 'at-home good parenting' has a significant positive effect on the achievement and adjustment of children even after all other factors influencing attainment – such as the quality of schools and even poverty – has been taken into consideration, and this is to be found across class and ethnic boundaries (Desforges and Abouchaar 2003).

Reinforcing the responsibilities of parents in addressing the offending and anti-social behaviour of their children is, therefore, a key objective of the youth justice system and is the basis of the parenting order. Family-focused work has been found notably to be more effective than interventions that focus solely upon parents or on young people (Kumpfer and Alvarado 1998) and family learning has also been shown to be effective in helping young people to move forward towards training and employment or reintegration into mainstream provision.

It is when their children become teenagers that parents experience demands that they often feel ill-equipped to deal with; while teenagers themselves are responding to physical, emotional and lifestyle changes that have a profound impact on them. Moreover, these challenges, for both parents and teenagers, can be located in the context of major shifts in the last decade in the social structure as well as in political responses to parenting, teenagers and the family (Coleman and Roker 2001). The changes external to families such as actual or relative poverty[1] can, therefore, intensify the changes within.

Parenting is, therefore, one of the key risk and protective factors in relation to the offending or anti-social behaviour of young people (Farrington 1992; Rutter *et al.* 1998) and the provision of support to parents can contribute to the reduction of offending and anti-social behaviour by young people (Alexander *et al.* 1976; Borduin *et al.* 1995; Wasserman *et al.* 1996; Henggeler *et al.* 1997; Gordon and Kacir 1998). Parents referred to parenting interventions in the contemporary youth justice system tend to present substantially higher levels of needs, in particular, managing the difficult behaviour of the child, setting boundaries, disciplining the child and improving school attendance, among others.[2]

As we saw in the previous chapter, section 8 of the CDA 1998 provides courts with powers to impose parenting orders but parenting programmes can be offered on a voluntary basis. Such programmes do, however, carry the risk that parents feel stigmatised – negatively labelled or blamed – and this is more likely to be the case for those referred via compulsory routes. Services working with parents on compulsory orders can therefore expect to meet considerable hostility and scepticism from the outset and it is has been found to be especially helpful when programmes focus on parenting strengths, rather than weaknesses. Parenting interventions within the youth justice system should, therefore, have clear aims and objectives related to identified need and to reducing parenting risk factors and strengthening protective factors (Kumpfer *et al.* 1996). Interestingly, psychodynamic interventions that focus on the child and its individual development, rather than structural family interventions, have been found to actually result in a deterioration of family functioning (Szapocznik *et al.* 1989).

Ghate and Hazel (2002) significantly note that these parenting risk and protective factors identified above need to be seen in the context of other invariably significant structural factors, such as impoverished neighbourhood, family poverty and poor housing, which may also impact considerably on parenting and family functioning. Thus, the available research shows that there is simply no one 'correct' model of parenting that will address the diverse needs of all parents and their children. It is, therefore, considered appropriate to choose from a menu of optional interventions following a full assessment of need (Stephenson *et al.* 2007).

Education, training and employment

Parsons and Howlett (2002) have identified educational failure and permanent exclusion or non-attendance at school as the risk factors with the highest correlation to youth offending, and longitudinal research has long established that children who are performing poorly from late junior school are more likely to become involved in offending than those performing adequately or well (see Wolfgang *et al.* 1972). Official statistics reviewed earlier in this book suggest that young people excluded from school commit 30 per cent of domestic burglaries and 40 per cent of street robberies.

Hodgson and Webb (2005) alert us to oversimplified deterministic interpretations of the link between school exclusions and offending by children and young people. In their sample, 82 per cent of the young people interviewed stated they were no more likely to offend subsequent to being excluded; while 55 per cent stated they were less likely to offend during their exclusion period. Often, this was because on being excluded, they were 'grounded' by their parents, thus alerting us to the importance of multiple risk factors and the inevitable interconnection between them.

The Cambridge longitudinal study, nevertheless, showed that between 44 per cent and 48 per cent of secondary school truants were offenders, compared with 14 to 16 per cent of non-truants (Robins and Hills 1996), while research among offenders in custody aged 17 to 20 has shown that almost one in four could not write their name and address correctly, more than two out of three could not fill in a job application form and a half had difficulty telling the time (Elliot and Voss 1974). This is bad news for most young people released from custody, for around half of all jobs require some basic maths and more than 90 per cent require communication skills (Literacy Working Group 1999). On release from prison, around 66 per cent of offenders have such poor literacy and numeracy skills that they are excluded from 96 per cent of jobs (Prison Service 1989). Moreover, adults with poor basic skills are more likely to end up in unskilled or semi-skilled, low-grade work; be unemployed, more often, and for longer; have children with poor basic skills; live in overcrowded conditions or be homeless; and have a criminal record. They are also less likely to receive even basic, on-the-job, training; vote; or participate in their local communities (Basic Skills Agency 2002). The Youth Justice Board consequently places a high priority on the education and training of young people at risk of reoffending.

Stephenson *et al.* (2007) observe that only 35 per cent of young people in the contemporary youth justice system, at any one time, may actually be in full-time education, training or employment, and note the existence of cases where young people have received no education for several years (see also Youth Justice Board 2003; Baker *et al.* 2002). Academic failure at school is widely recognised as being endemic among young offenders and, therefore, raising educational attainment is identified as one of the most effective means of reducing the risk factors associated with criminal behaviour. Ayers (1999) proposes that the route to rehabilitation for the vast majority of young people is through the attainment of very normal milestones – such as learning to read and write, gaining qualifications, getting a job, entering further education and training – often denied to them due to their marginalised status. Stephenson (2007) observes that there is a whole multitude of schemes and strategies that have been introduced in recent years with the intention of getting excluded and offending young people back into education, and subsequently, training and employment but there are, however, very limited research and evaluation findings to demonstrate their success.

Substance misuse

The relationship between substance misuse and offending by young people has long been established and was discussed in the second part of this book. The British Crime Survey 1998 found that 50 per cent of all young people under the age of 20 had used some kind of illegal drug but 70 per cent of those who were the subject of supervision orders reported substance misuse. The Audit Commission (1996) found that almost two-thirds of young male prisoners admitted to using drugs at some time, cannabis being the drug most often mentioned; moreover, 15 per cent of young offenders have been found to have a problem with either alcohol or illegal drugs with the figure rising to 37 per cent among those classed as persistent or serious offenders (DPAS and SCODA 2000; Nacro 2000).

A more recent Home Office study involving nearly 300 young people from YOTs across England and Wales found that almost all had used alcohol (91%) and tobacco (85%), with cannabis (86%) and ecstasy (44%) being the most commonly tried illegal drugs. There were, however, relatively few heroin or crack cocaine users, and use of these drugs was not generally that frequent (Hammersley *et al.* 2003). A total of 40 per cent or more of the sample felt that there was some relationship between their substance use and their offending, and while this does not suggest a simple causal relationship between drug use and offending behaviour, the authors found a strong correlation between the two. First, the factors relevant to the early onset and development of drug taking and involvement in juvenile crime were found to overlap significantly. Second, a strong association between the early onset of drug taking and the likelihood of a subsequent escalation into more problematic drug use was found. Third, it was proposed that drugs and crime experiences of young people may be mutually reinforcing.

These findings clearly have implications for the planning of youth justice interventions. First, it would appear that early intervention initiatives to address common risk factors will be of benefit to both drug prevention and crime reduction initiatives. Second, responses to known drug taking by young people who offend should, therefore, address in parallel those factors relevant to both drug taking and offending behaviour. Third, responses to all young people who offend should also be sensitive to their possible involvement with drugs and include the provision of appropriate services where needed (DPAS and SCODA 2000).

Mental health

Adolescence is a key developmental stage and has long been recognised as a time of major growth and change. The concept is – as we have seen in this book – culturally determined and adolescent disturbance must, therefore, be seen within the context of normal development within a particular culture during a certain time period. It is as a developmental stage fundamentally concerned with the negotiation of two specific and interrelated tasks. First, adjusting to the impact of puberty involves the adolescent in concerns about questions of sexual orientation and negotiating intimate relationships, separation from parents and the establishment of an individual identity. Second, during this period, there is a shift from accepting rules and boundaries imposed by others to setting them for oneself. Adolescents, therefore, begin to challenge the rules which adults set.

Definitions in 'mental health' can cause confusion about what is being described and communicated and here the term is used in a broad sense, as described by Hagell (2002), indicating 'a level of symptoms of mental ill health that have led to impairment in day-to-day life'. This term does not necessarily mean that young people are clearly diagnosable as having a major mental illness, but it does assume that they are affected enough by the poor status of their health to cause them problems.[3]

Several studies have conclusively shown that adolescents in prison and other secure establishments show very high rates of psychiatric disorder. Many young offenders have more than one psychiatric disorder and – especially those in secure conditions – often have a range of complex needs, while there is a consensus that this high prevalence rate of disorders can be explained by a range of factors (Rutter *et al.* 1998; Hagell 2002; Communities that Care 2001). First, risk factors in young people known to be associated with offending have also been shown to be strongly associated with mental health problems and these include family dysfunction/discord, exposure to poor parenting practices, including a lack of supervision, and harsh and erratic discipline. Over a third of young people in prison have been looked after by the local authority and as a group, young offenders report high levels of previous physical, sexual and emotional abuse (Boswell 1995). Schooling and employment factors include high rates of school exclusion and poor academic attainments and high levels of unemployment; individual child characteristics include learning difficulties and hyperactivity; with other factors including neighbourhood and community issues. Second, the reality of interactions with the criminal justice system may very well lead to anxiety and/or depression, particularly in children, who may be relatively unsupported by families and have few coping resources. Within prison, young people may experience further stress being separated from families and being exposed to further psychological and physical intimidation.

Implementing intervention

The previous group of key areas of effective practice focus on the issue of risk and protective factors in the lives of young people but the following category more specifically addresses the lives of apprehended young offenders and the role of contemporary youth justice interventions in their lives. These are: offending behaviour programmes; neighbourhood prevention; mentoring; restorative justice; intensive supervision and surveillance programmes; remand management; and resettlement.

Offending behaviour programmes

The prevention of offending behaviour may be undertaken at one of three levels: primary prevention includes long-term developmental projects to improve the overall life opportunities of disadvantaged families and children; secondary prevention includes work with children or young people at risk of involvement in delinquency; tertiary prevention entails work with adjudicated young people, that is, those who have already appeared before the courts and been convicted of crimes (Guerra *et al.* 1994).

Offending behaviour programmes are designed to prevent – or at least reduce – offending by children and young people and research evidence shows that they can make a significant contribution to the reduction of criminality. While such work is likely to be focused primarily on the tertiary level in most services, it may also be undertaken at the secondary level in some instances (Buckland and Stevens 2001; Nacro 2001a) and can be undertaken in secure establishments for young offenders, in YOTs or within voluntary-sector agencies.

The impact of offending behaviour programmes has been found to be on the whole positive (Lipsey 1995; Dowden and Andrews 1999) and when interventions have been studied in controlled experimental trials, they have resulted in a reduction in recidivism compared with control samples and therefore have been perceived as worthwhile in public policy terms (Lipsey 1999). Studies have, however, found substantial variability in outcomes depending on a range of other factors (Lipsey 1995; Lipsey and Wilson 1998) and it has been clearly established that there is no single solution to the problem of offending behaviour or in helping to reduce its frequency or severity. Thus, methods that might well work in one context, with one selected sample, may work less well in others. Decisions regarding the approach best adopted in a given setting for a particular group, therefore, need to consider a number of variables.

Effective interventions have been found to be those which focus on identified risk factors and utilise methods that actively engage young people in learning new skills or changing thought patterns or attitudes associated with offending (Andrews 1995). These factors are sometimes called 'criminogenic needs' or 'dynamic' risks because they may change over time, and the most effective programmes of intervention have been found to be those which employ interpersonal skills training, behavioural interventions such as modelling, graduated practice and role-playing, cognitive skills training, mentoring linked to individual counselling with the close matching of young people and mentors on key background variables, structured individual counselling within a reality therapy or problem-solving framework, and teaching family homes which involve specially trained staff acting in a parental role (Andrews *et al.* 1990; Hollin 1995; Lipsey and Wilson 1998; Redondo *et al.* 1999).

Significantly, punitive sanctions or other elements of a deterrence-based approach to the prevention of reoffending – including incarceration, boot camps, 'scared straight' and home confinement – have all been found to be ineffective. There is simply no evidence that they are a reliable means of achieving this end and their net effect has been sometimes to increase it (Gendreau *et al.* 1993; Baron and Kennedy 1998). Other programmes shown to be ineffective include those vocational training activities which have no associated links to real prospects of employment (and these are, in fact, associated with increased recidivism), wilderness or 'outdoor challenge' programmes (unless they include high-quality training or therapeutic aspects), open-ended individual counselling which is diffusely focused, or unstructured group programmes using experiential therapies or activities focused solely on personal development (Lipsey 1995; Lipsey and Wilson 1998; Wilson and Lipsey 2000; Petrosino *et al.* 2000). Effective offending behaviour programmes are, therefore, those that focus on the provision of long-term material benefits to young people such as proper employment opportunities and, thus, address significant structural issues in their lives.

Targeted neighbourhood prevention programmes

Stephenson *et al.* (2007) pertinently observe that crime does not affect everyone equally with perhaps 40 per cent of youth crime taking place in 10 per cent of neighbourhoods. These criminogenic localities are those which are characterised by major structural issues such as high unemployment, lack of investment in physical and social capital, and numerous risk factors, which impact on the lives of young people and the communities in which they live (Hope 2001). New Labour government policy has focused much attention on these geographical locations as part of its reintegrative tutelage strategy. Stephenson *et al.* (2007), nevertheless, observe that this plethora of government initiatives is not always seen as benign, with critics observing increased surveillance and social control over certain areas and, at the same time, the net-widening potential of some of these measures to draw increasing numbers of young people into the contemporary youth justice system (Smith 2003; Goldson and Muncie 2006). Social crime-reduction methods are those, however, that seek to change these underlying social conditions that permit – or even encourage – involvement in criminal behaviour through diversion from crime.

The Youth Inclusion Programme (YIP) and Splash projects are the flagship neighbourhood prevention programmes introduced by the YJB and both were established in response to the Audit Commission (1996) report which argued for preventative activity to be targeted at those young people most at risk and in areas of high deprivation and criminal activity by young people.

The YIP was established in 2000 by the YJB in 70 of the most deprived neighbourhoods and despite the voluntary nature of the project design aims to focus on the 50 most at risk 13- to 16-year-olds and engage them in a wide range of constructive activities. The membership of the core 50 changes and regular reviews ensure that young people move in or out of this category as appropriate. In order to discourage stigmatisation and labelling, many activities are open to other young people who live in the neighbourhood and, indeed, many young people in the core 50 are unaware of their status (Hopkins Burke and Orrock 2003).

In June 2003, the objectives of the YIP were revised with the overall aim to reduce youth crime in the local neighbourhood and there are three supporting targets. First, to ensure that at least 75 per cent of the identified target group (the core 50) are engaged with and that these receive at least five hours of appropriate interventions per week. Second, the reduction of arrest rates among the engaged target group by 70 per cent compared with the figure for the previous 12 months. Third, to ensure 90 per cent of those in the engaged group are in suitable full-time education, training or employment. Like many youth work projects, the YIP provides a wide range of activities, but it breaks with the idea of generic youth work provision and places its emphasis on evidence-led practice and focused project management (Stephenson et al. 2007).

Splash schemes have existed for a number of years and have targeted young people in the school holidays in order to deter them from crime and anti-social behaviour. They have been largely led by local police forces in partnership with agencies involved in youth provision. Splash Extra was launched in response to the Street Crime Initiative launched by the government in March 2002 and focuses on ten police force areas. Within this initiative, the YJB were asked to set up schemes in high-crime neighbourhoods adopting the original Splash model of delivery and extending the target age group to 9- to 17-year-olds (Hopkins Burke and Orrock 2003).

Peer influence on anti-social behaviour appears to be at its strongest during adolescence and in the Cambridge study, associations with delinquent friends at age 14 were found to be independently associated with an increased risk of convictions as a young adult, after controlling for other factors (Patterson and Yoerger 1997). Studies suggest that negative peer pressure occurs because anti-social young people tend to gravitate towards each other rather than additional peer pressure *per se* being a risk factor. Furthermore, young repeat offenders who desist from crime by the age of 19 were found less likely to associate with delinquent friends. One of the robust strategies of the aforementioned neighbourhood programmes is, therefore, to include offenders in activities with more law-abiding and compliant young people and in many cases – and in order to avoid labelling and stigmatisation – the most at-risk young people are unaware of their status. Work done with the families and community involvement also enhances the protective factors that combat negative peer pressure. Hawkins and Catalano (1992) found that when young people have a genuine stake in their families, schools and communities, they are less likely to get involved in anti-social acts that place their relationships in jeopardy. Honey and Mumford (1986) have suggested that peer-led approaches to changing behaviour are more credible to young people and have the added benefit of affecting the peer educators themselves, who may gain in self-esteem, self-confidence and social skills.

Mentoring

Stephenson *et al.* (2007) observe that mentoring in the contemporary youth justice system is a voluntary one-to-one relationship between a young person and a supportive adult. It is nevertheless more than simple befriending and the aim is to help bring about constructive changes in the life and behaviour of the young person. Shea (1992) proposes that a mentor can be defined 'as someone who helps others to achieve their potential'. Mentoring is, however, a natural part of child development and most young people will identify with one or more adults that provide them with support and guidance outside the family context. Young women are more likely to identify mentoring to be significant in their lives than young men (Blyth *et al.* 1982).

The revised disposal and sentencing options introduced by the CDA 1998 incorporate a number in which mentoring may play a part. Participation on a mentoring scheme is, however, voluntary and not part of an order to which a young person might be subject.[4] The main purpose of mentoring is to benefit the young person and this can only happen if their agenda is at the heart of the relationship. Successful mentoring relationships are, therefore, associated with, active listening, ongoing training for mentors, the establishment and maintenance of a 'youth driven' agenda, time to develop trusting relationships and reciprocity, and constructive attempts by the mentor to affect the behaviour of the young person (Brewer *et al.* 1995; Philip 1997; Scales and Gibbons 1996; St James Roberts and Samlal Singh 2001; Clayden and Stein 2002).

The role of the mentor is, as we have seen, to provide support, guidance and coaching to a young person (Brewer *et al.* 1995) and where interaction is 'youth driven' it is more likely to be successful (Styles and Morrow 1992). There is, however, some evidence that mentoring may be at its most effective where there is some attempt, not simply to establish a positive relationship between the mentor and the young person, but where the former seeks to reinforce positive patterns of behaviour by the latter through praise and/or reward (Fo and O'Donnell 1974; Tierney and Grossman, with Resch 1995).

Retention of young people in mentoring programmes has been found to be maximised where there is a goal-focused relationship (Brewer *et al.* 1995) and the framework and structure of this will depend on the age of the young person, level of maturity, risk or level of offending behaviour, developmental and cultural needs and issues particular to the locality. The learning needs of young people can be addressed in both group and one-to-one settings and in matching mentors and young people; while procedures should be developed that take into account the preferences of young people, that of their families and the volunteers (Clayden and Stein 2002). Matching along cultural or gender lines is sometimes not possible, nor in every case is it necessarily desirable. It is essential, however, that the cultural and other needs of the young person are recognised, respected and that an attempt should be made to meet them. The mentor must understand the cultural and community background of the young person (Rhodes *et al.* 1992; Rhodes *et al.* 1995).

Restorative justice

The active involvement of victims of crime in the youth justice process is a key element of the contemporary youth justice system. Actions to achieve these aims are usually called restorative justice and seek to balance the concerns of the victim and the community with the need to reintegrate the young person into society. They seek to assist the recovery of the victim and enable all parties with a stake in the justice process to participate in it (Marshall 1998) and also they have been shown to be effective in reducing re-offending by young people (Sherman and Strang 1997; Nugent *et al.* 1999; Street 2000), especially by violent young people (Strang 2000), and provide greater satisfaction for victims (Wynne and Brown 1998; Umbreit and Roberts 1996; Strang 2001). Compliance with reparation has been found to be generally higher in restorative schemes than through the courts (Marshall 1999).

The CDA 1998 incorporates the use of reparation to victims in final warnings, action plan orders and reparation orders (Home Office 1998). Restorative approaches to arranging reparation can also be used in the context of pre-court work, including final warnings and bail support.[5] The New Zealand conferencing system for young offenders enables restorative work to be undertaken as an alternative to the formal criminal justice system at any stage of the process, so serious and/or persistent offenders can be included where this is appropriate (Justice 2000).

Eight main theoretical principles of effective restorative justice can be identified. First, those directly affected by a crime, the victims, are involved in the process of determining the outcome, including how best to repair the harm done. Second, consideration of the wishes and needs of the victim is perceived to be more important than in traditional criminal justice procedures. Third, young people have to take responsibility for their actions and acknowledge what they have done in accordance with the rational actor model of criminal behaviour before entering the restorative process. Fourth, young people are helped to see that their actions have negatively affected the lives of other real human beings. Fifth, restorative work should address the specific cultural, religious, and language needs of all those involved. Sixth, all parties are entitled to express their feelings and contribute their views in a non-adversarial process. Seventh, all parties – including the perpetrator and the victim – can be helped to regain a sense of personal power and control over their lives. Eighth, positive outcomes for the victim and their community are valid objectives alongside change in the behaviour and attitudes of the offender (Youth Justice Board 2001b; Graef 2000; Marshall 1996; McCold and Wachtel 2000). Researchers have, nevertheless, emphasised a number of crucial tensions between the spirit of restorative justice and the practice of decision-making in the contemporary youth justice system. Haines and O'Mahoney (2006: 119) thus observe that:

> The growth in popularity and spread of restorative justice precisely at a time when attitudes towards young people find expression in generally more controlling and/or punitive measure (especially in England and Wales) both rest in, and at the same time expose, the crucial tension within restorative justice to be simultaneously both positive and punitive. In practice, the positive elements are more rhetorical whilst the punitive expressions are more materially apparent.

Intensive supervision and surveillance programmes

Intensive supervision and surveillance programmes (ISSPs) are targeted at that small minority of offenders we have previously identified in this book who are responsible for a disproportionately large number of offences. The eligibility criteria require the young person to be appearing in court, charged with or convicted of an offence, and having previously been charged, warned or convicted of offences committed on four or more separate dates within the previous twelve months, and to have received at least one community or custodial penalty. A young person can also qualify for ISSP if they are at risk of custody, because the current charge or sentence relates to an offence which is so serious that an adult could be sentenced to 14 years or more, or they have a history of repeat offending on bail and are at risk of a secure remand. There is some evidence, however, to suggest that the provision of intensive programmes to low-risk offenders can be counterproductive and they may actually lead to an increase in recidivism (Andrews *et al.* 1990). The accurate targeting of ISSP resources towards those who meet the eligibility criteria is, therefore, considered essential (Stephenson *et al.* 2007).

The ISSP programme content should incorporate five core modules covering essential areas of youth justice effective practice intervention identified above – education and training, restorative justice, offender behaviour, interpersonal skills and family support – with ancillary options based on individual circumstances and local resources, including drug or alcohol work or 'constructive leisure/

recreation' (Gray *et al.* 2005). In addition, those on ISSPs should also be subject to at least one form of surveillance. Smith (2007) observes that the framework and delivery requirements for the ISSP are highly prescriptive and this leaves little scope for the exercise of professional discretion by practitioners. The overall aim is, nevertheless, clearly to provide a demanding programme which reassures courts that it is an 'effective' alternative to custody.

Remand management and resettlement

Remand and pre-trial services exist primarily to divert those considered to be appropriate young people from unnecessary custodial remands and to manage them while they are awaiting trial, or sentence, including preventing and/or reducing offending and ensuring attendance at court. It has become widely accepted that the use of custody for young people is undesirable and damaging, with periods spent in custody being disruptive to family life, employment and the education of the young person, particularly when they are detained a long way from home, while custodial remands may also be emotionally damaging and increase health risks (Cavadino and Gibson 1993; Moore and Smith 2001). Moreover, the Prison Service prioritises security and containment rather than welfare (Woolf 1991) and prison is not a safe or appropriate environment for young people where they may be vulnerable and lack the necessary coping strategies to deal with the conditions of incarceration (Her Majesty's Inspectorate of Prisons 1997). Problems of vulnerability are exacerbated by intimidation, violence and bullying which are commonplace within the secure estate (Goldson 2002) and the incidence of self-harm and suicide is high among young people on remand (Liebling 1992).

Drug use is also widespread within penal establishments (Hucklesby and Wilkinson 2001); while the incidence of mental health problems is higher in prison establishments than in the population as a whole and young people with such difficulties may present a significant risk to themselves and others (Her Majesty's Inspectorate of Prisons 2000). Furthermore, there is evidence that custodial remands result in higher conviction rates, with a greater likelihood of incarceration on conviction (Cavadino and Gibson 1993). One factor which may explain this relationship is the difficulties of preparing a defence case when young people are in custody.

Safeguarding the rights of all unconvicted young people at every stage of the criminal justice process from arrest to final disposal is a key objective of remand management. This is an important component because research evidence suggests that young people are being remanded in custody unnecessarily (Goldson 2002) and this is a problem that has been exacerbated by heightened media interest in offending on bail and legislative change and consequently resulted in a rise in the number of young people subject to custodial remands (Home Office 2001). Other policy and legal changes, such as the introduction of electronic monitoring, have, on the other hand, increased the number, scope and restrictiveness of non-custodial remand options. This has increased the opportunities for diverting young people from custody but has, at the same time, increased the potential for 'net-widening' (Hucklesby 2001). This, therefore, increases the importance of assessing the least intrusive remand option possible in the individual circumstances.

An important impetus behind recent legislative changes relating to bail has been the concern over the number offences committed while on bail (Hucklesby and Marshall 2000). It has been argued that offending on bail contributes to a large proportion of the total number of offences committed (Avon and Somerset Constabulary 1991; Northumbria Police 1992; Hucklesby and Marshall 2000) and young people are believed to contribute to this problem disproportionately (Avon and Somerset Constabulary 1991; Northumbria Police 1992; Morgan and Henderson 1998). Several initiatives and changes to legislation have been introduced to tackle the problem of offending on bail and these include the introduction of electronic monitoring (Criminal Justice and Police Act 2001) and increasing the powers of the court to impose a secure remand on young people it believes have offended on bail (Criminal Justice and Police Act 2001). These measures make the granting of bail more difficult and, therefore, less likely. Reducing the incidence of offending on bail, nevertheless, remains a priority for the Youth Justice Board and a key objective of remand management.

Resettlement

Resettlement is formally defined as the effective reintegration of imprisoned offenders into the community after the sentence has been served (HM Inspectorates of Prisons and Probation 2001). Reoffending rates after custody are, however, notoriously high, and the highest of all for young men in their teens leaving custody with a history of residential burglary convictions (Home Office 1998) and those on short-term sentences (HM Inspectorates of Prisons and Probation 2001). These are among the most challenging people to reintegrate into the community and to set on a course that takes them away from their high-risk offending lifestyles. Research constantly demonstrates that many young offenders have dysfunctional families, very poor educational histories, mental health needs, and drug and alcohol problems (e.g. Hagell and Newburn 1994; Loeber and Farrington 1998; Rutter *et al.* 1998) and changing the way they behave and interact with their local communities is possibly the most difficult thing that youth justice practitioners can ever try to achieve.

In an ideal world, successful resettlement for these young people will include five crucial elements. First, there will be a cessation of offending, or at least a significant reduction in their criminal involvement to encompass lower-level offences committed less frequently and with less risk to others. Second, there will be engagement in employment, education or training activities, in a way that will lead to a new life away from offending. Third, there will be a full realisation of any benefit entitlement and general support will be provided with financial planning. Fourth, the process of reintegration will include inclusion back into the health and dental services, including if necessary, engagement in substance misuse programmes. Fifth, there will be settlement into stable accommodation – in the parental home, if suitable, or in private, local authority or similar accommodation. Sixth, there will be crucial support in building new and better relationships with family – both existing family and a new young family they may be fathering. Seventh, there will be engagement in some way with people who can provide long-term mentoring or other kinds of social support during the short-term future when opportunities, pressures and temptations may conspire to push the young person back into offending (Stephenson *et al.* 2007).

HM Inspectors of Prison and Probation (2001) pertinently observed that the term, 'resettlement', is in reality a misnomer, as many of these young people will never have been in a position where these objectives could have been met, even before they went into custody. In many cases, a serious attempt at resettlement after the first custodial sentence may be the first time that anyone has ever really tried to engage these young people or attempt to socially include them. This consequentially makes the challenge even greater.

It is clear that unless the underlying causes of criminality are addressed, offending behaviour will continue after release. Among these underlying causes are the poor parenting, exclusion from education, unstable living conditions and mental health problems we have previously identified. It is clear from this observation that successful resettlement and reintegration will play a crucial part in helping to prevent reoffending and in addition, in order to reduce risks to the public from offenders, it is a highly significant way of ensuring a decline in the crime rate. The existing evidence for reducing the crime rate by increasing incarceration as proposed by contemporary rational actor model proponents is not strong, while statisticians have shown that we would have to imprison a significant and unrealistic proportion of the population to see a meaningful reduction in crime levels (Tarling 1993; Spelman 1994), so investment in more effective resettlement and reintegration into the community would appear to be the only real answer. The research evidence nevertheless suggests that this is a far from easy task and we will reconsider the whole notion of reintegrative tutelage which is so central to the intellectual justifications for the contemporary youth justice system in the following concluding chapter.

Conclusions

The key areas of effective practice considered above provide the basis of the multi-agency contemporary youth justice system. New Labour neo-communitarianism clearly underpins an approach where the responsibilities of the individual are clearly located in the context of a community with rights. The significance of the left realist intervention model with its dual emphasis on a balanced intervention that focuses not just on the crimes committed by young people but also very much on the social causes of that criminality is clearly identified in the above interventions which also have clear resonance with the concepts of risk and the audit society. Clearly the proclaimed aim of the Youth Justice Board to seriously reduce youth offending is an ambitious, difficult and problematic project.

Stephenson *et al.* (2007) observe pertinently that if evidence-based youth justice is to be taken seriously by practitioners and key decision-makers in the contemporary system, then there has to be an accepted recognition of the limitations of the strategy. They observe quite correctly that:

> The basic contexts associated with offending such as poverty and childhood abuse may be very difficult to ameliorate. Devising interventions that are of an intensity, duration and sophistication that match the multiple challenges facing some young people, such as detachment from education and

employment, homelessness, substance misuse, and poor mental health is often beyond the resources available to a YOT let alone an individual practitioner.

(Stephenson *et al.* 2007: 255)

The following concluding chapter reconsiders the work of the contemporary youth justice system in the context of the inevitable structural constraints in which it can be located.

Notes

1 Absolute poverty measures the number of people living below a certain income threshold or the number of households unable to afford certain basic goods and services. Relative poverty measures the extent to which a household's financial resources falls below an average income threshold for the economy. Although living standards and real incomes have grown because of higher employment and sustained economic growth over recent years, the gains in income and wealth have been unevenly distributed across the population.

2 The term 'parent' includes birth parents (whether married or unmarried) and guardians or other carers, including step-parents, adoptive parents, foster parents, grandparents, older siblings or other relatives.

3 The term 'mental' health encompasses varied disorders such as emotional disorders, depression, post-traumatic stress disorder, conduct disorders, hyperkinetic (hyperactivity) disorders, personality disorders, persuasive developmental disorders, mental retardation/learning difficulties and specific learning difficulties. For further information about specific disorders, the reader is referred to a child psychiatry text (Goodman and Scott 1997; Black and Cottrell 1993).

4 The overall responsibility for the provision of mentoring programmes for young offenders – although they may be run by agencies outside of the formal youth justice system – lies with the local YOT.

5 Final warnings can be delivered in a restorative way by a police officer.

Chapter 12

Reflections on the management of contemporary youth crime

The previous chapter considered the work of the contemporary youth justice system in practice and involved an examination of the role and significance of identified key areas of effective practice. This concluding chapter reflects further on the effectiveness of that system in a wider structural context.

Armstrong (2005) observes that the very idea of children and young people being involved in criminal behaviour is of considerable concern to most of us on different levels. Thus, first, it quite simply challenges any belief we may have in the notion of childhood innocence and, perhaps, some fundamental beliefs we may have about the possibility of a 'good society'. Second, it generates in us a fear of lawlessness and the effects of a breakdown in socialisation. We therefore come to question the quality of our services for children, our support for parents and our investment in future generations; not least those of us who are parents ourselves. Yet it is also evident from the many self-report studies that have been undertaken in recent years that most young people these days are not involved in crime at any level (Communities that Care 2002; Flood-Page et al. 2000; MORI 2001, 2002, 2003).

The Home Office youth lifestyles survey (covering the period 1998–9), for instance, and which we encountered in the introduction to this book, found that 33 per cent of males aged 15–16 admitted committing at least one crime within the previous 12 months, with the percentage of females in the same age group who admitted having offended being predictably much lower (Flood-Page et al. 2000). The YJB survey for 2003 (MORI 2003) found that 26 per cent

223

of 11–16-year-olds in mainstream schools admitted committing an offence in the previous 12 months, although some children, such as those excluded from school (60 per cent of whom reported offending in the previous 12 months) were far more likely to report offending during this period than others (MORI 2003).

For those who do get involved in offending behaviour, the evidence from both reconviction and self-report studies has consistently indicated that the great majority of young people do continue to 'grow out' of it (MORI 2003) regardless of virtually continuous 'moral panics' that suggest the very opposite. Moreover, of those who do report offending, a much smaller proportion than previously report coming into contact with the criminal justice system. The YJB survey for 2003 found that 21 per cent of children and young people in mainstream schools say that they have been caught by the police at least once (MORI 2003) but the converse of that finding is that 79 per cent – or well over two-thirds – had not.

The evidence we have of the relationship between children and young people and criminality in the contemporary world would thus seem to contradict popular perceptions. Indeed, if we consider the 'fear of crime' from the perspective of the young person, what might be the most worrying, if perhaps ironic, observation about the crime statistics, is that young people are the group more likely to be victims of crime (Furlong and Cartmel 1997; Home Office 2002). Yet, as Nacro (2001) have observed, British public perceptions tend to overstate the extent of crime attributable to young people: thus, while 28 per cent believe that young people are responsible for more than half of all offences and a further 55 per cent believe that responsibility for crime is shared equally between adults and children, in fact during 1999, 76 per cent of detected crime was committed by persons over the age of 18, and those over 21 were responsible for almost 60 per cent. Furthermore, to locate these findings in their proper context, trend data from the British Crime Survey show quite clearly that offending by young people is significantly in decline. After a period of unparalleled increases in crime worldwide during the 1970s and 1980s, between 1992 and 1999 the number of 10–17-year-olds convicted or cautioned for an indictable offence in the UK fell from 143,400 to 120,400, while for those under 21 years of age the decline over the same period was from 278,900 to 208,700 (Home Office 2000).

It is significant, moreover, that many young people do not appear to possess a liberal 'let them grow out of it' attitude to criminality among their peers. It was explained at the conclusion of the second chapter that this text favours a variation on the Foucauldian carceral society orthodoxy where it is readily accepted that disciplinary and tutelage strategies are often implemented by philanthropists, moral entrepreneurs, professional agents and practitioners who often have little, or no idea, how their often, but sometimes less, humble discourse contributes to the grand overall disciplinary control matrix. The variation proposed in this text recognises, however, that there are further interests involved in the creation of that matrix and these significantly are ours. This hybrid – or left realist – perspective accepts the legitimacy of both neo-Marxist and social progress accounts because there were and are a multitude of motivations for both implementing and accepting the increasing surveillance and control of young people on the streets and elsewhere. But crucially among those who wish to see a rigorous intervention in the lives of those socially excluded young people who are overrepresented among the numbers of persistent offenders are both ourselves as parents – who invariably go to great lengths to ensure that our children do not come into contact with this socially excluded underclass, an evasiveness perfectly epitomised by our careful choice of school for our offspring – and perhaps more importantly our children themselves. It is the latter who want protection from what they widely perceive to be the dangerous, threatening elements in their age group who are the most likely to make them victims of crime.

A recent survey conducted by IPO-Mori for the Youth Justice Board (BBC 2007) showed that 60 per cent of young people between the ages of 10 and 17 years want to see more police on the beat as the best way to protect them from becoming a victim of crime at the hands of other young people. Moreover, 38 per cent called for harsher punishments for children and young people who offend. YJB Interim Chair Graham Robb said:

> It's positive that young people believe the police have a major role to play in keeping them safe. However, the underlying issue is that many young people don't feel protected outside the home and, in particular, they are afraid of other youngsters.

> This type of situation can lead some children to carry weapons for self protection and is something we must avoid at all costs. We all need to do more to make our children feel safe.

The decline in youth crime reflects a similar decrease in crime overall, both in the UK and in many other parts of the world during the same period (Young 1999). In case one should think that this decline in the crime rate might indicate a detection failure rather than any real decrease, it is worth noting that the British Crime Survey for the year 2000 also shows a decrease in victimisation of 15 per cent during the period 1995 to 1999. Thus, if less people are reporting victimisation it is reasonable to suppose that less crime is being committed (Home Office 2000).

It could be argued that changes in the youth crime rate have been brought about, or at least influenced, by the policies and actions of the contemporary youth justice system. The evidence, nevertheless, shows that the trend of decline was clearly evident before the establishment of that system. It is, therefore, difficult to disentangle the possible causes that lie behind social trends and the impact of particular policies. Indeed, in practice it is likely that the causal relationship between different factors impacting upon the trend in youth crime is going to be extremely complex. Armstrong (2005) observes that whatever the explanation for this downturn in offending behaviour by children and young people, there do appear to be some fairly sound grounds for optimism. Yet it is difficult to escape the conclusion that in the UK, as in some other parts of the world, any optimism about youth offending trends must be tempered by the presence of an extraordinary contradiction. At the very time that youth crime is seen to be dramatically falling there has been both a heightened profile given to the problem and a significant increase in the use of custodial sentencing as a means of dealing with this declining problem.

There is a serious possibility that increasing numbers of young people have simply desisted from involvement in offending behaviour in recent years because it is simply no longer a rational or 'cool' choice in a changed socio-economic context. It is a world where the only hope of legitimate material success is the adoption of an 'upward' strategy of educational attainment and this notion is further critically explored below. We are now going to consider the increasing policing and surveillance of those groups who continue to pursue a 'downward' strategy that has seen them absorbed into the ranks of social exclusion. In particular we are going to consider how a new industry of early intervention based upon an ideology of 'risk' has become a tool of governmentality in the lives of young people, their families and their schools, in some of our most deprived communities. For it is, in reality, these young people overrepresented among the numbers of persistent young offenders with a multiplicity of risk factors that predispose them to crime – the 3 to 4 cent identified in this book – that the young people recently surveyed by the YJB seek protection from.

Risk-based contemporary youth justice revisited

As we have seen, the contemporary youth justice system is very much founded on the notion of risk-focused prevention. From this perspective, it is argued that there is a strong correlation between the offending behaviour of young people and significant risk factors to be found in their life experiences; thus, dysfunction within or in relation to the family, school, community and the peer group of delinquent individuals (Hawkins *et al.* 1992), as well as in the personalities or genetic make-up of certain children (Farrington 1994; Rutter *et al.* 1998). It has therefore been proposed that early interventions which focus upon correcting these deficiencies are likely to reduce the likelihood of involvement in offending behaviour.

The most influential study on the identification of risk factors related to criminal behaviour has been the Cambridge study in delinquent development, a longitudinal study of 411 working-class males born in London in 1953 (Farrington 1995) and this has been cited previously in the book. The original sample has been followed up periodically from the age of eight and a strong correlation has been found between a number of risk factors – including low family income, large family size, poor housing, low intelligence, parental problems – and offending behaviour. This study has been extremely influential in reorienting thinking about youth crime in favour of a focus upon those psychogenic antecedents of criminal behaviour which are believed to lie in the immediate social environment of the child rather than in the structural characteristics of society itself. It has come to have a major influence on the policies of governments and has become integral to crime-reduction strategies in the UK, USA and elsewhere (see Graham and Bowling 1995; Utting 1996; Graham 1998), and in the former, this approach has, as we have seen, found particular favour with the Youth Justice Board (2001a).

Pitts (2001), nevertheless, alerts us to how the original findings of the 'Cambridge study' have been processed and refined by subsequent reports and have come to focus primarily on the family while ignoring wider structural issues. Indeed, this is seen as a good example of the ways in which governments employ social science creatively to support their positions. The original study actually discovered a multitude of risk factors – some in the immediate environment of the offender but others, such as a lack of employment opportunities, which can be located in the wider social structure – but, at the same time, had been unable to distinguish any 'cause' and 'effect' in what is, of course, a significantly complex reality. From that time onwards, the data from the original survey have come to be 'reinterpreted' and refined in subsequent documents. Thus, the Conservative Party discussion document *Tackling the Causes of Crime* published in 1996 identified eight 'key risk factors': parenting, truancy, drug abuse, lack of facilities, homelessness, unemployment, low income and – interestingly and honestly – the effects of economic recession. The influential Audit Commission report (1996) of the same year, nevertheless, refined these findings further into foreground familial and background factors. Factors such as family income, employment and the socio-economic status of neighbourhood were now relegated to the background factor category. Yet, a significant pamphlet written by New Labour 'insiders' (Utting *et al.* 1993) had independently identified that 'the tangled roots of delinquency lie, to a considerable extent, inside the family'. Pitts (2001) observes that this latter document came to significantly influence the influential New Labour policy document *No More Excuses* published in 1997 which unequivocally reduced the multiplicity of risk factors in the original study to three main groupings of parenting, schooling and peer influence. The key risk factors were now identified as being male, poor parental discipline, criminal parents and poor school performance. Structural social exclusion factors such as unemployment and poverty had disappeared from the spectrum altogether, with the focus now clearly on the individual child and their parents.

Armstrong (2005) observes that the risk factor model appears to have provided a two-fold legitimation of state intervention in the governance of children, families, schools and designated problematic communities. On the one hand, it provides a simplistic crime management system which – because it denies any social structural contribution to the construction and reproduction of offending behaviour – can focus its attention not on the causes of crime but rather on a policy of containment through the morality of 'blame'. On the other hand, the model is used to justify a whole paraphernalia of surveillance and intervention based on the assumption that youth crime is an outcome of dysfunctional individuals and communities and that these individuals can be identified through an assessment process determined by experts (see Kelly 2001; O'Malley 1992; Rose and Miller 1992; Stenson and Edwards 2003; Stenson and Watt 1999).

Armstrong (2005) observes that, significantly and problematically, such regulation has not been confined to the troublesome. Equally as important are the consequences of establishing criteria for 'normality' based upon a supposed scientific knowledge of the pathological or abnormal for maintaining the self-regulation of family life. These processes of governmentality, Armstrong argues, are embedded in the valuation of academic and professional judgements that masquerade as expertise. It is a masquerade because their science is decontextualised from the contested beliefs and values which give meaning and relevance to particular representations of normality and social order. Yet, the notion of 'risk' supports an anti-welfare rhetoric (Culpitt 1999) that legitimises the redistribution of social resources into a privatised world of individual responsibility and risk management. It is a language that has 'replac[ed] need as the core principle of social policy formation and welfare delivery' (Kemshall 2002: 1).

Armstrong (2005) further argues that what is lacking in these risk-analysis-based individualised accounts of criminal behaviour is: first, any sense of the significance of historically located, cultural and social forms in relation to the construction and negotiation of individual identities (as 'normal' or 'abnormal'); and, second, any discussion of the way in which social power is a factor, not only in the construction of 'risk' within society but also in the theorisation of 'risk' by social scientists themselves: thus, 'legitimacy is conferred almost exclusively on analysis at the individual level' (Susser 1998: 1). Armstrong (2005) observes that in this way, the representation of certain behaviours solely in terms of individual, or micro-social, dysfunction both hides from public view the social and cultural upheavals of the last 20 years while discouraging any attempt to understand the relationships between processes of social change and identity formation in young people.

Social exclusion and reintegrative tutelage reconsidered

We encountered earlier in the book the concept 'excluded tutelage', which was developed in order to make sense of an apparent – albeit relative, it was argued – success story in Conservative Party youth justice policy during the years 1979–97 (Hopkins Burke 1999). Thus, for many young people this was an era characterised very much by 'the stick' of coercion and discipline but rather weak on 'the carrot' of socio-economic opportunity. Thus, a fundamental outcome of economic and social policy during that period was the creation of a socially excluded underclass. Youth justice policies, in particular, and welfare policies, in general, had, at best, done nothing to alleviate that situation, and, at worst, managed to exacerbate the problem.

It is the notion of reintegration into the community that enables us to both explain and contextualise the youth justice strategy of the New Labour government elected in 1997, and distinguish its policies from those of its populist Conservative predecessors. It is in this way a distinctive strategy which we observed at the outset of this third part of the book to be a significant component of a wider set of neo-communitarian strategies that have sought to reintegrate those sections of the population that have become increasingly socially and economically excluded during the past 30 years. This unwritten and unspoken government strategy, which has been termed 'reintegrative tutelage' (Hopkins Burke 1999), nevertheless invites critical reconsideration in the context of recent recognition that prevailing discourses of transitions and social exclusion are no longer adequate to describe or explain the experiences of that substantial minority of young people who have become located in 'underclass locations' (Fergusson *et al.* 2000). Indeed, in this context, the whole notion of social reintegration appears to be a fatally flawed strategy in society as it is currently structured.

The educational and employment prospects for all young people have clearly changed dramatically in the past 30 years. Thus, in the early 1970s the majority left school at 16 and were able to secure full-time employment with seemingly relative ease. However, by the 1990s these young workers were replaced by full-time students, trainees, part-time workers and the unemployed working 'off the cards'.[1] Since Income Support benefit was abolished in 1988 for virtually all 16- and 17-year-olds, successive cohorts of that age group have been faced with an apparently wide range of options but each with its own limitations: to continue with schooling or further education; accept a place on a government-sponsored training scheme; enter the labour market (often on a part-time or short-term basis); or, if unemployed, stay dependent on their families. As a result, it has been widely acknowledged that 'adolescence' has been formally extended in most social classes. At the same time, while most young people have been faced with extensive choices, they have been denied the possibility of full independence.

One of the most conspicuous consequences of a contracting and deregulated youth labour market has been the expansion of what Furlong and Cartmel (1997: 17) describe as 'an army of reluctant conscripts to post-compulsory education'. Thus, whereas in the mid-1970s a third of 16-year-olds stayed on at school, by the mid-1990s it was nearer 80 per cent. A range of vocational courses (BTEC, NVQ and GNVQ) have been introduced in schools and colleges of further education but with limited success. About a third of those starting a full-time post-16 course leave early or fail the relevant examinations, while those entering youth training fare little better. Despite government claims that various forms of youth training have been designed to improve skills and subsequent employability, these schemes have been consistently considered by young people themselves to be 'slave labour', with employers operating 'try-out schemes' in which the work performance of young people is assessed and only the best are retained (Coffield *et al.* 1986; Lee *et al.* 1990; Banks *et al.* 1992). Youth training schemes have thus been received by young people with a combination of resistance, denial and ambivalence (Mizen 1995: 197–202). The experience of training has also become fragmented and individualised but, at the same time, remains stratified by class, gender and 'race' (Furlong and Cartmel 1997: 32). Thus, most disadvantaged and, in particular, those from minority ethnic groups, tend to be concentrated in schemes with low rates of subsequent employment.

The promised new opportunities simply failed to materialise for many young people, with the vast majority of schemes reinforcing and reproducing gender stereotypes in their provision of 'suitable' work for young men and women (Griffin 1985; Cockburn 1987; Wallace 1987). Furthermore, the free-market logic of deregulation did not help young people get into work, despite them being cheaper to employ. Demand in industrialised economies for skilled workers has meant that the young – especially those without qualifications – have been left behind. Brinkley (1997) showed that in the previous year the unemployment rate for under-25s was 14.8 per cent, which was almost twice the national average for all claimants. Unemployment has always hit the young hardest, particularly so those from ethnic minorities: thus while, in 1995, 15 per cent of white 16–25-year-olds were estimated to be unemployed, this compared quite favourably to the 51 per cent of African-Caribbean young men, 41 per cent of African-Caribbean young women, 34 per cent of Pakistani/Bangladeshi young men and 30 per cent of Indian young men (Runnymede Trust 1996).

These estimates, nevertheless, ignore a sizeable percentage of the population. Wilkinson (1995) found, in his Sunderland-based study, that between 5 and 10 per cent of 16- and 17-year-olds were neither in education or training nor in employment and they did not have any access to income support or any form of legitimate income. Officially, they did not exist. This could amount to some 100,000 young people nationally who occupy what Williamson (1997) has, not without criticism, termed 'status-zero'.

This was the context in which the New Labour government

in 1997 announced its Welfare-to-Work plans designed to take a quarter of a million under-25-year-olds 'off the dole'. Significantly, it was an extension of the former Conservative government's Job Seeker's Allowance and stipulated that if claimants refused to take up the proposed employment and training options they would lose all right to claim welfare benefits. After a four-month induction period, designed to facilitate entry into the labour market, the young unemployed were now to take up a private-sector job for which the employer or training organisation was to be subsidised, work with a voluntary organisation or an environmental taskforce, or take up full-time education and training.

Fergusson et al. (2000) identify three interpretations of the collective experiences of 16–19-year-olds over the past two decades. First, a transitions discourse was for many years the dominant discourse (Ashton and Field 1976) where this age range was seen as the critical period of transition, principally from student to employee, from adolescent to young adult and from a state of dependency to independence. From this perspective, post-16 activity is portrayed as a relatively rational process whereupon young people are matched to a range of possible places according to their preferences, their performance and the assessments of careers staff (Bates 1984). It is this effective matching that provides the foundations for careers which progress through further education, training and workplace experience. For the vast majority, it is argued, the period between 16 and 19 constitutes a relatively non-problematic linear transition from school to employment or further education/higher education.

Second, the markets and choice discourse is an outcome of the major restructuring of provision for 16–19-year-olds, from the late 1980s to the mid-1990s, in which providers are encouraged to open access and increase options in a competitive environment, and users are partially reconstructed as customers, with credit to spend and choices to exercise in pursuit of preferences and armed with information about the relative quality of institutions. This argument has impacted greatly on the first discourse by shifting responsibility for the transition away from careers guidance and towards the individual for mapping out their own education and training after the age of 16 (Hodkinson 1996).

Third, the social exclusion discourse is largely a product of the massive contraction of youth labour markets and has identified institutional arrangements as having failed to make adequate provision for those most vulnerable to market fluctuations. It is often combined with a discourse of disaffection where it is argued that they are cut off not only from traditional unilinear 'career' patterns, but also from finding a place in the market of studentships, jobs and training placements, either by structural factors like inadequate provision and family poverty, or by individual factors, such as an anti-educational culture on the part of the individual young person. These patterns of experience tend to be interpreted through a discourse of exclusion when the factors are thought to be structural and through a discourse of disaffection when they are represented as personal shortcomings or as dysfunctional behaviour. Thus, much policy since the election of New Labour in 1997 has focused on making provision for this group as part of their reintegrative tutelage strategy.

Fergusson *et al.* (2000) propose an alternative discourse where they argue that the transitions discourse remains largely plausible for interpreting the careers of many entrants to higher education, and for a small proportion of young people who leave school at 16 and proceed through well-established training routes into a range of vocational openings. Moreover, a social exclusion/disaffection discourse might well be appropriate for explaining the experiences of those who opt out or become 'status zero'. Fergusson *et al.* nevertheless observe that neither of these discourses are appropriate for explaining the experiences of a growing number of young people who appear to be neither 'in' nor 'out' and identify approximately a third of 16–18-year-olds who are seemingly engaged in a series of multiple trajectories. Such activities remain understandable in terms of a discourse of markets and choice, but the former is experienced in ways which not only fail to translate into 'transitions', but also do not permit exclusion or opting out. In the case of unsecured transitions, the processes of negotiating markets are, for some young people, resulting in dislocation from any hitherto identifiable mode of activity. For others, distinctive processes of marginalisation are being reproduced which cannot be attributed to structural exclusions or individualised disaffection alone. In contrast to social exclusion, which assumes a lack of means – or cultural capital – to take advantage of existing available opportunities, and to disaffection, which assumes an unwillingness to participate, a distinctive discourse of normalised dislocation identifies a partial lack of success at participation in a competitive environment, without any acknowledgment of structural or individual impediment.

Fergusson *et al.* (2000) argue that present 'quasi-market' systems actively encourage instability in the trajectories of a substantial minority of young people. Through generating powerful pressures which force young people to make particular rational choices, markets draw into particular modes of participation, young people who are either ill-informed about what they have committed themselves to, or are unable to identify or pursue a preferred option. The outcome is that options are found to be noticeably unsuitable, are pursued with little commitment and are short-lived. What is of particular interest is the nature of the pressures – and the complex mix of financial, social and cultural forces – which allow an apparently voluntary system of participation to result in unstable modes of activity.

Market-induced instability, it is argued, is experienced as a series of multiple relocations and unstable trajectories which occur within the context of a 'compulsory' market-driven inclusivity and which is characterised by default participation in education and resorting to part-time work. In short, there is a significant blurring of boundaries between those who have taken a conscious 'upward solution' of education and career pursuit progression and those who have taken a 'downward solution' of *laissez-faire* non-participation, albeit in the latter case invariably by default. There is, therefore, a significant group in the middle who are sufficiently motivated to take an upward trajectory but are unable to acquire sufficient cultural capital to obtain a stable successful economic location. Such young people with significantly weakened social bonds are very much at risk of being absorbed into the readily available offending subcultures we have encountered in this book even though they have few other risk factors present in their lives.

In short, the whole notion of reintegrative tutelage on which the whole New Labour neo-communitarian strategy is founded seems to be based on rather fragile socio-economic foundations, with the economy unable to provide accessible legitimate sustainable opportunities for increasingly large sections of young people. Thus, in these circumstances, the notion of restorative justice on which the whole neo-communitarian contemporary youth justice strategy is based is also equally problematic.

Restorative justice revisited

We have seen previously that it is the purpose of restorative justice to bring together victims, offenders and communities to decide on a response to a particular crime. The intention is to put the needs of the victim at the centre of the criminal justice system and to finding positive solutions to crime by encouraging offenders to take responsibility for their actions. Victims may, therefore, request a restorative justice approach to make an offender realise how the crime has affected their life, find out information to help put the crime behind them, for example, why it was the offender targeted them, and to openly forgive the offender.

Whereas 'traditional justice' is about punishing offenders for committing offences against the state, restorative justice, on the other hand, is about offenders making amends directly to the people, organisations, and the communities they have harmed. The New Labour government has, therefore, supported restorative justice because it is seen as giving victims a greater voice in the criminal justice system, it allows victims to receive an explanation and more meaningful reparation from offenders, makes offenders accountable by allowing them to take responsibility for their actions and, it is proposed, builds community confidence that offenders are making amends for their wrongdoing. We saw in the previous chapter that restorative justice is a key element of the contemporary youth justice system and research has shown that this strategy has had some success in reducing reoffending by young people and providing greater satisfaction for victims but there are, nevertheless, significant concerns about the legitimacy and efficacy of restorative justice in practice.

First, there have been concerns raised about the boundary between the negotiatory practices of restorative justice and the workings of the criminal justice system: thus, on one hand, it is argued, the due-process safeguards for rights, equality and proportionality could all be lost, while, on the other hand, the power of judicial agencies can undermine and subvert the aims of restorative practices (Messmer and Otto 1992). Some argue, therefore, for completely separate and parallel systems, neither interfering with the other. Others have countered and argued that this would not lead to restorative justice at all, because all gains would be destroyed by the alienating and negative effects of adversarial justice. It is, nevertheless, difficult to see how two independent systems can coexist for there is bound to be some influence each way and thus the problem cannot be avoided. Even though restorative justice involves a greater or lesser degree of devolution of control to individual citizens and communities, it is now generally accepted that it can and should be integrated as far as possible with legal justice as a complementary process that improves the quality, effectiveness and efficiency of a 'whole justice' (Marshall 1997). Restorative justice, therefore, becomes an instrument of the neo-communitarian state-dominated contemporary youth justice system rather than having any significant independence from it.

A second limitation to any restorative justice practice which attempts to involve communities is the relative availability of resources and skills. Communities are not the integrated entities with high levels of mechanical solidarity that they once were in those antipodean communities where restorative justice has been shown to be successful. In our contemporary post-industrial society, there is a greater emphasis on individual privacy and autonomy, and major social divides occur between cultures and age groups, without the interdependency of an ideal organic solidarity. Greater community involvement would therefore inevitably mean increased education, training and practical resources, and more would need to be provided in some areas of significant deprivation than in others.

A third, very closely related, and highly significant limitation for restorative justice is the continuing existence of social injustice and inequality in and between communities. While problems such as these continue, the degree to which communities can be supportive, caring and controlling is seriously restricted. Social divisions also make voluntary participation less likely or less effective. If restorative justice involves the community as a major player, there simply needs to be a community with which the young person can identify and belong. The degree to which effective communities exist depends largely on other social policies apart from criminal justice and there are, therefore, implications for education, housing, community development, employment opportunities, welfare, health and the environmental services on which the contemporary youth justice system and the strategy of reintegrative tutelage is so dependent.

Gray (2005) observes that responsibilisation through restorative justice interventions is one of the main technologies of risk management but the whole ethos, as we have observed above, envisages more than just holding young people responsible for their offending. It also professes a commitment to the restoration of victim–offender relations and the reintegration of young offenders into mainstream community life. Gray observes, however, that the principles of restorative justice have been narrowly interpreted within the contemporary youth system to give undue weight to the responsibilisation of young offenders by challenging perceived deficits in their moral reasoning without any real attempt to legitimately challenge the exclusionary socio-economic constraints that severely limit their choices and ability to successfully reintegrate into mainstream society. The outcome has been that restorative justice has simply become bound to the interests of reinforcing 'moral discipline' rather than engaging with 'social justice' and the reinvigoration of community on which restorative justice and reintegrative tutelage are theoretically founded.

Proponents argue that the reinvigoration of community through restorative justice mechanisms can facilitate strong bonds of social control: 'strong communities can speak to us in moral voices' and they allow 'the policing *by* communities rather than the policing *of* communities' (Strang 1995: 217). Nevertheless, as Crawford and Clear (2003) observe, alternative justice systems, through necessity, presuppose an existing degree of informal control upon which mutuality, reciprocity and commitment can be re-formed. Moreover, Braithwaite (1989: 100) observes that informal control processes, such as reintegrative shaming, which some community conferences seek to engender, are more conducive to – and more effective when drawing upon – communitarian cultures. The paradox is that in urban, individualistic and anonymous cultures, such as those that exist in most Western towns and cities, informal control mechanisms such as shaming lack potency. The appeal to revive or transform community has arisen at exactly the moment when it appears most absent, when Durkheimian anomie or normlessness is rampant (Durkheim 1933). For some, this paradox provides the basis for the attraction of restorative and community justice.

The whole notion of community is, however, complex and extends beyond the more traditional definitions based on locality and embraces a multiplicity of groups and networks to which, it is believed, we all belong (Strang 1995: 16). This conception thus does not rely upon a fixed assumption of where a community will be found. Rather, it builds upon the notion of 'communities of care' – that is, the networks of obligation and respect between the individual and everyone who cares about the person the most – and these are significantly not bounded by geography (Braithwaite and Daly 1994: 195).

These communities of care are considered more relevant to contemporary modern living in urban societies because they provide a developed notion of 'community' where membership – or social identity – is personal and does not necessarily carry any fixed or external attributes of membership. The fact that such communities do not carry any connotations of coercion or forced membership is one of the distinctive appeals of the concept (Crawford and Clear 2003) and from this perspective, there is an assumption that people can move freely between communities if they disagree with their practices and values and/or remain within a community but dissent from the dominant moral voice that exists. This is, nevertheless, a significantly problematic situation for, on the one hand, these contemporary 'light' communities are held up as examples of how they can allow sufficient space for individual or minority dissent, innovation and difference but, on the other hand, they are also seen as insufficient with regard to informal control.

Crawford and Clear (2003) observe that this all raises the question of exactly what is meant by the claim to 'restore' or 'reintegrate' communities as proposed by the proponents of both community and restorative justice (see: Braithwaite 1998; Clear and Karp 1999; Van Ness and Strong 1997). For the very notion of restoring communities suggests a return to some pre-existing state and appears to involve a nostalgic urge to return to a mythical age of genuine human identity, connectedness, and reciprocity. It certainly does seem questionable that the concept of community constitutes a dynamic force for democratic renewal that challenges existing inequalities of power and the differential distribution of life opportunities and pathways to crime that characterise our society.

Crawford and Clear (2003) argue that in order to consider the genuine potential of restorative and community justice it is necessary to avoid the idealistic perceptions of many proponents and confront the empirical realities of most communities. The ideal of unrestricted entry to, and exit from, communities needs to be reconciled with the existence of relations of dominance, exclusion and differential power. The reality is that many stable communities contain very high levels of mechanical solidarity, they tend to resist innovation, creation and experimentation, and shun diversity (Hopkins Burke and Pollock 2004). These communities may well be able to come together for informal social control but the way these processes play out lacks inclusive qualities and offender-sensitive styles. These communities can be, and often are, pockets of intolerance and prejudice. They can be coercive and tolerant of bigotry and discriminatory behaviour. Weaker individuals – and minority groups – within such communities often experience them not as a home of connectedness and mutuality but as the foundations of inequalities that sustain and reinforce relations of dependence (for example, with regard to gender role and the tolerance of domestic violence or child abuse). Such communities are, therefore, often hostile to minorities, dissenters and outsiders, and can tolerate and even encourage deviant and offending behaviour.

Communities are quite simply hierarchical formations which are structured upon lines of power, dominance and authority. They are intrinsically exclusive – as social exclusion presupposes processes of exclusion – and many solidify and define themselves around notions of 'otherness' that are potentially infused with racialised overtones. Challenging and disrupting established community order, its assumptions and power relations might, therefore, be a more fundamental aspect of a progressive restorative justice programme and transforming communities may be a more appropriate strategy than the restoration of atavistic communities. The related question begged by this assertion is whether transforming communities is either feasible or an appropriate task of restorative justice in the contemporary youth justice system.

Towards the future

It is clear from the discussion in this book that patterns of offending by children and young people and the nature of the response by the authorities are closely linked to significant socio-economic circumstances. I have previously proposed that the 'third way' neo-communitarian crime-control strategy of New Labour with its theoretical roots in left realism is a legitimate long-term strategy for both understanding crime and criminal behaviour in all its many manifestations and for the development of flexible strategies for dealing with a complex and ambiguous social problem (Hopkins Burke 2005, 2007). Moreover, it was argued that for this to be a successful and widely accepted long-term strategy capable of surviving a change of government, it must have strong social foundations and, therefore, embrace the essential tenets of a contemporary new-liberalism, that is, a liberalism where there is respect for the rights and responsibilities of both individuals and communities while at the same time recognising that crime is real problem which impacts hugely and negatively on the lives of real people, be they victims or offenders, and moreover that it is not inappropriate or illiberal to intervene in such activities or deal with the consequences of those actions in a rigorous way.

There are, however, legitimate concerns among many respected researchers and commentators that the rigour might have gone too far. Certainly, since gaining office in 1997, New Labour has claimed a commitment to rebuilding a strong civic society where 'rights and duties go hand in hand' (Blair 2002) and the broad social policy agenda of the government has sought to emphasise individual responsibilities and obligations to that civic society in accordance with the central tenets of communitarianism. Jamieson (2005) notes that with the publication of the White Paper: *Respect and Responsibility: Taking a Stand Against Anti-Social Behaviour* (Home Office 2003), the 'respect' agenda now comprises a central component of the government pursuit of a 'responsive inclusive citizenship' (Squires and Stephen 2005). The non-remitting assault against anti-social behaviour in our communities has moreover been a cornerstone of the respect agenda and at the centre of that civilising tutelage project has been young people.

The Crime and Disorder Act 1998 had been the primary piece of legislation responsible for introducing the Anti-social Behaviour Order (ASBO) into the mainstream criminal justice and social policy arena. Alongside this legislation 'guidance ... appeared to anticipate up to 5000 orders per year but, by March 2004, the overall total had still not reached 2500' (Squires 2006: 145). The outcome was further legislation to encourage their use. Thus, the Police Reform Act 2002 was 'designed to make the ASBO more widely available and easier to obtain and non-statutory *Acceptable Behavioural Contracts* (ABCs) have been adopted ... with the proviso that non-compliance is likely to result in an ASBO' (Jamieson 2005: 185). The following year brought the introduction of the Anti-Social Behaviour Act 2003 with the aim to 'push the boundaries of control still further, with an eclectic mix of environmental enforcement and new constraints on tenants, parents and young people' (Burney 2005: 72). Alongside this piece of legislation there was the launch of the Home Office Anti-social Behaviour Unit. This increased focus on anti-social behaviour through the creation of legislation and departments seems to have achieved the outcome the government wanted (Squires 2006: 145).

Young people are currently the main targets in the government's battle against crime and disorder, social disorganisation and, most notably, anti-social behaviour (Squires and Stephen 2005). This overzealous focus on anti-social behaviour also 'signals exclusion and rejection' (Burney 2005: 2); instead of empowering and uniting the community, it ostracises certain families or individuals, while also pitting the community against the individual, as the former effectively has to police the latter to make sure they comply with the requirements of the order. This allows for the development of resentment and division rather than the creation of a strong inclusive community.

When a young person becomes the subject of an ASBO, the community in which they live may be informed through the local newspapers, or through the distribution of leaflets, and this publicity includes information regarding the restrictions that are placed on the activities of the young person and a photographic image, so that the person is easily recognised when they are encountered. Not only is this contrary to a long-established principle in youth justice established by the Children and Young Persons Act 1933 s.49 which places significant restrictions on the naming of a young person who is involved in criminal proceedings (Fionda 2005), but also it is a classic example of 'disintegrative, rather than reintegrative, shaming because it does nothing constructive for the individual to ensure their reintegration into the community, but serves to alert a mistrusting community to their misbehaviour and places them under the surveillance of their neighbours' (Fionda 2005: 243).

Jamieson (2005) observes that the authoritarian penal populism of the 'respect' agenda – of which the anti-social behaviour order agenda has such a central part – has a particular electoral appeal within a risk-conscious society. Thus, the punitive emphasis of responses to 'anti-social' and criminal behaviour provides an opportunity to reassure the public that firm measures are in place to deal with such behaviours. Jamieson nevertheless argues that while such interventionist measures may well provide some respite from troublesome behaviour in the short term – and may even serve to deter involvement in such activities – the legitimacy, justification and desirability of the 'respect' agenda are questionable. The denigration inherent in the derogatory rhetoric and punitive emphasis of that agenda promotes profoundly negative portrayals of the parents, children and young people primarily targeted (Burney 2005; Squires and Stephen 2005). The danger of this strategy, it is observed, is that it not only encourages intolerance and hostility, but also serves to obscure the often complex and diverse needs underlying 'parenting deficits' and 'anti-social' and 'criminal' behaviour. Furthermore, the emphasis on – and enforcement of – individual responsibility masks the reality that the government and the 'law-abiding' community can be implicated in the causes of 'anti-social' and 'criminal' behaviour (Hudson 2003). The government and the 'law-abiding' majority also have responsibilities, not least the responsibility for ensuring that social justice extends to all members of society. As Squires and Stephen (2005) astutely observe, 'respect and responsibility is a two-way street – it cannot be demanded of children (or of adults for that matter) who have not the wherewithal or the appropriate opportunities to demonstrate responsibility'. The New Labour agenda has, therefore, developed an increasingly authoritarian character – using an expanding central state apparatus to deliver outcomes – rather than giving encouragement to the relatively autonomous powers of civil society to deliver progress as suggested by communitarianism (see Driver and Martell 1997; Jordan 1998).

A non-adulterated left realist criminological agenda – which, in short, proposes a balance of intervention challenging both criminal behaviour and the conditions which facilitate and nurture it (Hopkins Burke 2005) – is, however, very much in accordance with the propositions of a 'new' liberalism and it has been observed elsewhere that the essential baseline for the formulation of this proposed contemporary social solidarity will of necessity involve a reduction in socio-economic inequality at the same time as recognition and celebration of the diversity of contemporary society (Hopkins Burke 2007).

It is the work of Durkheim and his observations on the moral component of the division of labour in society that provides the theoretical foundations of this 'new' liberalism and a legitimate social context for community: that is, a political vision which actively promotes both the rights and responsibilities of both individuals and communities but in the context of an equal division of labour. It is this latter element that deviates significantly from the orthodoxy promoted by Amitai Etzioni – and which has been embraced and distorted in the UK by New Labour with its enthusiasm for a strong dictatorial central state apparatus to enforce its agenda – and provides us with the basis of a genuine moral communitarianism, founded on notions of consensual interdependency with others we all recognise and identify as fellow citizens and social partners, and not as potential legitimate crime targets. Linked to this notion of moral communitarianism in the context of youth justice is a need to reconsider notions of risk and how we and young people in particular understand it.

Armstrong (2005) observes that criminological studies of risk have simply ignored the ways in which young people negotiate and interact within their social worlds and have simply underestimated, or even ignored, the importance of (sub) cultures and the structural context that we encountered in the second part of this book. The outcome has been an almost total absence of any consideration of the social construction of risk. Yet, as Armstrong so rightly observes, the experience and management of social exclusion, for example, may significantly impact on the types of risk the young person is willing to take. As France (2000: 36) notes, 'being "different" may bring with it more substantial and immediate risks that have everyday consequences for young people's lives'.

Armstrong (2005) proposes that if we want to seriously engage with the perspectives of young people there is a need for new approaches to the study of risk and offending. Such research should, therefore, explore the pathways of children and young people in different contexts, looking at how 'risk' and 'resilience' to risk are constructed and understood by those involved. Such a research strategy would involve a focus on the biographical experiences of individuals and the social construction of their behaviour, a consideration of how children understand and explain their own behaviour and an exploration of the geographical, social, cultural and historical worlds in which their lives are given meaning.

The future of youth justice

The Youth Justice Board was at the outset given extensive powers, political access and a broad brief involving a degree of financial control and responsibility for the promulgation of national standards and targets, service development, training, and inspection and audit. Pitts (2003) observes that while, at first sight, the YJB appears to have been given unprecedented autonomy and power, a closer examination reveals a significantly different story. The YJB, in fact, faces four closely interconnected problems. First, there has been an unprecedented politicisation of youth crime under New Labour. Second, there has been an excessive link between the political and administrative spheres (Pitts 2001). Third, there has been the unwillingness of government to give the YJB a role in policy formation. Fourth, there was the tendency of the then Prime Minister (Tony Blair) to suddenly take control of a particular criminal justice issue at short notice and make it his own for short-term political gain. Pitts (2003: 14) observes that:

> As a result, alongside the difficult task of transforming the youth justice system, the YJB constantly has to cobble together responses to whatever the issue of the week may be, while also serving as an apologist for these off-the-cuff initiatives, some of which appear to undermine the Board's key objectives. This attempt to 'run with the hare and the hounds' has led some Board members to threaten to resign, and others to publicly castigate the field for its failure to live in the 'real world of hard political choices'.

Pitts further observes that the youth justice specialists recruited to serve as a link between the Board and the YOTs are required to press practitioners to implement otherwise sound policies too hastily, or to meet politically driven – and hence frequently changing   priorities and targets. He argues that many of these problems could be ameliorated, if not resolved, by the de-politicisation of the contemporary youth justice system although it is accepted that this is unlikely to happen in the present political climate. Pitts (2003) observes that such a depoliticised and autonomous supervising agency could become the champion and supporter of the youth justice system, its staff and its clients, from attempts by government to exploit them to political advantage. In such a scenario, he observes, the Board would gain the unequivocal support of the practitioners and managers who are precisely the people it needs to promote its agenda and realise its vision.

The Youth Justice Board is extremely unlikely to be replaced in the foreseeable future, even in the event of a change in government, and abolition would probably be inappropriate. The evidence reviewed in this book suggests a promising start with even greater potential but greater independence and autonomy from a controlling, however well-meaning government, would provide it with greater widespread credibility, and moreover, such an agenda would coincide appropriately with the requirements of the 'new liberal' moral communitarian agenda outlined above.

Pitts (2003: 17) provides us with a template for an optimum Youth Justice Board – or autonomous supervising agency – which would be fully compatible with the proposed moral communitarian agenda. First, it is proposed that there should be a powerful neutral autonomous element in youth justice policy-making that avoids short-term political imperatives and contingencies. Second, the supervising agency should be a robust, principled, non-political governmental policy adviser. Third, the agency should promote and champion the rights of children and young people. Fourth, the agency should challenge the political and media exploitation of youth crime and young offenders, and unrealistic political pressure for results. Fifth, the agency should be a perceptive strategic planner of youth justice services. Sixth, there should be an attentive, engaged and robust manager of the juvenile secure estate, committed to the realisation of relevant international rights conventions within its institutions and practice standards developed in residential child care (Warner 1992). Seventh, the agency should be a forum for debate and original thinking in the youth justice arena which embraces the whole range of informed opinion, theory and research findings on relevant issues. Eighth, it should an instigator and disseminator of apolitical evidence of good practice and the sponsor and defender of experimentation and innovation. Ninth, it should be a facilitator of dialogue within and between practice and the academy.[2] Tenth, it should be the purveyor of coherent and consistent standards and priorities. Eleventh, it should be a facilitator of service development, training and support for the youth justice professions. Twelfth, the agency needs to be an innovative evaluator, devising data-collection methods relevant to local situations and ensuring that data held by partner agencies are compatible and accessible. Pitts (2003) proposes that such a revitalised Youth Justice Board, pursuing these goals – or something very much similar to them – would almost certainly gain greater respect, influence and support. The cost, which could well turn out to be a long-term benefit, would be a distancing from, and occasional conflict with, government.

There is, however, an additional qualification that needs to be made if a properly independent contemporary youth justice system is to be introduced in the foreseeable future. It must simply deliver, to some measurable and widely acceptable extent, on its central aim of reducing youth offending and, at the same time, it must be seen to deliver on an efficient, cost-effective basis. We live in a world where results are important and the customer expects value for money. In this case the customer is the general public which clearly wants to see reductions in criminality and certainly among children and young people.

Pitts (2003) interestingly cites the Bank of England's monetary policy committee as an example of a key governmental function given to an independent agency in the interests of the state and one providing an appropriate model for the introduction of an autonomous contemporary youth justice system. That body clearly has significant public support – not least among key economic players – and there a widespread, invariably unspoken expectation that it will do the right thing in the public interest without favour when called upon to make a tough decision. Moreover, the evidence to date suggests that it has not shirked that duty even when causing (at least) short-term political damage to the government, as has been the case with interest-rate increases. It is, however, not clear that the public has such confidence in a contemporary youth justice system which is clearly perceived to be a quasi-welfare agency regardless of the protestations of liberal and left-wing critics. It therefore seems indisputable that given proper independence of government it would need to visibly deliver on its key aims and provide value for money. Whatever negative observations we might make about quality assurance, accountability and the audit society, these systems are an inevitable part of the real non-negotiable contemporary world and for any foreseeable future. Quite simply, the public wants to see that its money is being well spent and this clear, understandable expectation needs to be acknowledged by those involved in youth justice, whether practitioners, researchers or commentators. This would be the basis of public trust and provide an independent youth justice system with the opportunity to serve children and young people well in a moral communitarian society.

Notes

1 The term 'off the cards' was widely used among those working illegally while claiming welfare benefits and thus not having their National Insurance cards stamped by their employer.
2 This is a role akin to that played by the Office of Juvenile Justice and Delinquency Prevention in the United States Department of Justice.

References

Aichhorn, A. (1925) *Wayward Youth.* New York: Viking Press.

Akers, R.L. (1985) *Deviant Behaviour: A Social Learning Approach.* 3rd edn, Belmont, CA: Wadsworth.

Akers, R.L. (1992) 'Linking Sociology and Its Specialities', *Social Forces,* 71: 1–16.

Akers, R.L. (1997) *Criminological Theories: Introduction and Evaluation.* Los Angeles, CA: Roxbury.

Akers, R.L., Krohn, M.D., Lanza-Kaduce, L. and Radosevich, M. (1979) 'Social Learning and Deviant Behaviour: A Specific Test of a General Theory', *American Sociological Review,* 44: 635–55.

Akester, K. (2000) The Changing Face of Youth Justice, *New Law Journal,* 21 Apr., 566.

Alexander, J., Barton, C., Schiavo, R. and Parsons, B. (1976) 'Systems-behavioural Interventions with Families of Delinquents: Therapists, Characteristics, Family Behaviour and Outcome', *Journal of Consulting and Clinical Psychology,* 44: 656–64.

All-Party Group on Alcohol Misuse (1995) *Alcohol and Crime: Breaking the Link.* London: HMSO.

Allsopp, J.F. and Feldman, M.P. (1975) 'Extroversion, Neuroticism and Psychoticism and Antisocial Behaviour in Schoolgirls', *Social Behaviour and Personality,* 2: 184.

Allsopp, J.F. and Feldman, M.P. (1976) 'Personality and Antisocial Behaviour in Schoolboys', *British Journal of Criminology,* 16: 337–51.

Anderson, E. (1990) *Street Wise.* Chicago: University of Chicago Press.

Anderson, S., Kinsey, R., Loader, I. and Smith, C. (1994) *Cautionary Tales: Young People, Crime and Policing In Edinburgh.* Aldershot: Avebury.

Andrews, D. (1995) 'The Psychology of Criminal Conduct and Effective Treatment', in J. McGuire (ed.) *What Works: Reducing Re offending: Guidelines from Research and Practice.* Chichester: John Wiley and Sons.

Andrews, D., Hollins, C., Raynor, P., Trotter, C., Armstrong, B. (2001) *Sustaining Effectiveness in Working with Offenders*. Cardiff: The Cognitive Centre Foundation.

Andrews, D.A., Zinger, I., Hoge, R.D., Bonta, J., Gendreau, P. and Cullen, F.T. (1990) 'Does Correctional Treatment Work? A Clinically Relevant and Psychologically Informed Meta-analysis, *Criminology*, 28: 369–404.

Andry, R.G. (1957) 'Faulty Paternal and Maternal Child Relationships, Affection and Delinquency', *British Journal of Delinquency* VIII: 34–48.

Annison, J. (2005) 'Risk and Protection' in T. Bateman and J. Pitts (eds) *The RHP Companion to Youth Justice*. Lyme Regis: Russell House Press.

Aries, P. (translation Robert Baldick) (1962) *Centuries of Childhood: A Social History of Family*. New York: Alfred A. Knopf.

Armstrong, D. (2005) 'A Risky Business? Research, Policy, Governmentality and Youth Offending', *Youth Justice*, 4(2): 100–16.

Ashford, M. (1998) 'Making Criminals out of Children: Abolishing the Presumption of Doli Incapax, *Criminal Justice*, 16(16).

Ashford, M. and Chard, A. (2000) *Defending Young People in the Legal System*. London: Legal Action Group.

Ashton, D.N. and Field, D. (1976) *Young Workers*. London: Hutchinson.

Ashworth, A., Gardner, J., Morgan, R., Smith, A.T.H., Von Hirsch, A. and Wasik, M. (1998) 'Neighbouring on the Oppressive: The Government's "Anti-social Behaviour Order" Proposals', *Criminal Justice*, 16(1): 7–14.

Audit Commission (1996) *Misspent Youth: Young People and Crime*. London: Audit Commission.

Audit Commission (2006) *Strategic Plan*. London: HMSO.

Avon and Somerset Constabulary (1991) *The Effect of 'Re-Offending' on Bail on Crime in Avon and Somerset*. Bristol: Avon and Somerset Constabulary.

Aye Maung, N. (1995) *Young People, Victimisation and the Police: British Crime Survey Findings on the Experiences and Attitudes of 12–15 year olds*. Home Office Research Study 140. London: HMSO.

Ayers, C. (1999) 'Assessing Correlates of Onset, Escalation, De-escalation and Desistance of Delinquent Behaviour', *Journal of Quantitative Criminology*, 15(3).

Bail Support Policy and Dissemination Unit (2000). *First Evaluation Report: Evaluation of Projects Funded Under the Youth Justice Board: Bail Support and Supervision Grants*. Swansea: Nacro Cymru.

Bailey, V. (1987) *Delinquency and Citizenship: Reclaiming the Young Offender 1914–48*, Oxford: Clarendon Press.

Baker, K., Jones, S., Merrington, S. and Roberts, C. (2005) *Further Development of ASSET*. London: Youth Justice Board.

Baker, K., Jones, S. Roberts, C. and Merrington, S. (2002) *Validity and Reliability of ASSET*. London: Youth Justice Board.

Balding, J. and Shelley, C. (1993) *Very Young Children in 1991/2*. Exeter: University of Exeter Schools Health Education Unit.

Baldwin, J.D. (1990) 'The Role of Sensory Stimulation in Criminal Behaviour, with Special Attention to the Age Peak in Crime', in L. Ellis and H. Hoffman (eds) *Crime in Biological, Social, and Moral Contexts*. New York: Praeger.

Ball, C. (1998) 'R v B *(Young Offender: Sentencing Powers)*: Paying Due Regard to the Welfare of the Child in Criminal Proceedings', *Child and Family Law Quarterly*, 10: 4: 417–24.

Ball, C. (2000) 'The Youth Justice and Criminal Evidence Act 1999 Part I: A Significant Move Towards Restorative Justice, or a Recipe for Unintended Consequences?', *Criminal Law Review*, 211–22.

Bandura, A. and Walters, R.H. (1959) *Adolescent Aggression*. New York: Ronald Press.

Banks, M., Bates, I., Breakwell, G., Bynner, J., Emler, N., Jamieson, L. and Roberts, K. (1992) *Careers and Identities*. Buckingham: Open University Press.

Barclay, G.C. (1995) *The Criminal Justice System in England and Wales 1995*, London: Home Office, Research and Statistics Department

Baron, S.W. and Kennedy, L.W. (1998) 'Deterrence and Homeless Male Street Youths', *Canadian Journal of Criminology*, 40: 27–60.

Barry, A., Osborne, T. and Rose, N. (1996) *Foucault and Political Reason: Liberalism, Neo-Liberalism and Rationalities of Government*. London: UCL Press.

Basic Skills Agency (2002) *Basic Skills and Social Exclusion: Findings from a Study of Adults Born in 1970*. London: Centre for Longitudinal Studies, Institute of Education.

Bateman, T. (2005) 'Reducing Child Imprisonment: A Systemic Challenge', *Youth Justice*, 5(2): 91–104.

Bateman, T. (2006) 'Youth Crime and Justice: Statistical "Evidence", Recent Trends and Responses', in B. Goldson and J. Muncie (eds) *Youth Crime and Justice*. London: Sage, 65–77.

Bateman, T. and Pitts, J. (2005) 'Conclusion: What the Evidence Tells Us', in T. Bateman and J. Pitts (eds) *The RHP Companion to Youth Justice*. Lyme Regis: Russell House.

Bates, I. (1984) 'From Vocational Guidance to Life Skills: Historical Perspectives on Careers Education', in I. Bates, J. Clarke, P. Cohen, D. Finn, R. Moore and P. Willis (eds) *Schooling for the Dole?* Basingstoke: Macmillan.

Bauman, Z. (1998) *Work, Consumerism and the New Poor*. Buckingham: Open University Press.

Bauman, Z. (2000) 'Social Uses of Law and Order', in D. Garland and R. Sparks (eds) *Criminology and Social Theory*. Oxford: Oxford University Press.

Beccaria, C. (1963, first English edition 1767) *On Crimes and Punishments*, (translated by H. Paolucci). Indianapolis: Bobbs-Merrill Educational.

Beck, U. (1992) *Risk Society: Towards a New Modernity*. New Delhi: Sage.

Becker, G.S. (1968) 'Crime and Punishment: An Economic Approach', *Journal of Political Economy*, 76(2): 169–217.

Becker, H. (1963) *Outsiders: Studies in the Sociology of Deviance.* New York: Free Press.

Becker, H. (1967) 'Whose Side Are We On?', *Social Problems,* 14(3): 239–47.

Beinart, S. Anderson, B., Lee, S., Utting, D. (2002) *Youth at Risk? A National Survey of Risk Factors and Problem Behaviour Among Young People in England, Scotland and Wales.* London: Communities that Care.

Bell, C. (1999) 'Appealing for Justice for Children and Young People: A Critical Analysis of the Crime and Disorder Bill 1998', in B. Goldson (ed.) *Youth Justice: Contemporary Policy and Practice.* Aldershot: Ashgate.

Belson, W.A. (1975) *Juvenile Theft: The Causal Factors.* London: Harper and Row.

Bennett, T. (2000) *Drugs and Crime: The Results of the Second Developmental Stage of the New-Adam Programme,* Home Office Research Study 2005. London: Home Office.

Bennett, T., Holloway, K. and Williams T. (2001) *Drug Use and Offending: Summary Results from the First Year of the NEW-ADAM Research Programme,* Findings 148. London: Home Office.

Bentham, J. (1970) *An Introduction to the Principles of Morals and Legislation,* edited by J.H. Burns and H.L.A. Hart. London: Athlone Press.

Bernard, T.J. (1983) *The Consensus-Conflict Debate.* New York: Columbia University Press.

Binfield, C. (1973) *George Williams and the YMCA: A Study in Victorian Social Attitudes.* London: Heinemann.

Blair, T. (1998) *The Third Way: New Politics for the New Century.* London: The Fabian Society.

Blair, T. (2002) 'My Vision for Britain', *The Observer,* Sunday 10 November. www.observer.co.uk/crimedebate/story/0,12079,837223.00.html

Blanch, M. (1979) 'Imperialism, Nationalism and Organized Youth', in J. Clarke *et al.* (eds) *Working Class Culture.* London: Hutchinson.

Blyth, D.A., Hill, J.P. and Thiel, K.S. (1982) 'Early Adolescents, Significant Others: Grade and Gender Differences in Perceived Relationships with Familial and Nonfamilial Adults and Young People', *Journal of Youth and Adolescence,* 11: 425–50.

Bocock, R. (1986) *Hegemony.* London: Tavistock.

Borduin, C., Mann, B., Cone, L., Henggeler, S., Fucci, B., Blaske, D. and Williams, R. (1995) 'Multisystemic Treatment of Serious Juvenile Offenders: Long Term Prevention of Criminality and Violence', *Journal of Consulting and Clinical Psychology,* 34: 105–13.

Boswell, G. (1995) *Violent Victims: The Prevalence of Abuse and Loss in the Lives of Section 53 Offenders.* London: The Prince's Trust.

Bottomley, K. and Pease, K. (1986) *Crime and Punishment: Interpreting the Data.* Milton Keynes: Open University Press.

Bottoms, A. (1974) 'On the Decriminalization of the Juvenile Court', in R. Hood (ed.) *Crime, Criminology and Public Policy.* London: Heinemann.

Bottoms, A. (1977) 'Reflections on the Renaissance of Dangerousness', *The Howard Journal,* 16(2): 70–96.

Bottoms, A. (2005) 'Methodology Matters', *Safer Society*, Summer: 10–12.

Bowlby, J. (1952) *Maternal Care and Mental Health*. New York: World Health Organisation.

Box, S. (1981) *Deviance, Reality and Society*, 2nd edn, London: Rinehart and Winston.

Box, S. (1983) *Power, Crime and Mystification*. London: Tavistock.

Box, S. (1987) *Recession, Crime and Punishment*. London: Macmillan.

Braithwaite, J. (1989) *Crime, Shame and Reintegration*. Cambridge: Cambridge University Press.

Braithwaite, J. (1998) 'Restorative Justice', in M. Tonry (ed.) *Handbook of Crime and Punishment*. New York: Oxford University Press.

Braithwaite, J. and Daly, K. (1994) 'Masculinities, Violence and Communitarian Control', in T. Newburn and E.A. Stanko (eds) *Just Boys Doing Business? Men, Masculinities and Crime*. London: Routledge, pp. 189–213.

Brake, M. (1980) *The Sociology of Youth Cultures and Youth Sub-cultures*. London: Routledge and Kegan Paul.

Brake, M. (1985) *Comparative Youth Culture*. London: Routledge.

Brand, S. and Price, R. (2000) *The Economic and Social Costs of Crime*, Research Study 217. London: Home Office.

Bray, R. (1907) *The Town Child*. London: Fisher Unwin.

Brewer, D.D., Hawkins, J.D., Catalano, R.F. and Neckerman, H.J. (1995) 'Preventing Serious, Violent and Chronic Juvenile Offending: A Review of Evaluations of Selected Strategies in Childhood, Adolescence, and the Community', in J.C. Howell, B. Krisberg, J.D. Hawkins and J.J. Wilson (eds) *Serious, Violent and Chronic Juvenile Offenders: A Sourcebook*. Thousand Oaks, CA: Sage.

Brinkley, I. (1997) 'Underworked and Underpaid', *Soundings*, 6: 161–71.

Brown, S. (1998) *Understanding Youth and Crime*. Buckingham: Open University Press.

Buckland, G. and Stevens, A. (2001) *Review of Effective Practice with Young Offenders in Mainland Europe*. European Institute of Social Services, University of Kent at Canterbury.

Bunt, S. (1975) *Jewish Youth Work in Britain: Past, Present, and Future*. London: Bedford Square Press.

Burgess, R.L. and Akers, R.L. (1968) 'A Differential Association-Reinforcement Theory of Criminal Behaviour', *Social Problems*, 14: 128–47.

Burney, E. (2005) *Making People Behave: Anti-social Behaviour, Politics and Policy*. Cullompton: Willan.

Burt, C. (1945) *The Young Delinquent*. London: University of London Press.

Butler, I. and Drakeford, M. (1997) 'Tough Guise: The Politics of Youth Justice', *Probation Journal*, 44: 216–19.

Callinicos, A. (2001) *Against the Third Way: An Anti-Capitalist Critique*. Cambridge: Polity Press.

Campbell, B. (1993) *Goliath: Britain's Dangerous Places*. London: Methuen.

Campbell, B. (1999) 'Criminalising Children', *Community Care,* 29 Jul. 14.

Campbell, S. (2002) *A Review of Anti-social Behaviour Orders,* Home Office Research Series 236. London.

Campbell, S. and Harrington, V. (2000) *Youth Crime: Findings from the 1998/99 Youth Lifestyles Survey,* Home Office Research Findings 126, London: Home Office.

Carew, R. (1979) 'The Place of Knowledge in Social Work Activity', *British Journal of Social Work,* 19(3): 349–64.

Carpenter, M. (1853) *Juvenile Delinquents: Their Condition and Treatment,* London: Cash.

Cavadino, P. (1997a) 'Government Plans for Youth Justice', *Childright,* 141: 4–5.

Cavadino, P. (1997b) 'Goodbye Doli, Must We Leave You?' *Child and Family Law Quarterly,* 9(2): 165–71.

Cavadino, M. and Dignan, J. (1997) *The Penal System: An Introduction.* London: Sage.

Cavadino, P. and Gibson, B. (1993) *Bail: The Law, Best Practice and the Debate.* Winchester: Waterside Press.

CDCU (Central Drugs Co-ordination Unit) (1995) *Tackling Drugs Together: A Strategy for England 1995–1998.* London: HMSO.

Chambliss, W.J. (1969) *Crime and the Legal Process.* New York: McGraw-Hill.

Chapman, T. (2000) *Time to Grow.* Lyme Regis: Russell House.

Chapman, T. and Hough, M. (1998) *Evidence Based Practice: A Guide to Effective Practice.* London: H.M. Inspectorate of Probation/Home Office.

Charlton, B.G. (1999) 'The Ideology of "Accountability"', *Journal of the Royal College of Physicians of London,* 33: 33–5.

Charlton B.G. (2001) 'Clinical Governance: A Quality Assurance Audit System for Regulating Clinical Practice, in A. Miles (ed.) *Clinical Governance: Encouraging Excellence or Imposing Control?* London: Aesculaepius Medical Press.

Childright (1998) 'The Crime and Disorder Bill: Will it Really Curb Youth Crime', *Childright,* 143: 8–9.

Chilton, R.J. and Markle, G.E. (1972) 'Family Disruption, Delinquent Conduct, and the Effect of Subclassification', *American Sociological Review,* 37: 93–108.

Christiansen, K.O. (1968) 'Threshold of Tolerance in Various Population Groups Illustrated by Results from the Danish Criminologic Twin Study', in A.V.S. de Reuck and R. Porter (eds) *The Mentally Abnormal Offender.* Boston: Little, Brown.

Clapham, B. (1989) 'A Case of Hypoglycaemia', *The Criminologist,* 13: 2–15.

Clarke, J. (1975) *Ideologies of Control of Working Class Youth.* University of Birmingham: Centre for Contemporary Cultural Studies.

Clarke, J. and Cochrane, A. (1998) 'The Social Construction of Social Problems', in E. Saraga (ed.) *Embodying the Social Construction of Difference.* London: Routledge/Open University.

Clarke, R.V.G. (1980) '"Situational" Crime Prevention: Theory and Practice', *British Journal of Criminology*, 20: 132–45.

Clarke, R.V.G. (1987) 'Rational Choice Theory and Prison Psychology', in B.J. McGurk *et al.* (eds) *Applying Psychology to Imprisonment: Theory and Practice*. London: HMSO.

Clarke, R.V.G. and Mayhew, P. (eds) (1980) *Designing Out Crime*. London: HMSO.

Clayden, J. and Stein, M. (2002) *Mentoring for Care Leavers*. The Prince's Trust: London.

Clear, T.R. and Karp, D.R. (1999) *The Community Justice Ideal: Preventing Crime and Achieving Justice*. Boulder, CO: Westview.

Cloward, R.A. (1959) 'Illegitimate Means, Anomie and Deviant Behaviour', *American Sociological Review*, (April) 24: 164–76.

Cloward, R.A. and Ohlin, L.E. (1960) *Delinquency and Opportunity: A Theory of Delinquent Gangs*, New York: Free Press.

Cockburn, C. (1987) *Two-Track Training: Sex Inequalities and YTS*. London: Macmillan.

Coffield, F., Borrill, C. and Marshall, S. (1986) *Growing Up at the Margins*, Milton Keynes: Open University Press.

Cohen, A.K. (1955) *Delinquent Boys: The Culture of the Gang*. New York: Free Press.

Cohen, L.E. and Felson, M. (1979) 'Social Inequality and Predatory Criminal Victimization: An Exposition and Test of a Formal Theory', *American Sociological Review,* 44: 588–608.

Cohen, L.E., Kluegel, J. and Land, K. (1981) 'Social Inequality and Predatory Criminal Victimisation: An Exposition and Test of a Formal Theory', *American Sociological Review*, 46: 505–24.

Cohen, M. (1998) 'The Monetary Value of Saving a High-risk Youth', *Journal of Quantitative Criminology*, 14: 5–33.

Cohen, P. (1972) 'Sub-Cultural Conflict and Working Class Community', *Working Papers in Cultural Studies*, No. 2, Birmingham: CCCS, University of Birmingham.

Cohen, S. (1973) *Folk Devils and Moral Panics*. Oxford: Martin Robertson.

Cohen, S. (1980) *Folk Devils and Moral Panics*, 2nd edition. Oxford: Martin Robertson.

Cohen, S. (1985) *Visions of Social Control*. Cambridge: Polity Press.

Coid, J., Carvell, A., Kittler, Z., Healey, A. and Henderson, J. (2000) *Opiates, Criminal Behaviour and Methadone Treatment*, RDS Occasional Paper. London: Home Office.

Coleman, C. and Moynihan, J. (1996) *Understanding Crime Data*. Buckingham: Open University Press.

Coleman, J. and Roker, D. (2001) 'Setting the Scene: Parenting and Public Policy', in J. Coleman and D. Roker (eds) *Supporting Parents of Teenagers, A Handbook for Professionals*. London: Jessica Kingsley.

Coleman, J.C. and Warren-Adamson, C. (1992) *Youth Policy in the 1990's: The Way Forward*. London: Routledge.

Collins, J.J. (1988) 'Alcohol and Interpersonal Violence: Less than Meets the Eye', in A. Weiner and M.E. Wolfgang (eds) *Pathways to Criminal Violence*, Newbury Park, CA: Sage.

Communities that Care (2001) *The Risk and Protective Factors for Youth Crime – Prevalence, Salience, and Reduction*. London: Youth Justice Board.

Communities that Care (2002) *Youth At Risk? A National Survey of Risk Factors, Protective Factors and Problem Behaviour Among Young People in England, Scotland and Wales*. London: Communities that Care.

Conklin, J.E. (1977) *Illegal but Not Criminal*. New Jersey: Spectrum.

Cornish, D.B. and Clarke, R.V.G. (1986) *The Reasoning Criminal*. New York: Springer-Verlag.

Corrigan, P. (1979) *The Smash Street Kids*. London: Paladin.

Cortes, J.B. and Gatti, F.M. (1972) *Delinquency and Crime: A Biopsychological Approach*. New York: Seminar Press.

Coulshed, V. and Orme, J. (1998) *Social Work Practice: An Introduction*, 3rd edition. Basingstoke: Macmillan Press.

Coupland, D. (1992) *Generation X: Tales for an Accelerated Culture*. London: Abacus.

Crawford, A. and Clear, T.R. (2003) 'Community Justice: Transforming Communities through Restorative Justice?' in E. McLaughlin, R. Fergusson, G. Hughes and L. Westmarland, *Restorative Justice: Critical Issues*. London: Sage/Open University.

Crawford, A. and Newburn, T. (2003) *Youth Offending and Restorative Justice*. Cullompton: Willan.

Crimmens, D. and Pitts, J. (2000) *Positive Residential Practice, Learning the Lessons of the 1990s*. Lyme Regis: Russell House.

Croall, H. (1992) *White-collar Crime*. Buckingham: Open University Press.

Croall, H. (2001) *Understanding White-collar Crime*, Crime and Justice Series. Buckingham: Open University Press.

Crowther, C. (1998) 'Policing the Excluded Society', in R.D. Hopkins Burke, *Zero Tolerance Policing*, Leicester: Perpetuity Press.

Culpitt, I. (1999) *Social Policy and Risk*. London: Sage.

Cunningham, H. (1980) *Leisure in the Industrial Revolution*. London: Croom Helm.

Curtis, L.A. (1975) *Violence, Race and Culture*, Lexington, Massachusetts: Heath.

Dahrendorf, R. (1985) *Law and Order*, London: Stevens.

Dale, D. (1984) 'The Politics of Crime', *Salisbury Review*, October.

Darlington, Y. and Osmond, J.L. (2001) *Using Knowledge in Practice*. Brisbane: University of Queensland.

Davidoff, L. (1976) 'The Rationalization of Housework', in D.L. Barker and S. Allen (eds) *Dependence and Exploitation in Work and Marriage*. Harlow: Longman.

Davidson, N. (2006) 'Chernobyl's 'Nuclear Nightmares', *Horizon*, London: BBC, http://news.bbc.co.uk/1/hi/sci/tech/5173310.stm.

Davies, B. (1982) 'Juvenile Justice in Confusion', *Youth and Policy*, 1(2).

Davies, B. and Gibson, A. (1967) *The Social Education of the Adolescent*. London: University of London Press.

Davis, J. (1990) *Youth and the Condition of Britain*. London: Athlone Press.

Day-Sclater, S. and Piper, C. (2000) 'Re-moralising the Family? Family Policy, Family Law and Youth Justice', *Child and Family Law Quarterly*, 12(2): 135–51.

Dawes, F. (1975) *A Cry from the Streets: The Boys Club Movement in Britain*. Hove: Wayland.

De Luca, J.R. (ed) (1981) *Fourth Special Report to the US Congress on Alcohol and Health*. Rockville, Maryland: National Institute on Alcohol Abuse and Alcoholism.

Dennis, N. and Erdos, G. (1992) *Families Without Fatherhood*. London: Institute of Economic Affairs.

Dennis, N., Henriques, F. and Slaughter, C. (1956) *Coal is Our Life*. London: Eyre & Spottiswoode.

Department of Health (2005) *Smoking, Drinking and Drug Use among Young People in England in 2004*. London: Department of Health.

DHSS (1981) *Offending by Young People: A Survey of Recent Trends*. London: DHSS.

Diduck, A. (1999) 'Justice and Childhood: Reflections on Refashioned Boundaries', in M. King (ed.) *Moral Agendas for Children's Welfare*. London: Routledge.

Dignan, J. (1999) 'The Crime and Disorder Act and the Prospects for Restorative Justice', *Criminal Law Review*, 48–60.

Dignan, J. (2000) 'Victims, Reparation and the Pilot YOTs', *Justice of the Peace*, 164: 296–7.

Donajgrodzki, A. (1977) *Social Control in Nineteenth Century Britain*. London: Croom Helm.

Donald, J. (1985) 'Beacons of the Future', in V. Beechey and J. Donald (eds) *Subjectivity and Social Relations*. Milton Keynes: Open University Press.

Donzelot, J. (1980) *The Policing of Families: Welfare versus the State*. London: Hutchinson University Library.

Dowden, C. and Andrews, D.A. (1999) 'What Works in Young Offender Treatment: A Meta-analysis', *Forum on Corrections Research*, 11: 21–4.

Downes, D. (1966) *The Delinquent Solution*, London: Routledge & Kegan Paul.

Downes, D. and Rock, P. (1998) *Understanding Deviance*. 3rd edn, Oxford: Oxford University Press.

DPAS and SCODA (2000) *Drugs and Young Teams and Youth Offending Teams*. London: DPAS and SCODA.

Drakeford, M. and McCarthy, K. (2000) 'Parents, Responsibility and the New Youth Justice', in B. Goldson (ed.) *The New Youth Justice*. Lyme Regis: Russell House.

Driver, S. and Martell, L. (1997) 'New Labour's Communitarianisms', *Critical Social Policy*, 52: 27–46.

Dugdale, R.L. (1877) *The Jukes*. New York: Putnam.

Dunkel, F. (1996) 'Juvenile Delinquents', in W. Carney (ed.) *Juvenile Delinquents and Young People in Danger in an Open Environment*. Winchester: Waterside Press.

Durkheim, E. (1933, originally 1893) *The Division of Labour in Society*. Glencoe: Free Press.

Durkheim, E. (1964 originally published 1915) *The Elementary Forms of Religious Life*. Glencoe: Free Press.

Dyhouse, C. (1981) *Girls Growing Up in Late Victorian and Edwardian England*. London: Routledge and Kegan Paul.

Eagar, W. McG (1953) *Making Men: A History of Boys' Clubs and Related Movements*. London: University of London Press.

Edmunds, M., Hough, M. and Turnbull, P.J. (1999) *Doing Justice to Treatment: Referring Offenders to Drug Treatment Services*, Drugs Prevention Initiative Paper No. 2. London: Home Office.

Ehrenkranz, J. Bliss, E. and Sheard, M.H. (1974) 'Plasma Testosterone: Correlation with Aggressive Behaviour and Social Dominance in Man', *Psychosomatic Medicine*, 36: 469–83.

Elias, N. (1978) *The Civilising Process, Vol. 1: The History of Manners*. Oxford: Blackwell.

Elias, N. (1982) *The Civilising Process, Vol. 2: State-Formation and Civilisation*. Oxford: Blackwell.

Elliot, P.S. and Voss, H.L. (1974) *Delinquency and Drop-out*. Toronto: Lexington.

Elliot, D., Ageton, S. and Canter, J. (1979) 'An Integrated Theoretical Perspective on Delinquent Behaviour', *Journal of Research in Crime and Delinquency*, 16: 126–49.

Ellis, L. and Coontz, P.D. (1990) 'Androgens, Brain Functioning, and Criminality: The Neurohormonal Foundations of Antisociality', in L. Ellis and H. Hoffman (eds) *Crime in Biological, Social, and Moral Contexts*. New York: Praeger.

Emanuel, E. (1991) *The Ends of Human Life: Medical Ethics in a Liberal Polity*. Cambridge, MA: Harvard University Press.

Erikson, K. (1962) 'Notes on the Sociology of Deviance', *Social Problems*, 9: 309–14.

Ericson, R.V. and Haggerty, D. (1997) *Policing the Risk Society*. Oxford: Clarendon Press.

Erooga, M. and Masson, H. (1999) *Children and Young People who Sexually Abuse Others*. London: Routledge.

Etzioni, A. (1993) *The Spirit of Community: The Reinvention of American Society*, New York: Touchstone.

Etzioni, A. (ed.) (1995) *New Communitarian Thinking: Persons, Virtues, Institutions and Communities*. Charlottesville: University of Virginia Press.

Evans, K. and Alade, S. (2001) *Vulnerable Young People and Drugs: Opportunities to Tackle Inequalities*. London: DrugScope.

Eysenck, H.J. (1959) *Manual of the Maudsley Personality Inventory*. London: University of London Press.

Eysenck, H.J. (1970) *Crime and Personality*. London: Granada.

Eysenck, H.J. (1977) *Crime and Personality*. 3rd edn, London: Routledge & Kegan Paul.

Fagan, J. (1990) 'Intoxication and Aggression', in M. Tonry and J.Q. Wilson (eds) *Crime and Justice: A Review of Research*, 13, Chicago: University of Chicago Press.

Family Policy Studies Centre (1998) *The Crime and Disorder Bill and the Family*. London: Family Policy Studies Centre.

Farrington, D. (1978) 'Family Backgrounds of Aggressive Youths', in L. Hersov *et al.*, *Aggressive and Anti-social Behaviour in Childhood and Adolescence*. London: Pergamon Press.

Farrington, D. (1992, 1996) *Understanding and Preventing Youth Crime*. York: Joseph Rowntree Foundation.

Farrington, D.P. (1992a) 'Juvenile Delinquency', in J.C. Coleman (ed.) *The School Years*, 2nd edn. London: Routledge.

Farrington, D.P. (1992b) 'Explaining the Beginning, Progress and Ending of Anti-social Behaviour from Birth to Adulthood', in J. McCord (ed.) *Facts, Frameworks and Forecasts: Advances in Criminological Theory, Vol 3*, New Brunswick, NJ: Transaction.

Farrington, D.P. (1994) 'Human Development and Criminal Careers', in M. Maguire, R. Morgan and R. Reiner (eds) *The Oxford Handbook of Criminology*. Oxford: Clarendon.

Farrington, D.P. (1994) 'Introduction', in D.P. Farrington (ed.), *Psychological Explanations of Crime*. Aldershot: Dartmouth.

Farrington, D. (1995) 'The Twelfth Jack Tizard Memorial Lecture: The Development of Offending and Antisocial Behaviour from Childhood: Key Findings from the Cambridge Study in Delinquent Development', *Journal of Child Psychology and Psychiatry*, 36: 929–64.

Farrington, D.P. (1996) *Understanding and Preventing Youth Crime*. York: Joseph Rowntree Foundation.

Feeley, M. and Simon, J. (1996) 'Actuarial Justice: The Emerging New Criminal Law', in D. Nelkin (ed.) *The Future of Criminology*. Thousand Oaks, CA: Sage.

Feest, J. (1990) *New Social Strategies and the Criminal Justice System*. Brussels: Council of Europe.

Feldman, M.P. (1977) *Criminal Behaviour: A Psychological Analysis*. Bath: Pitman Press.

Felson, M. (1998) *Crime and Everyday Life*, 2nd edn. Thousand Oaks, CA: Pine Forge.

Fergusson, R., Pye, D., Esland, G., McLaughlin, E. and Muncie, J. (2000) 'Normalised Dislocation and the New Subjectivities in Post-16 Markets for Education and Work', *Critical Social Policy*, 20(3): 283–305.

Ferri, E. (1895) *Criminal Sociology*, London: Unwin.

Field, F. (1989) *Losing Out: The Emergence of Britain's Underclass*. Oxford: Blackwell.

Fionda, J. (1999) 'New Labour, Old Hat: Youth Justice and the Crime and Disorder Act 1998', *Criminal Law Review*, 36–47.

Fionda, J. (2005) *Devils and Angels*. Oxford: Hartley Publishing.

Fishbein, D.H. and Pease, S.E. (1990) 'Neurological Links between Substance Abuse and Crime', in L. Ellis and H. Hoffman (eds) *Crime in Biological, Social, and Moral Contexts*. New York: Praeger.

Flanzer, J. (1981) 'The Vicious Circle of Alcoholism and Family Violence', *Alcoholism*, 1(3): 30–45.

Fletcher, H. (2005) *ASBOs: An Analysis of the First 6 Years*. London: ASBOConcern/Napo.

Flood-Page C., Campbell, S., Harington, V. and Miller, J. (2000) *Youth Crime Findings from the 1998/99 Youth Lifestyles Survey*, Home Office Research Study 209. London: Home Office.

Fo, W.S.O. and O'Donnell, C.R. (1974) 'The Buddy System: Relationship and Contingency Conditioning in a Community Intervention Program for Youth with Nonprofessionals as Behaviour Change Agents', *Journal of Consulting and Clinical Psychology*, 42: 163–9.

Foucault, M. (1971) *Madness and Civilisation: A History of Insanity in the Age of Reason*. London: Tavistock.

Foucault, M. (1976) *The History of Sexuality*. London: Allen Lane.

Foucault, M. (1977) *Discipline and Punish – the Birth of the Prison*. London: Allen Lane.

Foucault, M. (1980) *Power/Knowledge: Selected Interviews and Other Writings 1972–77* (ed. C. Gordon). Brighton: Harvester Press.

France, A. (2000) 'Towards a Sociological Understanding of Youth and Their Risk Taking', *Journal of Youth Studies*, 3(3): 317–31.

Fraser, D. (1973) *The Evolution of the British Welfare State*. London: Macmillan.

Freud, S. (1920) *A General Introduction to Psychoanalysis*. New York: Boni and Liveright.

Freud, S. (1927) *The Ego and the Id*. London: Hogarth.

Freud, S. (1933) *New Introductory Lectures on Psychoanalysis*. New York: W.W. Norton.

Friedlander, K. (1947) *The Psychoanalytic Approach to Juvenile Delinquency*. London: Kegan Paul.

Friedlander, K. (1949) 'Latent Delinquency and Ego Development', in K.R. Eissler (ed.) *Searchlights on Delinquency*. New York: International University Press: 205–15.

Furlong, A. and Cartmel, F. (1997) *Young People and Social Change*. Buckingham: Open University Press.

Fyfe, N.R. (1995) 'Law and Order Policy and the Spaces of Citizenship in Contemporary Britain, *Political Geography*, 14 (2): 177–89.

Gardner, H. (1993) *Frames of Mind: The Theory of Multiple Intelligences*. New York: Basic Books.

Garland, D. (1985) *Punishment and Welfare: A History of Penal Strategies*. London: Gower.

Garland, D. (1996) 'The Limits of the Sovereign State: Strategies of Crime Control in Contemporary Society', *British Journal of Criminology*, 34(4): 445–71.

Garland, D. (2001) *The Culture of Control*. Oxford: Oxford University Press.

Garofalo, R. (1914) *Criminology*. Boston: Little, Brown.

Gelsthorpe, L. and Morris, A. (1994) 'Juvenile Justice 1945–1992', in M. Maguire, R. Morgan and R. Reiner (eds), *The Oxford Handbook of Criminology*. Oxford: Clarendon Press.

Gelsthorpe, L. (1999) 'Parents and Criminal Children', in A. Bainham, S. Day Sclater and M. Richards (eds) *What is a Parent? A Socio-legal Analysis*. Oxford: Hart.

Gelsthorpe, L. and Morris, A. (1999) 'Much Ado About Nothing: A Critical Comment on Key Provisions Relating to Children in The Crime and Disorder Act 1998', *Child and Family Law Quarterly*, 11(3): 209–21.

Gendreau, P., Paparozzi, M., Little, T. and Goddard, M. (1993). 'Does "Punishing Smarter" Work? An Assessment of the New Generation of Alternative Sanctions in Probation', *Forum on Corrections Research*, 5: 31–4.

Ghate, D. and Ramella, M. (2002) *Positive Parenting*. London: Youth Justice Board.

Gibbens, T.C.N. (1963) *Psychiatric Studies of Borstal Lads*. Oxford: Oxford University Press.

Gibbons, D.C. (1970) *Delinquent Behaviour*. Englewood Cliffs, NJ: Prentice-Hall.

Gibbs, J. (1975) *Crime, Punishment, and Deterrence*. New York: Elsevier.

Gibson, B. (1994) *The Youth Court: One Year Onwards*. London: Waterside Press.

Giddens, A. (1990) *Consequences of Modernity*. Cambridge: Polity Press.

Giddens, A. (1994) *Beyond Left and Right: The Future of Radical Politics*. Cambridge: Polity Press.

Giddens, A. (1998) *The Third Way*. Cambridge: Polity Press.

Giddens, A. (1999) 'Risk and Responsibility', *Modern Law Review*, 62(1): 1–10.

Gilliom, J. (1994) *Surveillance, Privacy and the Law: Employee Drug Testing and the Politics of Social Control*. Michigan: University of Michigan Press.

Gillis, G.R. (1974) *Youth and History*. London: Academic Press.

Giroux, H.A. (1983) *Theory and Resistance in Education*, London: Heinemann.

Gittins, D. (1985) *The Family in Question. Changing Households and Familiar Ideologies*. London: Macmillan.

Glendon, M.A. (1991) *Rights Talk: The Impoverishment of Political Discourse*. New York: Free Press.

Glueck, S. and Glueck, E. (1950) *Unravelling Juvenile Delinquency*. Oxford: Oxford University Press.

Goddard, H.H. (1914) *Feeblemindedness: Its Causes and Consequences*. New York: Macmillan.

Godfrey, C., Eaton, G., McDougall, C. and Culyer, A. (2002) *The Economic and Social Costs of Class A Drug Use in England and Wales, 2000*. London: Home Office.

Goldson, B. (1997) 'Children, Crime, Policy and Practice: Neither Welfare nor Justice', *Children and Society*, 11(2): 77–88.

Goldson, B. (1999) 'Re-visiting First Principles and Re-stating Opposition to Child Incarceration', *Ajjust*, 44: 4–9.

Goldson, B. (2000a) "Children in Need" or "Young Offenders"? Hardening Ideology, Organisational Change and New Challenges for Social Work with Children in Trouble', *Child and Family Social Work*, 5(3): 255–65.

Goldson, B. (2000b) 'Youth Justice and Criminal Evidence Bill Part I: Referrals to Youth Offender Panels', in L. Payne (ed.) *Child Impact Statements 1998/99*. London: National Children's Bureau and UNICEF.

Goldson, B. (2002) *Vulnerable Inside: Children in Secure and Penal Settings*. London: The Children's Society.

Goldson, B. (2006) 'Penal Custody: Intolerance, Irrationality and Indifference', in B. Goldson and J. Muncie (eds) *Youth Crime and Justice*. London: Sage, pp. 139–56.

Goldson, B. and Peters, E. (2002) *The Children's Society National Remand Review Initiative: Final Evaluation Report (1/12/1999 – 30/11/1999)*. London: The Children's Society.

Goldson, B. and Jamieson, J. (2002) 'Youth Crime, the "Parenting Deficit" and State Intervention: A Contextual Critique', *Youth Justice*, 2(2): 82–99.

Goldson, B. and Muncie, J. (eds) (2006) *Youth Crime and Justice*. London: Sage.

Goldthorpe, J.H. (1968–9) *The Affluent Worker in The Class Structure*, 3 Vols. Cambridge: Cambridge University Press.

Goodman, R. and Scott, S. (1997) *Child Pschiatry*. Oxford: Blackwell.

Gordon, R.A (1986) 'Scientific Justification and the Race-IQ-Delinquency Model', in T. Hartnagel and R. Silverman (eds) *Critique and Explanation: Essays in Honor of Gwynne Nettler*. New Brunswick, NJ: Transaction.

Gordon, D. and Kacir, C. (1998) *Effectiveness of an Interactive Parent Training Program for Changing Adolescent Behavior for Court-Referred Parents*, Unpublished Manuscript. University of Ohio: Athens.

Goring, C. (1913) *The English Convict: A Statistical Study*. London: HMSO.

Gottfredson, M.R. and Hirschi, T. (1990) *A General Theory of Crime*. Stanford, CA: Stanford University Press.

Graef, R. (2000) *Why Restorative Justice?* London: Calouste Gulbenkian Foundation.

Graham, J. (1998) 'What Works in Preventing Criminality', in P. Goldblatt and C. Lewis (eds) *Reducing Offending*, Home Office Research Study No 187. London: HMSO.

Graham, J. and Bowling, B. (1995) *Young People and Crime*, Home Office Research Study No. 145. London: HMSO.

Gramsci, A. (1971) *Selections from Prison Notebooks* (edited and translated by Q. Hoare and C.N. Smith). London: Lawrence and Wishart.

Gray, P. (2005) 'The Politics of Risk and Young Offenders' Experiences of Social Exclusion and Restorative Justice', *British Journal of Criminology*, 45(6), 938–57.

Gray, E. Taylor, E., Roberts, C., Merrington, S., Fernandez, R. and Moore, R. (2005) *Intensive Supervision and Surveillance Programme: The Final Report*. London: Youth Justice Board.

Greenwood, J. (1869) *The Seven Curses of London: Scenes from the Victorian Underworld* (1981 edn). Oxford: Blackwell.

Griffin, C. (1985) *Typical Girls?* London: Routledge.

Griffin, C. (1997) 'Representations of the Young', in J. Roache and S. Tucker (eds) *Youth In Society*. London: Sage.

Grygier, T. (1969) 'Parental Deprivation: A Study of Delinquent Children', *British Journal of Criminology*, 9: 209.

Guerra, N.G., Tolan, P.H. and Hammond, W.R. (1994) 'Prevention and Treatment of Adolescent Violence', in L.D. Eron, J.H. Gentry and P. Schlegel (eds) *Reason to Hope: A Psychosocial Perspective on Violence and Youth*. Washington, DC: American Psychological Association.

Hagedorn, J. (1992) 'Gangs, Neighbourhoods, and Public Policy', *Social Problems*, 38 (4): 529-42.

Hagell, A. (2002) *The Mental Health of Young Offenders*. London: The Mental Health Foundation.

Hagell, A. and Newburn, T. (1994) *Persistent Young Offenders*. London: Policy Studies Institute.

Haines, K. (2000) 'Referral Orders and Youth Offender Panels: Restorative Approaches and the New Youth Justice', in B. Goldson (ed.) *The New Youth Justice*. Lyme Regis: Russell House.

Haines, K. and O'Mahony, D. (2006) 'Restorative Approaches, Young People and Youth Justice, in B. Goldson and J. Muncie (eds) *Youth Crime and Justice*. London: Sage.

Hall, G.S. (1905) *Adolescence, Its Psychology and its Relations to Physiology, Anthropology, Sociology, Sex, Crime, Religion and Education*. New York: Appleton.

Hall, G.S. (1906) *Youth: Its Regime and Hygiene*. New York: Appleton.

Hall, M. and Schwarz, B. (eds) (1985) *Crises in the British State 1880–1930*. London: Hutchinson.

Hall, S., Critcher, C., Jefferson, T., Clarke, J. and Roberts, B. (1978) *Policing the Crisis: Mugging, the State and Law and Order*. London: Macmillan.

Hallet, C. and Hazel, N. (1998) *The Evaluation of the Children's Hearings in Scotland, Volume 2, The International Context*. Edinburgh: Scottish Office.

Hardyment, C. (1983) *Dream Babies: Child Care from Locke to Spock*. London: Jonathan Cape.

Hammersley, R., Marsland, L. and Reid M. (2003) *Home Office Research Study 261: Substance Use by Young Offenders: The Impact of the Normalisation of Drugs Use in the Early Years of the 21st Century*. London: Home Office Research, Development and Statistics Directorate.

Hare, D.R. (1982) 'Psychopathy and Physiological Activity during Anticipation of An Aversive Stimulus in a Distraction Paradigm', *Psychophysiology*, 19: 266–80.

Harris, R. and Webb, D. (1987) *Welfare, Power and Juvenile Justice*. London: Tavistock.

Hartless, J., Ditton, J., Nair, G. and Phillips, S. (1995) 'More Sinned Against than Sinning: A Study of Young Teenager's Experiences of Crime', *British Journal of Criminology*, 35(1): 114–33.

Harvey, D. (1989) *The Condition of Postmodernity: An Enquiry into the Origins of Cultural Change*. Oxford: Blackwell.

Harvey, I. (2000) 'Youth Culture, Drugs and Criminality', in J. Pickford, J. (ed.) *Youth Justice: Theory and Practice*. London: Cavendish.

Hawkins, J.D. and Catalano R.F. (1992) *Communities that Care: Action for Drug Abuse Prevention*. San Francisco: Josey Bass.

Hawkins, J.D., Catalano, R.F. and Miller, J.Y. (1992) 'Risk and Protective Factors for Alcohol and Other Drug Problems in Adolescence and Early Adulthood: Implications for Substance Abuse Prevention', *Psychological Bulletin*, 112: 64–105.

Haydon, D. and Scraton, P. (2000) 'Condemn a Little More, Understand a Little Less: The Political Context and Rights Implications of the Domestic and European Rulings in the Venables-Thompson Case', *Journal of Law and Society*, 27(3): 416–48.

Hayes, M. and Williams, C. (1999) '"Offending" Behaviour and Children Under 10', *Family Law*, May: 317–20.

Healy, W. and Bronner, A.F. (1936) *New Light on Delinquency and its Treatment*, New Haven: Yale University Press.

Hebdige, D. (1976) 'The Meaning of Mod', in S. Hall and T. Jefferson (eds.) *Resistance Through Rituals: Youth Sub-cultures in Post-war Britain*. London: Hutchinson: 118–43.

Hebdige, D. (1979) *Subculture: The Meaning Of Style*. London: Methuen.

Hendricks, H. (1986) 'Personality and Psychology: Defining Edwardian Boys', *Youth and Policy*, 18.

Hendricks, H. (1990a) 'Constructions and Reconstructions of British Childhood: An Interpretive Study 1800 to the Present', in A. James and A. Prout (eds) *Constructing and Reconstructing Childhood*. London: The Falmer Press.

Hendricks, H. (1990b) *Images of Youth: Age, Class and the Male Youth Problem 1880–1920*. Oxford: Clarendon.

Henggeler, S., Melton, G., Brondino, M., Scherer, D. and Hanley, J. (1997) 'Multisystemic Therapy with Violent and Chronic Juvenile Offenders and their Families: The Role of Treatment Fidelity in Successful Dissemination', *Journal of Consulting and Clinical Psychology*, 65: 821–33.

Henggeler, S.W., Schoenwald, S.K., Borduin, C.M., Rowland, M.D. and Cunningham, P.B. (1998) *Multisystemic Therapy for Anti-social Behaviour in Children and Adolescents*. New York: Guilford Press.

Henle, M. (1985) 'Rediscovering Gestalt Psychology', in S. Koch and D.E. Leary (eds), *A Century of Psychology as a Science*. New York, NY: McGraw-Hill.

Her Majesty's Inspectorate of Prisons for England and Wales (2000) *Unjust Desserts: A Thematic Review by HM Chief Inspector of Prisons for the Treatment and Conditions for Unsentenced Prisoners in England and Wales*. London: Home Office.

Herrnstein, R.J. and Murray, C. (1994) *The Bell Curve*. New York: Basic Books.

HM Inspectorate of Prisons and Probation (2001) *Through the Prison Gate: A Joint Thematic Review*. London: HM Prison Service.

Hindelang, M. (1979) 'Sex Differences in Criminal Activity', *Social Problems*, 27: 15–36.

Hine, J. and Celnick, A. (2001) *A One Year Reconviction Study of Final Warnings*. Sheffield: University of Sheffield.

Herschi, T. (1995) 'The Family', in J.Q. Wilson and J. Petersilia (eds) *Crime*. San Francisco: ICS Press.

Herschi, T. (1969) *Causes of Delinquency*. Berkeley, CA: University of California Press.

Hirschi, T. and Hindelang, M.J. (1977) 'Intelligence and Delinquency: A Revisionist Review', *American Sociological Review*, 42: 572–87.

Hobbs, D. (1995) *Bad Business*. Oxford: Oxford University Press.

Hobbs, D. (1998) *Doing the Business: Entrepreneurship, the Working Class and Detectives in East London*. Oxford: Clarendon Press.

Hodgson, P. and Webb, D. (2005) 'Young People, Crime and School Exclusions: A Case of Some Surprises', *The Howard Journal*, 44(1): 12–28.

Hodkinson, P. (1996) 'Careership: The Individual, Choices and Markets in the Transition to Work', in J. Avis, M. Bloomer, G. Esland, D. Gleeson and P. Hodkinson (eds) *Knowledge and Nationhood*. London: Cassell.

Hoffman, M.L. and Saltzstein, H.D. (1967) 'Parent Discipline and the Child's Moral Development', *Journal of Personality and Social Psychology*, 5: 45.

Hogg, E. (2000) The New Approach to Parental Responsibility: Practical Application. *Justice of the Peace*. 164. 735–8.

Hogg, J.G. (1999) 'Crime and Disorder Act: First Crack in the Threshold', *Family Law*, Aug, 574–7.

Hoghughi, M.S. and Forrest, A.R. (1970) 'Eysenck's Theory of Criminality: An Examination with Approved Schoolboys', *British Journal of Criminology* 10: 240.

Holdaway, S., Davidson, N., Dignan, J., Hammersley, R., Hine, J. and Marsh, P. (2001) *New Strategies to Address Youth Offending: The National Evaluation of the Youth Justice Board's Final Warning Projects*. London: Youth Justice Board.

Hollin, C.R. (1990a) 'Social Skills Training with Delinquents: A Look at the Evidence and Some Recommendations for Practice', *British Journal of Social Work*, 20: 483–93.

Hollin, C.R. (1990b) Cognitive-Behavioural Interventions with Young Offenders. Elmsford, NY: Pergamon Press.

Hollin, C.R. (1995) 'The Meaning and Implications of Programme Integrity', in J. McGuire (ed.) *What Works: Reducing Re-offending: Guidelines from Research and Practice*. Chichester: John Wiley & Sons.

Home Office (1980) *Young Offenders*, Cmnd 8045. London: HMSO.

Home Office (1991) *Safer Communities: The Local Delivery of Crime Prevention Through the Partnership Approach (Morgan Report)*. London: Home Office.

Home Office (1993) *Criminal Statistics in England and Wales 1992*. London: HMSO.

Home Office (1997) *No More Excuses – A New Approach to Tackling Youth Crime in England and Wales*. London: HMSO.

Home Office (1998) *Youth Justice: The Statutory Principal Aim Of Preventing Offending by Children and Young People*. London: Home Office.

Home Office (1998a) *The Crime and Disorder Act 1998*. London: Home Office.

Home Office (1998b) *Criminal Statistics*. London: Home Office

Home Office (2000) *British Crime Survey*. London: HMSO.

Home Office (2000a) *Fighting Violent Crime Together: An Action Plan*. London: Home Office.

Home Office (2000b) *British Crime Survey*. London: HMSO.

Home Office (2001) *Criminal Careers of Those Born Between 1953 and 1978*, Home Office Statistical Bulletin, 4/2001.

Home Office (2002) *British Crime Survey*. London: HMSO.

Home Office (2003) *Respect and Responsibility – Taking a Stand Against Anti-Social Behaviour*. London: Home Office.

Home Office (2004) *Defining and Measuring Anti-social Behaviour*. London: Home Office.

Home Office (2005) *Criminal Statistics*. London: Stationery Office.

Home Office/Lord Chancellor's Department (2002) *Criminal Justice System Business Plan – 2002–2003*. London: Home Office/Lord Chancellor's Department.

Honey, P. and Mumford, A. (1986) *The Manual of Learning Styles*. Maidenhead: Peter Honey.

Hood, R. (1965) *Borstal Re-Assessed*. London: Heinemann.

Hooton, E.A. (1939) *The American Criminal: An Anthropological Study.* Cambridge, MA: Harvard University Press.

Hopkins Burke, R.D. (1998) 'A Contextualisation of Zero Tolerance Policing Strategies' in R.D. Hopkins Burke (ed.) *Zero Tolerance Policing.* Leicester: Perpetuity Press.

Hopkins Burke, R.D. (1999) *Youth Justice and the Fragmentation of Modernity.* Scarman Centre for the Study of Public Order Occasional Paper Series: University of Leicester.

Hopkins Burke, R.D. (2001) *An Introduction to Criminological Theory.* Cullompton: Willan.

Hopkins Burke, R.D. (2003) 'Policing Bad Behaviour: Interrogating the Dilemmas', in J. Rowbotham and Kim Stevenson (eds) *Behaving Badly? Offensive Behaviour and 'Crime'.* London: Ashgate.

Hopkins Burke, R.D. (ed.) (2004a) *'Hard Cop/Soft Cop': Dilemmas and Debates in Contemporary Policing.* Cullompton: Willan.

Hopkins Burke, R.D. (2004b) 'Policing Contemporary Society', in R.D. Hopkins Burke, *'Hard Cop/Soft Cop': Dilemmas and Debates in Contemporary Policing.* Cullompton: Willan Publishing.

Hopkins Burke, R.D. (2004c) 'Policing Contemporary Society Revisited' in R.D. Hopkins Burke, *'Hard Cop/Soft Cop': Dilemmas and Debates in Contemporary Policing.* Cullompton: Willan.

Hopkins Burke, R.D. (2005) *An Introduction to Criminological Theory,* 2nd edn. Cullompton: Willan.

Hopkins Burke, R.D. (2007) 'Moral Ambiguity, the Schizophrenia of Crime and Community Justice', *British Journal of Community Justice,* 5(1): 43–64.

(Hopkins) Burke, R.D. and Hopkins (Burke), K.J. (1995) 'The Differential Needs of Young People in Local Authority Care', paper given to conference organised by Susie Lamplugh Trust on Child Victims, British Telcom Centre, London (January).

Hopkins Burke, R.D. and Morrill, R. (2002) 'Anti-social Behaviour Orders: An Infringement of the Human Rights Act 1998?' *The Nottingham Law Journal,* 2(2): 1–16.

Hopkins Burke, R.D. and Morrill, R. (2004) 'Human Rights v. Community Rights: The Case of the Anti-Social Behaviour Order', in R.D. Hopkins Burke (ed.) *'Hard Cop/Soft Cop': Dilemmas and Debates in Contemporary Policing.* Cullompton: Willan.

Hopkins Burke, R.D. and Pollock, E. (2004) 'A Tale of Two Anomies: Some Observations on the Contribution of (Sociological) Criminological Theory to Explaining Hate Crime Motivation', *Internet Journal of Criminology:* http://www.flashmousepublishing.com/Hopkins%20Burke%20&%20Pollock%20-%20A%20Tale%20of%20Two%20Anomies.pdf: 18.

Hopkins Burke, R.D. and Sunley, R. (1996) *'Hanging Out' in the 1990s: Young People and the Postmodern Condition,* Occasional Paper II, Scarman Centre of the Study of Public Order, University of Leicester.

Hopkins Burke, R.D. and Sunley, R. (1998) 'Youth Subcultures in Contemporary Britain', in K. Hazelhurst and C. Hazelhurst (eds) *Gangs and Youth Subcultures: International Explorations*. New Brunswick, NJ: Transaction Publishers.

Howard League for Penal Reform, The (2005) *Abolish ASBOs for Children*: www.howardleague.org/index.php?id=222&0

Hoyles, M. and Evans, P. (1989) *The Politics of Childhood*. London: Journeyman Press.

Hucklesby, A. (2001) 'Police Bail and the Use of Conditions', *Criminal Justice*, 1(4): 441.

Hucklesby, A. and Marshall, E. (2000) 'Tackling Offending on Bail', *Howard Journal of Criminology*, 29(2): 150–70.

Hucklesby, A. and Wilkinson, C. (2001) 'Drug Misuse in Prisons: Some Comments on the Prison Service Drug Strategy', *Howard Journal of Criminology*, 40(3): 347–63.

Hudson, B. (2003) *Justice in the Risk Society: Challenging and Re-affirming Justice in Late Modernity*. London: Sage.

Hughes, G. (1998) *Understanding Crime Prevention: Social Control, Risk and Late Modernity*. Buckingham: Open University Press.

Humphries, S. (1981) *Hooligans or Rebels?* Oxford: Blackwell.

Hutchings, B. and Mednick, S.A. (1977) 'Criminality in Adoptees and their Adoptive and Biological Parents: A Pilot Study', in S.A. Mednick and K.O. Christiansen (eds) *Biosocial Bases of Criminal Behaviour*. New York: Gardner.

Idriss, M.M. (2001) 'The Power to Impose Curfew Orders', *Justice of the Peace*, 165: 58–62.

Institute of Alcohol Studies (2005a) *Adolescents and Alcohol*. St Ives, Cambridge: IAS.

Institute of Alcohol Studies (2005b) *Alcohol and Crime*. St Ives, Cambridge: IAS.

Jackson, S.E. (1999) 'Family Group Conferences and Youth Justice: The New Panacea?', in B. Goldson (ed.) *Youth Justice: Contemporary Policy and Practice*. Aldershot: Ashgate.

Jamieson, J. (2005) 'New Labour, Youth Justice and the Question of Respect', *Youth Justice*, 5(3): 180–93.

Jefferis, B.J.M.H., Power, C. and Manor, O. (2005) 'Adolescent Drinking Level and Adult Binge Drinking in a National Cohort', *Addiction*, 100 (4): 543–9.

Jeffery, C.R. (1979) *Biology and Crime*. Beverly Hills, CA: Sage.

Jeffs, T. (1979) *Young People and the Youth Service*. London: Routledge & Kegan Paul.

Jeffs, T. and Smith, M. (eds) (1988a) *Welfare and Youth Work Practice*. London: Macmillan.

Jenks, C. (1996) *Childhood*. London: Routledge.

Jessor, R. and Jessor, S. (1997) *Problem Behaviour and Psychosocial Development: A Longitudinal Study of Youth*. New York: Academic Press.

Jones, D.W. (2002) 'Questioning New Labour's Youth Justice Strategy: A Review Article', *Youth Justice*, 1(3): 14–26.

Jones, S. (1993) *The Language of the Genes*. London: Harper Collins.

Jones, S. (2001) *Criminology*, 2nd edn, London: Butterworths.

Jordan, B. (1998) 'New Labour, New Community?', *Imprints*, 3(2): 113–31.

Justice (2000) *Restoring Youth Justice: New Directions in Domestic and International Law and Practice*. London: Justice.

Katz, J. (1986) 'What Makes Crime "News"?', in R. Collins (ed.) *Media, Culture, and Society: A Critical Reader*. Thousand Oaks, CA: Sage.

Katz, J. (1988) *Seductions of Crime: Moral and Sensual Attractions in Doing Evil*. New York: Basic Books.

Kazdin, A. (1996) 'Combined and Multimodal Treatments in Child and Adolescent Psychotherapy: Issues, Challenges and Research Directions, *Clinical Psychology: Science and Practice'*, 3(1): 69–100.

Kelly, P. (2001) 'The Post Welfare State and the Government of Youth at Risk', Special Issue of *Social Justice, In the Aftermath of Welfare Reform*, 28 (4): 96–113.

Kemshall, H. (2002) *Risk, Social Policy and Welfare*. Buckingham: Open University Press.

Kendler, H.H. (1985) 'Behaviourism and Psychology: An Uneasy Alliance', in S. Koch and D.E. Leary (eds) *A Century of Psychology as Science*. New York: McGraw-Hill.

Kershaw, C., Budd, T., Kinshott, G., Mattinson, J., Mayhew, P. and Myhill, A. (2000) *The 2000 British Crime Survey*. London: Home Office.

Keverne, E.B., Meller, R.E. and Eberhart, J.A. (1982) 'Social Influences on Behaviour and Neuroendocrine Responsiveness in Talapoin Monkeys', *Scandinavian Journal of Psychology*, 1: 37–54.

Klinefelter, H.F., Reifenstein, E.C., Albright, F. (1942) 'Syndrome Characterized by Gynecomastia, Aspermatogenesis without Aleydigism and Increased Excretion of Follicle-Stimulating Hormone', *Journal of Clinical Endocrinology*, 2: 615–27.

Kolvin, I., Miller, F.J.W., Scott, D.M., Gatzanis, S.R.M. and Fleeting, M. (1990) *Continuities of Deprivation?* Aldershot: Avebury.

Kreuz, L.E. and Rose, R.M. (1972) 'Assessment of Aggressive Behaviour and Plasma Testosterone in a Young Criminal Population', *Psychosomatic Medicine*, 34: 321–33.

Krisberg, B. (1974) 'Gang Youth and Hustling: The Psychology of Survival', *Issues in Criminology*, 9 (Spring 1): 115–31.

Kulik, J.A. and Kulik, C.-L.C. (1989) 'Meta-analysis in Education', *International Journal of Educational Research*, 13: 221–340.

Kumpfer, K. and Alvarado, R. (1998) 'Effective Family Strengthening Interventions', *Juvenile Justice Bulletin*, Nov 1998, Office of Juvenile Justice Delinquency Prevention, Office of Justice Programmes, US Department of Justice.

Kumpfer, K., Molgaard, V. and Spoth, R. (1996) 'The Strengthening Families Program: The Prevention of Delinquency and Drug Use', in R.D.V. Peters and R.J. McMahon (eds) *Preventing Childhood Disorders, Substance Abuse and Delinquency*. Thousand Oaks, CA: Sage.

Labour Party (1996) *New Labour, New Life for Britain*. London: The Labour Party.

Labour Party (2006) *Labour: The Future for Britain*. London: The Labour Party, http://www.labour.org.uk/home.

Lange, J. (1930) *Crime as Destiny*. London: Allen and Unwin.

Larder, D. (2000) *Psychiatric Morbidity among Young Offenders in England and Wales*. London: Office for National Statistics on behalf of the Department of Health and the National Assembly for Wales.

Lauritsen, J., Laub, J. and Sampson, R. (1992) 'Conventional and Delinquent Activities: Implications for the Prevention of Violent Victimisation Among Adolescents, *Criminology*, 7: 91–108.

Lea, J. (1999) 'Social Crime Revisited', *Theoretical Criminology*. London: Sage.

Lea, J. and Young, J. (1984) *What Is To Be Done About Law and Order?* London: Penguin.

Lee, D., Marsden, D., Rickman, P. and Duncombe, J. (1990) *Scheming for Youth: a Study of YTS in the Enterprise Culture*. Milton Keynes: Open University Press.

Lemert, E. (1951) *Social Pathology: A Systematic Approach to the Theory of Sociopathic Behavior*. New York: McGraw-Hill.

Lesser, M. (1980) *Nutrition and Vitamin Therapy*. New York: Bantam.

Levitas, R. (1996) The Concept of Social Exclusion and the New Durkheimian Hegemony, *Critical Social Policy*, 16(1): 5–20.

Liazos, A. (1972) 'The Poverty of the Sociology of Deviance: Nuts, Sluts and Perverts', *Social Problems*, 20: 103–20.

Liebling, A. (1992) *Suicides in Prison*. Routledge: London.

Liddle, M. and Solanki, J. (2000) *Missed Opportunities: Key Findings and Implications from an Analysis of the Backgrounds and Life Experiences of a Sample of Persistent Young Offenders in Redbridge*. London: NACRO.

Liebling, A. (1996) 'Suicide and Suicide Attempts Amongst Young Prisoners: The UK Experience', in A. Liebling and T. Ward (eds) *Deaths in Custody: Care for People at Risk*. London: Whiting and Bach.

Lipsey, M.W. (1992) 'Juvenile Delinquency Treatment: A meta-analytic Inquiry into the Viability of Effects', in T. Cook, H. Cooper, D.S. Cordray, H. Hartmann, L.V. Hedges, R. J. Light, T.A. Louis and F. Mosteller, *Meta-analysis for Explanation*. New York: Sage.

Lipsey, M. (1995) 'What do We Learn from 400 Research Studies on the Effectiveness of Treatment with Juvenile Delinquents?', in J. McGuire (ed.) *What Works: Reducing Re-offending – Guidelines from Research*. London: John Wiley and Sons.

Lipsey, M.W. (1999) 'Can Rehabilitative Programs Reduce the Recidivism of Juvenile Offenders? An Inquiry into the Effectiveness of Practical Programs', *Virginia Journal of Social Policy and the Law*, 6: 611–41.

Lipsey, M.W. and Wilson, D.B. (1998) 'Effective Intervention for Serious Juvenile Offenders: A Synthesis of Research', in R. Loeber and D.P. Farrington (eds) *Serious and Violent Offenders: Risk Factors and Successful Interventions*. Thousand Oaks, CA: Sage

Literacy Working Group (1999) *A Fresh Start: Improving Literacy and Numeracy*. London: The Literacy Working Group.

Little, A. (1963) 'Professor Eysenck's Theory of Crime: An Empirical Test on Adolescent Offenders', *British Journal of Criminology*, 4: 152.

Loeber, R. and Farrington, D. (1998) *Serious and Violent Juvenile Offenders: Risk Factors and Successful Interventions*. Thousand Oaks, CA: Sage.

Loeber, R. and Stouthamer-Loeber, M. (1986) 'Family Factors as Correlates and Predictors of Antisocial Conduct Problems and Delinquency', in N. Morris and M. Tonry (eds) *Crime and Justice*, Vol. 7. Chicago: University of Chicago Press.

Lombroso, C. (1876) *L'uomo delinquente (The Criminal Man)*. Milan: Hoepli.

Lyotard, J.DF. (1984) *The Postmodern Condition: A Report on Knowledge*. Manchester: Manchester University Press.

McCold, P. and Wachtel, T. (2000) 'Restorative Justice Theory Validation', Paper Presented at the Fourth International Conference on Restorative Justice for Juveniles, Tubingen, Germany, 1–4 October.

McCord, J. (1982) 'A Longitudinal Review of the Relationship between Paternal Absence and Crime', in J. Gunn and D.P. Farrington (eds) *Abnormal Offenders, Delinquency, and the Criminal Justice System*. Chichester: Wiley.

McCord, W., McCord, J. and Zola, I.K. (1959) Origins of Crime: *A New Evaluation of the Cambridge-Somerville Youth Study*. New York: Columbia University Press.

McEwan, A.W. (1983) 'Eysenck's Theory of Criminality and the Personality Types and Offences of Young Delinquents', *Personality and individual Differences*, 4: 201–4.

McEwan, A.W. and Knowles, C. (1984) 'Delinquent Personality Types and the Situational Contexts of their Crimes', *Personality and Individual Differences*, 5: 339–44.

Macdonald, G. (1998) 'Promoting Evidence-based Practice in Child Protection', *Clinical Child Psychology and Psychiatry*, 3(1): 123–36.

McGuire J. (2000) *Cognitive-Behavioural Approaches: An Introduction to Theory and Research*. London: Home Office.

McGurk, B.J. and McDougall, C. (1981) 'A New Approach to Eysenck's Theory of Criminality', *Personality and Individual Differences*, 13: 338–40.

McLauglin, E. and Muncie, J. (1994) 'Managing the Criminal Justice System', in J. Clarke *et al.* (eds) *Managing Social Policy*. London: Sage.

Macleod, D.I. (1983) *Building Character in the American Boy: Boy Scouts, YMCA and their Forerunners*. Madison, WI: University of Wisconsin Press.

Mannheim, H. (1948) *Juvenile Delinquency in an English Middletown*. London: Kegan Paul, Turner, Trubner and Co. Ltd.

Mannheim, H. (1955) *Group Problems in Crime and Punishment*. London: Routledge & Kegan Paul.

Manning, M. (2005) 'The New Public Management and Its Legacy', Administrative and Civil Service Reform website at http://www1. worldbank.org/publicsector/civilservice/debate1.htm.

Marshall, G., Roberts, S. and Burgoyne, C. (1996) Social Class and the Underclass in Britain and the USA. *British Journal of Sociology*, 47(10): 22–44.

Marshall, T. (1996) 'The Evolution of Restorative Justice in Britain', *European Journal on Criminal Policy and Research*, 4: 21–43.

Marshall, T.F. (1997) 'Seeking the Whole Justice', in S. Hayman, (ed.) *Repairing the Damage: Restorative Justice in Action*. London: ISTD.

Marshall, T. (1998) *Standards for Restorative Justice*. London: Restorative Justice Consortium.

Marshall, T. (1999) *Restorative Justice: An Overview*. London: Home Office (Occasional Paper).

Martin, G. and Pear, J. (1992) *Behaviour Modification: What It Is and How to Do It*. 4th edn, Englewood Cliffs, NJ, Prentice-Hall.

Martinson, R. (1974) 'What Works? – Questions and Answers About Prison Reform', *The Public Interest*, 35: 22–54.

Marx, K. (1887) *Capital*, Vol. 1 (1961 edn). Moscow: Foreign Languages Publishing House.

Matthews, R. and Young, J. (eds) (1986) *Confronting Crime*. London: Sage.

Matthews, R. and Young, J. (eds) (1992) *Issues in Realist Criminology*. London: Sage.

Matza, D. (1964) *Delinquency and Drift*. New York: Wiley.

Mawby, R. (1979) 'The Victimisation of Juveniles: A Comparative Study of Three Areas of Publicly Owned Housing in Sheffield', *Journal of Crime and Delinquency*, 16(1): 98–114.

Maxson, C.L. and Klein, M.W. (1990) 'Street Gang Violence: Twice as Great or Half as Great?' in C.R. Huff (ed.) *Gangs in America*. Newbury Park, CA: Sage.

May, M. (1973) 'Innocence and Experience: The Evolution of the Concept of Juvenile Delinquency in the Mid-nineteenth Century', in J. Muncie, G. Hughes and E. McLaughlin (eds) (2002) *Youth Justice: Critical Readings*. London: Sage.

Mayhew, P., Clarke, R.V.G., Sturman, A. and Hough, J.M. (1976) *Crime as Opportunity*. London: HMSO.

Mays, J.B. (1954) *Growing Up in the City: A Study of Juvenile Delinquency in an Urban Neighbourhood*. Liverpool: Liverpool University Press.

Mazur, A. (1998) *A Hazardous Inquiry: The Rashemon Effect at Love Canal*. Cambridge, MA: Harvard University Press.

Mears, D. and Kelly, W. (1998) 'Assessment and Intake Processes in Juvenile Justice Processing: Emerging Policy Considerations', *Crime and Delinquency*, 45(4).

Mednick, S.A. (1977) 'A Biosocial Theory of the Learning of Law-Abiding Behavior', in S.A. Mednick and K.O Christiansen (eds) *Biosocial Bases of Criminal Behavior*. New York: Gardner.

Mednick, S.A., Gabrielli, T., William, F. and Hutchings, B. (1984) 'Genetic Influences on Criminal Convictions: Evidence from an Adoption Cohort', *Science*, 224.

Mednick, S.A., Pollock, V. Volavka, J. and Gabrielli, W.F. (1982) 'Biology and Violence', in M.E. Wolfgang and N.A. Weiner (eds) *Criminal Violence*. Beverly Hills, CA: Sage.

Mednick, S.A., Moffit, T.E. and Stack, S. (eds) (1987) *The Causes of Crime: New Biological Approaches*. Cambridge: Cambridge University Press.

Meltzer, H., Gatward, R., Goodman, R. and Ford, T. (2000) *Mental Health of Children and Adolescents in Great Britain*. London: Office for National Statistics on behalf of the Department of Health, the Scottish Health Executive and the National Assembly for Wales.

Menard, S. and Morse, B. (1984) 'A Structuralist Critique of the IQ-Delinquency Hypothesis: Theory and Evidence', *American Journal of Sociology*, 89: 1347–78.

Merton, R. (1938) 'Social Structure and Anomie', *American Socialogical Review*, 3(5): 321–37.

Messmer, H. and Otto, H. (1991) *Restorative Justice on Trial: Pitfalls and Potentials of Victim Offender Mediation*. Norwell, MA: Kluwer.

Miller, W.B. (1958) 'Lower Class Culture as a Generalising Milieu of Gang Delinquency' *Journal of Social Issues*, 14: 5–19.

Miller, W.R. (1990) 'When the United States Has Failed to Solve Its Youth Gang Problem', in C.R. Huff (ed.) *Gangs in America*, Newbury Park, CA: Sage, pp. 263–87.

Mizen, P. (1995) *The State, Young People and Youth Training*. London: Mansell.

Monaghan, G. (2000) 'The Courts and the New Youth Justice', in B. Goldson (ed.) *The New Youth Justice*. Lyme Regis: Russell House.

Monahan, T.P. (1957) 'Family Status and the Delinquent Child: A Reappraisal and Some New Findings', *New Forces*, 35: 250–66.

Montagu, L. (1904) 'The Girl in the Background', in E.J. Urwick (ed.) *Studies in Boy Life in our Cities*. London: Dent.

Moore, J.W. (1991) *Going Down to the Barrio*. Philadelphia: Temple University Press.

Moore, S. and Smith, R. (2001) *The Pre-Trial Guide: Working with Young People from Arrest to Trial*. London: The Children's Society.

Morash, M. and Rucker, L. (1989) 'An Exploratory Study of the Connection of Mother's Age at Childbearing to her Children's Delinquency in Four Data Sets', *Crime and Delinquency*, 35: 45–58.

Morgan, P. (1975) *Child Care: Sense and Fable*. London: Temple Smith.

Morgan, P. (1978) *Delinquent Fantasies*. London: Temple Smith.

Morgan, P.M. and Henderson, P.F. (1998) *Remand Decisions and Offending on Bail: Evaluation of the Bail Process Project*. London: Home Office.

MORI (2000) *Youth Survey 2000*, Research conducted for the Youth Justice Board. London: Youth Justice Board.

MORI (2001) *Youth Survey 2001 for the Youth Justice Board for England and Wales*. London: YJB.

MORI (2002) *Youth Survey 2002 for the Youth Justice Board for England and Wales*. London: YJB.

MORI (2003) *Youth Survey 2003*. London: Youth Justice Board.

Morris, A. and Gelsthorpe, L. (2000) 'Something Old, Something Borrowed, Something Blue but Something New? A Comment on the Prospects for Restorative Justice under the Crime and Disorder Act 1998', *Criminal Law Review*, 18–30.

Morris, A. and Giller, H. (1987) *Understanding Juvenile Justice*. London: Croom Helm.

Morris, A., Giller, H., Szwed, E. and Geach, H. (1980) *Justice for Children*. London: Heinemann.

Morris, R.J. (1979). *Class and Class Consciousness in the Industrial Revolution 1780–1850*. London: Macmillan.

Morris, T.P. (1957) *The Criminal Area: A Study in Social Ecology*. London: Routledge & Kegan Paul.

Morrison, W. (1995) *Theoretical Criminology: From Modernity to Post-modernity*. London: Cavendish.

Morse, S.M. (1997a) 'Immaturity and Irresponsibility', *Journal of Criminal Law and Criminology*, 88.

Morse, S.M. (1997b) 'Delinquency and Desert', *The ANNALS of the American Academy of Political and Social Science*, 564, No. 1, 56–80.

Muller, P. (1973) 'Childhood's Changing Status Over the Centuries', in L.M. Brockman, J.H. Whiteley, and J.P. Zubak (eds) *Child Development: Selected Readings*. Toronto: McClelland and Stewart.

Muncie, J. (1984) *The Trouble with Kids Today: Youth and Crime in Postwar Britain*. London: Hutchinson.

Muncie, J. (1990) '"Failure Never Matters": Detention Centres and the Politics of Deterrence', *Critical Social Policy*, 28: 53–66.

Muncie, J. (1999a) *Youth and Crime*. London: Sage.

Muncie, J. (1999b) 'Auditing Youth Justice', *Prison Service Journal*, 126: 55–9.

Muncie, J. (1999c) Institutionalized Intolerance: Youth Justice and the 1998 Crime and Disorder Act, *Critical Social Policy*, 19(2): 147–75.

Muncie, J. (2004) *Youth and Crime*, 2nd edn. London: Sage.

Murray, C. (1990) *The Emerging British Underclass*. London: Institute of Economic Affairs: Health and Welfare Unit.

Murray, C. (1994) *Underclass: The Crisis Deepens*. London: Institute of Economic Affairs.

Musgrove, F. (1964) *Youth and the Social Order*. London: Routledge and Kegan Paul.

NACRO (1998) *Wasted Lives: Counting the Cost of Juvenile Offending*. London: Nacro/Prince's Trust.

NACRO (2000) *Young People, Drug Use, and Offending*. London: Nacro.

NACRO (2001a) *Directory of Offending Behaviour Programmes*. London: Youth Justice Board.

NACRO (2001b) *Some Facts about Young People who Offend*. London: Nacro.

NACRO (2003) *Some Facts About Young People Who Offend – 2001, Nacro Youth Crime Briefing*. London: Nacro.

NAPO (National Association of Probation Officers) (1998) *Briefing on the Crime and Disorder Bill*. London: NAPO.

Naess, S. (1959) 'Mother–Child Separation and Delinquency', *British Journal of Delinquency*, 10: 22.

Naess, S. (1962) 'Mother-Child Separation and Delinquency: Further Evidence', *British Journal of Criminology*, 2: 361.

Narey, M. (1997) *Review of Delay in the Criminal Justice System: A Report*. London: Home Office.

National Prison Survey (1992) *Main Findings*, Home Office Research Study No. 128, London: HMSO.

Nava, M. (1984) 'Youth Service Provision, Social Order and the Question of Girls', in A. McRobbie & M. Nava (eds), *Gender and Generation*. London: Macmillan.

Nelken, D. (1994) 'Reflexive Criminology?' in D. Nelken (ed.) *The Futures of Criminology*. London: Sage.

Nelken, D. and Andrews, L. (1999) 'DNA Identification and Surveillance Creep', *Sociology of Health and Illness*, 21 (5): 689–706.

Neubacher, F., Walker, M., Valkova, H. and Krajewski, K. (1999) 'Juvenile Delinquency in Central European Cities: A Comparison of Registration and Processing Structures in the 1990s', *European Journal on Criminal Policy and Research*, 7: 533–58.

Newburn, T. (1995) *Crime and Criminal Justice Policy*. London: Longman.

Newburn, T. (1998) 'Tackling Youth Crime and Reforming Youth Justice: The Origins and Nature of "New Labour" Policy', *Policy Studies*, 19(3): 199–213.

Newburn, T. (2002) 'Young People, Crime, and Youth Justice', in M. Maguire, R. Morgan and R. Reiner, *The Oxford Handbook of Youth Justice*. Oxford: Oxford University Press.

Norris, C. and Armstrong, G. (1999) *The Maximum Surveillance Society: The Rise of CCTV*, Oxford: Berg.

Northcott, J. (1991) *Britain in 2010*. London: Policy Studies Institute.

Northumbria Police (1992) *Bail and Multiple Offending*. Newcastle: Northumbria Police.

Nugent, W., Umbreit, M., Winnamaki L. and Paddock, J. (1999) 'Participation in Victim Offender Mediation Reduces Recidivism', *Connections* (VOM Association), 3, Summer.

Nutley, S. M., Davies, H. T. O. & Tilley, N. (2000) Editorial: Getting research into practice, Public Money and Management, 20(4), 3–6. Furniss, J. & Nutley, S. M. (2000) Implementing what works with offenders – the Effective Practice Initiative, *Public Money and Management*, 20(4), 35–42.

Nye, F.I. (1958) *Family Relationships and Delinquent Behaviour*. New York: Wiley.

Office for National Statistics (2001) *Psychiatric Morbidity Among Adults Living in Private Households, 2000*. London: ONS.

Olwens, D. (1987) 'Testosterone and Adrenaline: Aggressive and Antisocial Behaviour in Normal Adolescent Males', in S.A. Mednick, T.E. Moffit and S. Stack (eds) *The Causes of Crime: New Biological Approaches*. Cambridge: Cambridge University Press.

O'Malley, P. (1992) 'Risk, Power and Crime Prevention', *Economy and Society*, 21(3): 252–75.

PA Consulting Group/Youth Justice Board (2002a) *Repeat Young Offenders in London*. London: PA Consulting Group/Youth Justice Board.

PA Consulting Group/Youth Justice Board (2002b) *Bringing Repeat Young Offenders to Justice*. London: PA Consulting Group/Home Office.

Padfield, N. (1998) 'No More Excuses', *New Law Journal*, Apr. 17: 561–3.

Parenti, C. (2000) *Lockdown America*. London: Verso.

Parker, H. (1974) *View From the Boys*. Newton Abbot: David and Charles.

Parsons, T. (1951) *The Social System*. London: Routledge & Kegan Paul.

Parsons, C. and Howlett, K. (2002) *A Review of the Relationship between Non-attendance at School and Youth Offending*. London: Youth Justice Board.

Patterson, G.R. and Yoerger, K. (1997) 'A Developmental Model for Late-onset Delinquency', in D.W. Osgood (ed.) *Motivation and Delinquency: Nebraska Symposium on Motivation*. Lincoln, NE: University of Nebraska Press.

Pearson, G. (1983) *Hooligan – A History of Respectable Fears*. London: Macmillan.

Persky, H., Smith, K.D. and Basu, G.K. (1971) 'Relation of Psychological Measures of Aggression and Hostility to Testosterone Production in Man', *Psychosomatic Medicine*, 33: 265–75.

Pethick, E. (1898) 'Working Girls Clubs', in W. Reason (ed.) *University and Social Settlements*. London: Methuen.

Petrosino, A., Turpin-Petrosino, C. and Finckenauer, J.O. (2000) 'Well-meaning Programs Can Have Harmful Effects! Lessons from Experiments of Programs Such as Scared Straight', *Crime and Delinquency*, 46: 354–79.

Philip, K. (1997) *New Perspectives on Mentoring: Young People, Youth Work and Mentoring.* Unpublished PhD thesis, University of Aberdeen.

Piaget, J. (1977) *The Department of Thought.* New York: Viking Press.

Pickford, J. (2000) 'Introduction: A New Youth Justice for a New Century?', in J. Pickford (ed.) *Youth Justice: Theory and Practice.* London: Cavendish.

Pickford, J. (ed.) (2000b) *Youth Justice: Theory and Practice.* London, Cavendish.

Pihl, R.O. (1982) 'Hair Element Levels of Violent Criminals', *Canadian Journal of Psychiatry*, 27: 533–45.

Pihl, R.O. and Peterson, J.B. (1993) 'Alcohol/Drug Use and Aggressive Behaviour', in S. Hodgins (ed.) *Moral Disorder and Crime.* Newbury Park, CA: Sage.

Pinchbeck, I. and Hewitt, M. (1973) *Children in English Society*, Vol. 2. London: Routledge & Kegan Paul.

Pinchbeck, I. and Hewitt, M. (1981) 'Vagrancy and Delinquency in an Urban Setting', in M. Fitzgerald, G. McLennan and J. Pawson (eds) *Crime and Society – Readings In History and Theory.* London: Routledge and Kegan Paul/Open University Press.

Piper, C. (1999) 'The Crime and Disorder Act 1998: Child and Community "Safety" ', *Modern Law Review*, 62(3): 397–408.

Pitts, J. (1982) 'Policy, Delinquency and the Practice of Youth Control 1964–81', *Youth and Policy*, 1(1).

Pitts, J. (1986) 'Black Young People and Juvenile Crime: Some Unanswered Questions', in R. Matthews and J. Young (eds) *Confronting Crime.* London: Sage.

Pitts, J. (1988) *The Politics of Juvenile Crime.* London: Sage.

Pitts, J. (1996) 'The Politics and Practice of Youth Crime'. in E. McLaughlin and J. Muncie (eds) *Controlling Crime.* London: Sage in Association with the Open University.

Pitts, J. (2000) The New Youth Justice and the Politics of Electoral Anxiety, in Goldson, B. (ed.) *The New Youth Justice.* Lyme Regis: Russell House Publishing.

Pitts, J. (2001a) *The New Politics of Youth Crime: Discipline or Solidarity.* Basingstoke: Macmillan/Palgrave.

Pitts, J. (2001b) 'Korrectional Karaoke: New Labour and the Zombification of Youth Justice', *Youth Justice*, 1(2): 3–16.

Pitts, J. (2003a) 'Youth Justice in England and Wales', in R. Matthews and J. Young, *The New Politics of Crime and Punishment.* Cullompton: Willan.

Pitts, J. (2003b) 'Changing Justice', *Youth Justice*, 3 (1): 5–20.

Platt, A. (1969) 'The Rise of the Child-Saving Movement', The Annals, 381.

Pollock, L.A. (1983) *Forgotten Children: Parent Child Relations from 1500—1900.* Cambridge: Cambridge University Press.

Power, M. (1997) *The Audit Society: Rituals of Verification.* Oxford: Oxford University Press.

Pratt, J. (1989) 'Corporatism: The Third Model of Juvenile Justice', *British Journal of Criminology*, 29: 236–54.

Presdee, M. (2000) *Cultural Criminology and the Carnival of Crime*. London: Routledge.

Price, W.H. and Whatmore, P.B. (1967) 'Behaviour Disorders and Patterns of Crime Among XYY Males Identified at a Maximum Security Hospital', *British Medical Journal*, 1: 533.

Prinz, R.J., Roberts, W.A. and Hantman, E. (1980) 'Dietary Correlates of Hyperactive Behaviour in Children', *Journal of Consulting and Clinical Psychology*, 48: 760–85.

Prison Service (1989) *The 1998/99 Prison Service Annual Report*. London: The Prison Service.

Pritchard, C. (2001) *A Family-Teacher-Social Worker Alliance*, RDS Occasional Paper No. 78. London: Home Office.

Pryce, K. (1979) *Endless Pressure: A Study of West Indian Life-styles in Bristol*. Harmondsworth: Penguin.

Quinney, R. (1970) *The Social Reality of Crime*. Boston: Little, Brown.

Raloff, J. (1983) 'Locks – A Key to Violence', *Science News*, 124: 122–36.

Ramdin, R. (1987) *The Making of the Black Working Class in Britain*. Aldershot: Wildwood House.

Reckless, W.C. (1967) *The Crime Problem*. New York: Apple-Century-Crofts.

Reddy, L.A. and Pfeiffer, S. (1997) 'Effectiveness of Treatment Foster Care with Children and Adolescents: A Review of Outcome Studies', *Journal of the American Academy of Child and Adolescent Psychiatry*, 36: 581–8.

Redl, F. and Wineman, D. (1951) *Children Who Hate*. New York: Free Press.

Redondo, S., Sánchez-Meca, J. and Garrido, V. (1999) 'The Influence of Treatment Programmes on the Recidivism of Juvenile and Adult Offenders: A European Meta-analytic Review', *Psychology, Crime and Law*, 5: 251–78.

Reid, K. (1997) 'The Abolition of Cautioning? Juveniles in the "Last Chance" Saloon', *The Criminal Lawyer*, Dec. 4–8.

Reiss, A.J. (1951) 'Delinquency as the Failure of Personal and Social Controls', *American Sociological Review*, 16: 213–39.

Rhodes, J., Ebert, L. and Fischer, K. (1992) 'Natural Mentors: An Overlooked Resource in the Social Networks of Adolescent Mothers', *American Journal of Community Psychology*, 20 (4): 445–61.

Rhodes, J., Contreras, J.M. and Mangelsdorf, S.C. (1995) 'Natural Mentor Relationships among Latina Adolescent Mothers, Psychological Adjustment, Moderating Processes and the Role of Early Parental Acceptance', *American Journal of Community Psychology*, (22): 211–28.

Robins, L.N. and Hills, S.Y. (1966) 'Assessing the Contribution of Family Structure, Class and Peer Groups to Juvenile Delinquency', *Journal of Criminal Law, Criminology and Police Science*, 578: 325–34.

Rohrer, R. (1982) 'Lost in the Myths of Crime', *New Statesman*, 22 January.

Rojek, C. (1985) *Capitalism and Leisure Theory*. London: Tavistock.

Rose, N. and Miller, P. (1992) 'Political Power Beyond the State: Problematics of Government', *British Journal of Sociology*, 43(2), 173–205.

Rose, R.M., Bernstein, I.S. Gorden, T.P. and Catlin, S.E. (1974) 'Androgens and Aggression: A Review and Recent Findings in Primates', in R.L. Holloway (ed.) *Primate Aggression: Territoriality and Xenophobia*. New York: Academia Press.

Rose, N. (1999) *Powers of Freedom: Reframing Political Thought*. Cambridge: Cambridge University Press.

Rosen, Q. (1994) 'Knowledge Use in Direct Practice', *Social Service Review*, 68 (4): 561–77.

Rosenthal, M. (1986) *The Character Factory. Baden Powell and the Origins of the Boy Scout Movement*. London: Collins.

Ross, P. (2003) 'Marxism and Communitarianism', *Imprints* 6(3): 215–43.

Rousseau, J.-J. (1911) *Emile*. London: Dent.

Rowe, D.C. (1990) 'Inherited Dispositions Toward Learning Delinquent and Criminal Behaviour: New Evidence', in L. Ellis and H. Hoffman (eds) *Crime in Biological, Social and Moral Contexts*. New York: Praeger.

Rowe, D.C. and Rogers, J.L. (1989) 'Behaviour Genetics, Adolescent Deviance, and "d": Contributions and Issues', in G.R. Adams, R. Montemayor and T.P. Gullotta (eds), *Advances in Adolescent Development*. Newbury Park, CA: Sage, pp. 38–67.

Joseph Rowntree Foundation (1995) *Income and Wealth: Report of the JRF Inquiry Group, Summary*. York: Joseph Rowntree.

Runnymede (1996) *Runnymede Bulletin*, No. 292, February: 6–7.

Russell, C.E.B. (1905) *Manchester Boys, Sketches of Manchester Lads at Work and Play*. Manchester: Neil Richardson (reprint 1984).

Russell, C.E.B. and Rigby, L.M. (1908) *Working Lads' Clubs*. London: Macmillan.

Rutherford, A. (1978) 'Decarceration of Young Offenders in Massachusetts', in N. Tutt (ed.) *Alternative Strategies for Coping with Crime*. Oxford: Blackwell/ Martin Robertson.

Rutherford, A. (1992) *Growing Out of Crime*, 2nd edn. London: Waterside Press.

Rutter, M. (1981) *Maternal Deprivation Reassessed*. Harmondsworth: Penguin.

Rutter, M. and Giller, H. (1983) *Juvenile Delinquency: Trends and Perspectives*. Harmondsworth: Penguin.

Rutter, M., Giller, H. and Hagell, A. (1998) *Anti-social Behaviour by Young People*. Cambridge: Cambridge University Press.

Sampson, R.J., Raudenbushs, S.W. and Earls, F. (1997) 'Neighborhood and Violent Crime: A Multi-level Study of Collective Efficacy', *Science*, 277: 918–23.

Sanderson, I. (2000) 'Evaluation in Complex Policy Systems', *Evaluation. The International Journal of Theory, Research and Practice*, 6(4): 433–54.

Saunders, W. (1984) *Alcohol Use in Britain; How Much is Too Much?* Edinburgh: Scottish Health Education Unit.

Scales, M. and Gibbons, R. (1996) 'Extended Family Members and Unrelated Adults in the Lives of Young Adolescents: A Research Agenda', *Journal of Early Adolescence*, 16(4): 365–89.

Scarmella, T.J. and Brown, W.A. (1978) 'Serum Testosterone and Aggressiveness in Hockey Players', *Psychosomatic Medicine*, 40: 262–75.

Schalling, D. (1987) 'Personality Correlates of Plasma Testosterone Levels in Young Delinquents: An Example of Person-Situation Interaction', in S.A. Mednick, T.E. Moffit and S.A. Stack (eds) *The Causes of Crime: New Biological Approaches*. Cambridge: Cambridge University Press.

Scheff, T.J. (1994) *Microsociology: Discourse, Emotion and Social Structure*. University of Chicago Press: Chicago.

Sclater, S.D. and Piper, C. (2000) 'Remoralising the Family? Family Policy, Family Law and Youth Justice', *Child and Family Law Quarterly*, 12(3): 135–51.

Scraton, P. (1985) *The State of the Police*. London: Pluto.

Scraton, P. and Chadwick, K. (1996 originally 1992) 'The Theoretical Priorities of Critical Criminology', in J. Muncie, E. McLaughlin, and M. Langan (eds) (1996) *Criminological Perspectives: A Reader*. London: Sage.

Scruton, R. (1980) *The Meaning of Conservatism*. Harmondsworth: Pelican.

Scruton, R. (1985) *Thinkers of the New Left*. London: Longman.

Scruton, R. (2001) *The Meaning of Conservatism*, 3rd edn. Houndmills: Palgrave.

Shah, S.A. and Roth, L.H. (1974) 'Biological and Psychophysiological Factors in Criminality', in D. Glaser (ed.) *Handbook of Criminology*. London: Rand McNally.

Shaw, C. and McKay, H.D. (1972, originally 1931) *Juvenile Delinquency and Urban Areas*. Chicago: University of Chicago Press.

Shea, G.F. (1992) *Mentoring: A Guide to the Basics*. London: Kogan Page.

Sheldon, B. (1995) *Cognitive-Behavioural Therapy: Research, Practice and Philosophy*. London: Routledge.

Sheldon, W.H. (1949) *Varieties of Delinquent Youth*. London: Harper.

Sherman, L. and Strang, H. (1997) 'Restorative Justice and Deterring Crime', *RISE Working Papers*, Canberra: Australian National University.

Shoenthaler, S.J. (1982) 'The Effects of Blood Sugar on the Treatment and Control of Antisocial Behaviour: A Double-Blind Study of an Incarcerated Juvenile Population', *International Journal for Biosocial Research*, 3: 1–15.

Sim, J. Scraton, P. and Gordon, P. (1987) 'Introduction: Crime, the State, and Critical Analysis', in P. Scraton, (ed.) (1987) *Law, Order and the Authoritarian State: Readings in Critical Criminology*. Milton Keynes: Open University Press.

Simon, B. (1965) *Education and the Labour Movement 1870–1920*. London: Lawrence and Wishart.

Smith, D.E. and Smith, D.D. (1977) 'Eysenck's Psychoticism Scale and Reconviction', *British Journal of Criminology*, 17: 387.

Smith, R. (2003) *Youth Justice: Ideas, Policy, Practice*. Cullompton: Willan.

Smith, R. (2006) 'Actuarialism and Early Intervention in Contemporary Youth Justice', in B. Goldson and J. Muncie (eds) *Youth Crime and Justice*. London: Sage.

Smith, R. (2007) *Youth Justice: Ideas, Policy, Practice*, 2nd edn. Cullompton: Willan.

Spelman, W. (1994) *Criminal Incapacitation*. New York: Plenum.

Spergel, I.A. (1964) *Racketsville, Slumtown, Haulburg*, Chicago: UniversitySpringhall, J. (1977) *Youth, Empire and Society: British Youth Movements 1883–1940*. London: Croom Helm.

Spergel, I.A. (1964) *Racketsville, Slumtown, Haulburg*. Chicago: University of Chicago Press.

Spergel, I.A. (1995) *The Youth Gang Problem: A Community Approach*. Oxford: Oxford University Press.

Springhall, J. (1977) *Youth, Empire and Society: British Youth Movements 1883–1940*. London: Croom Helm.

Springhall, J. (1986) *Coming of Age: Adolescence in Britain 1860—1960*. Dublin: Gill and Macmillan.

Springhall, J., Fraser, B. and Hoare, M. (1983) *Sure and Steadfast: A History of the Boys Brigade 1883–1983*. London: Collins.

Squires, P. (2006) *Understanding Community Safety*. Bristol: The Policy Press.

Squires, P. and Stephen, D.E. (2005) *Rougher Justice: Anti-social Behaviour and Young People*. Cullompton: Willan.

Stanley, M. (1890) *Clubs for Working Girls*. London: Macmillan.

Stedman Jones, G. (1984) *Outcast London: A Study in Relationships Between Classes in Victorian Society*, 2nd edn. Harmondsworth: Penguin.

Stenson, K. and Edwards, A. (2003) 'Crime Control and Local Governance: The Struggle for Sovereignty in Advanced Liberal Polities', *Contemporary Politics*, 9(2): 203–17.

Stenson, K. and Watt, P. (1999) 'Governmentality and the Death of the Social? A Discourse Analysis of Local Government Texts in the South-east of England', *Urban Studies*, 36(1): 189–201.

Stephenson, M. (2005) *Young People and Offending: Education, Youth Justice and Social Inclusion*. Cullompton: Willan.

Stephenson, M., Giller, H. and Brown, S. (2007) *Effective Practice in Youth Justice*. Cullompton: Willan Publishing.

Stern, V. (1998) *A Sin Against the Future: Imprisonment in the World*. London: Penguin.

Stewart, D., Gossop, M., Marsden, J. and Rolfe, A. (2000) 'Drug Misuse and Acquisitive Crime Among Clients Recruited to the National Treatment Outcome Research (NTORS)', *Criminal Behaviour and Mental Health*, 10, 13–24.

St James Roberts, I. and Samlal Singh, C. (2001) *Can Mentors Help Primary School Children with Behaviour Problems?* Home Office Research Study No. 233. London: Home Office.

Strachan, R. and Tallant, C. (1997) 'Improving Judgement and Appreciating Biases Within the Risk Assessment Process', in H. Kemshall and J. Pritchard (eds) *Good Practice in Risk Assessment and Risk Management 2*. London: Jessica Kingsley.

Strang, H. (1995) 'Replacing Courts With Conferences', *Policing*, 11(3): 21–30.

Strang, H. (2000) *Victim Participation in a Restorative Justice Process: The Canberra Reintegrative Shaming Experiments*, PhD Dissertation, Law Program, Research School of Social Sciences. Canberra: Australian National University.

Strang, H. (2001) *Repair or Revenge: Victim Participation in Restorative Justice*. Oxford: Oxford University Press.

Street, R. (2000) Restorative Justice Steering Group, *Review of Existing Research*. London: Home Office (unpublished).

Street, R. (2001) 'Restorative Justice – Time to Take Stock?', *Criminal Justice Matters*, 46: 32–3.

Styles, M. and Morrow, K. (1992) *Understanding How Elders and Youth Form Relationships: A Study of Four Linking Lifetimes Projects*. Philadelphia: Public/Private Ventures.

Susser, M. (1998) 'Does Risk Factor Epidemiology put Epidemiology at Risk? Peering into the Future', *Journal of Epidemiology and Community Health*, http://proquest.umi.com/pqdlink?

Sutherland, E.H. (1939) *Principle of Criminology*. Chicago: Lippincott.

Sutherland, E.H. (1947) *Principles of Criminology*, 4th edn. Philadelphia: Lippincott.

Sweatman, A. (1863) 'Youth Clubs and Institutes', reproduced in F. Booton, (ed.) (1985) *Studies in Social Education, Vol. 1 1860–1890*. Hove: Benfield Press.

Sykes, G. and Matza, D. (1957) 'Techniques of Neutralization: A Theory of Delinquency', *American Sociological Review*, (22): 664–70.

Szapocznik, J., Rio, A., Murray, E., Cohen, R., Scopetta, M.A., Rivas-Vasquz, A., Hervis, O.E. and Poseda, V. (1989) 'Structural Family versus Psychodynamic Child Therapy for Problematic Hispanic Boys', in *Journal of Consulting and Clinical Psychology*, 57(5): 571–8.

Tappan, P.W. (1960) *Crime, Justice and Correction*. New York: McGraw-Hill.

Tarde, G. (1969) 'On Communication and Social Influence', in T. Clark (ed.) *Gabriel Tarde on Communication and Social Influence*. Chicago: University of Chicago Press.

Tarling, R. (1993) *Analysing Offending: Data, Models and Interpretations*. London: HMSO.

Taylor, C.S. (1990) *Dangerous Society*. East Lansing, MI: Michigan State University Press.

Taylor, I. (1997) 'The Political Economy of Crime', in M. Maguire, R. Morgan and R. Reiner (eds) *The Oxford Handbook of Criminology*, 2nd edn. Oxford: Clarendon Press.

Taylor, I., Walton, P. and Young, J. (1973) *The New Criminology: For a Social Theory of Deviance*. London: Routledge & Kegan Paul.

Taylor, L., Lacey, R. and Bracken, D. (1979) *In Whose Best Interests: The Unjust Treatment of Children in Courts and Institutions*. London: Cobden Trust/Mind.

Thane, P. (1981) 'Childhood in History', in M. King, (ed.) *Childhood, Welfare and Justice*. London: Batsford.

Thane, P. (1982) *The Foundations of the Welfare State*. Harlow: Longman.

Thomas, D.W. and Hyman, J.M. (1978) 'Compliance, Theory, Control Theory and Juvenile Delinquency', in M. Krohn and R.L. Acker (eds) *Crime, Law and Sanctions*. London: Sage.

Thomas, T. (2005) 'The Continuing Story of the ASBO', *Youth and Policy*, 87, 1–14, Spring.

Thompson, K. (1986) *Beliefs and Ideology*. London: Tavistock.

Thompson, P. (1975) *The Edwardians: The Remaking of British Society*. London: Weidenfeld and Nicholson.

Thompson, W.E., Mitchell, J. and Doddler, R.A. (1984) 'An Empirical Test of Hirschi's Control Theory of Delinquency, *Deviant Behavior*. 5: 11–22.

Thorpe, D., Green, C.J. and Smith, D. (1980) *Punishment and Welfare*, Occasional Papers in Social Administration, No. 4, University of Lancaster.

Tierney, J.P. and Grossman, J.B. with Resch, N.L. (1995) *Making a Difference: An Impact Study of Big Brothers/Big Sisters*. Philadelphia, PA: Public/Private Ventures.

Titmus, R. (1974) *Social Policy*. London: Allen and Unwin.

Tolman, E.C. (1959) 'Principles of Purposive Behaviour', in S. Koch and D.E. Leary (eds), *A Century of Psychology as a Science*. New York, NY: McGraw-Hill.

Trasler, G. (1967) *The Explanation of Criminality*. Routledge & Kegan Paul.

Trasler, G. (1986) 'Situational Crime Control and Rational Choice: A Critique', in K. Heal and G. Laycock (eds) *Situational Crime Prevention: From Theory into Practice*. London: HMSO.

Trinder, L. and Reynolds, S. (eds) (2000) *Evidence-based Practice: A Critical Appraisal*. Oxford: Blackwell Science.

Trotter, C. (1999) *Working with Involuntary Clients: A Guide to Practice*. London: Sage.

Turk, A.T. (1969) *Criminality and the Social Order*. Chicago: Rand-McNally.

Tutt, N. (1981) 'A Decade of Policy', *British Journal of Criminology*, 21(4): 246–56.

Tzannetakis, T. (2001) 'Neo-Conservative Criminology', in McLaughlin and J. Muncie (eds) *The Sage Dictionary of Criminology*. London: Sage.

UKADCU (United Kingdom Anti-Drugs Co-ordinating Unit) (1998) *Tackling Drugs to Build a Better Britain: The Government's 10-year Strategy for Tackling Drug Misuse*. London: The Stationery Office.

Umbreit, M. and Roberts, A. (1996). *Mediation of Criminal Conflict in England: An Assessment of Services in Coventry and Leeds*. Rochester, Minnesota: Center for Restorative Justice and Mediation, University of Minnesota.

Urwick, E.J. (ed.) (1904) *Studies of Boy Life in our Cities*. London: Dent.

Utting, D. (1996) *Reducing Criminality Among Young People: A Sample of Relevant Programmes in the UK*, Home Office Research Study No. 161. London: HMSO.

Utting, W. (1997) *People Like Us: The Report of the Review of the Safeguards of Children Living Away from Home*. London: The Stationery Office.

Utting, D. and Vennard, J. (2000) *What Works with Young Offenders in the Community?* Ilford: Barnado's.

Utting, W., Bright, J. and Hendrickson, P. (1993) *Crime and the Family, Improving Child Rearing and Preventing Delinquency*, Paper No. 16. London: Family Policy Studies Centre.

Van Ness, D. and Strong, K.H. (1997) *Restoring Justice*. Cincinnati, OH: Anderson Publishing.

Virkkunen, M. (1987) 'Metabolic Dysfunctions Amongst Habitually Violent Offenders: Reactive Hypoglycaemia and Cholesterol Levels', in S.A. Mednick, T.E. Moffit and S.A. Stack (eds) *The Causes of Crime: New Biological Approaches*. Cambridge: Cambridge University Press.

Vold, G.B. (1958) *Theoretical Criminology*. Oxford: Oxford University Press.

Vold, G.B., Bernard, T.J. and Snipes, J.B. (1998) *Theoretical Criminology*, 4th edn. Oxford: Oxford University Press.

Von Hirsch, A., Ashworth, A., Wasik, M., Smith, A.T.H., Morgan, R. and Gardner, J. (1995) 'Overtaking on the Right', *New Law Journal*: 1501.

Walker, M. (1983) 'Some Problems in Interpreting Statistics Relating to Crime', *Journal Of the Royal Statistical Society Series A*, 146, part 3: 282–93.

Walklate, S. (1998) '"No More Excuses!" Young People, Victims and Making Amends', *Policy Studies*, 19(3): 213–22.

Wallace, C. (1987) *For Richer, For Poorer: Growing Up In and Out of Work*. London: Tavistock.

Walsh, C. (1999) 'Imposing Order: Child Safety Orders and Local Child Curfew Schemes', *Journal of Social Welfare and Family Law*, 21(2): 135–49.

Walvin, J. (1982) *A Child's World: A Social History of Childhood 1800–1914*. Harmondsworth: Penguin.

Warner, N. (1992) *Choosing with Care – The Report of the Committee of Inquiry into the Selection: Development and Management of Staff in Children's Homes*. London: HMSO.

Warner, N. (1999) 'Implementing the Youth Justice Reforms', *Youth Justice: A Conference for the Bedfordshire & Hertfordshire, & Kent, East & West Sussex Area Committees: Conference Report*, para 5–37.

Warner, N. (2003) *Tackling Anti-social Behaviour*. London: Youth Justice Board.

Wasik, M. (1999) Reparation: Sentencing and the Victim. *Criminal Law Review*, 470–9.

Wasserman, G., Miller, L., Pinner, E. and Jaramillo, B. (1996) 'Parenting Predictors of the Development of Conduct Problems in High-risk Boys', *Journal of the American Academy of Child and Adolescent Psychiatry*, 35: 1227–36.

Waters, I., Moore, R., Roberts, C. and Merrington, S. (2003) *Intensive Supervision and Surveillance Programmes for Persistent Young Offenders in England and Wales*. Oxford: Centre for Criminological Research.

Wedd, S. (2000) 'The Criminal Lawyers Reaction to Youth Court Referral Orders', *Criminal Practitioners Newsletter* (Law Society), Oct. 1–2.

Weiner, M.J. (1990) *Reconstructing the Criminal Culture, Law and Policy in England, 1830–1914*. Cambridge: Cambridge University Press.

West, D.J. (1967) *The Young Offender*. New York: International Universities Press.

West, D.J. (1969) *Present Conduct and Future Delinquency*. London: Heinemann.

West, D.J. and Farrington, D.P. (1973) *Who Becomes Delinquent?* London: Heinemann.

Westergaard, J. (1995) *Who Gets What? The Hardening of Class Inequality in the Late Twentieth Century*. Cambridge: Polity Press.

White, J. (1980) *Rothschild Buildings: Life in an East End Tenement Block 1887–1920*. London: Routledge and Kegan Paul.

Wilcox, A. (2003) 'Evidence-based Youth Justice? Some Valuable Lessons from and Evaluation for the Youth Justice Board', *Youth Justice*, 3(1): 21–35.

Wilkins, L. (1964) *Social Deviance*. London: Tavistock.

Wilkinson, C. (1995) *The Drop-Out Society: Young People on the Margin*. Leicester: Youth Work Press.

Williamson, H. (1997) 'Status Zero Youth and the Underclass', in R. MacDonald (ed.) *Youth, the 'Underclass' and Social Exclusion*. London: Routledge.

Willis, P. (1977) *Learning to Labour*. London: Saxon House.

Wills, T.A., Vaccaro, D., McNamara, G. and Hirky, E.A. (1996) 'Escalated Substance Use: A Longitudinal Grouping Analysis from Early to Middle Adolescence', *Journal of Abnormal Psychology*, April: 166–80.

Wilmott, P. (1966) *Adolescent Boys in East London*. London: Routledge & Kegan Paul.

Wilson, H. (1980) 'Parental Supervision: A Neglected Aspect of Delinquency', *British Journal of Criminology*, 20: 315–27.

Wilson, J.Q. and Herrnstein, R.J. (1985) *Crime and Human Nature*. New York: Simm and Schuster.

Wilson, S.J. and Lipsey, M.W. (2000) 'Wilderness Challenge Programs for Delinquent Youth: A Meta-analysis of Outcome Evaluations', *Evaluation and Program Planning*, 23: 1–12.

Wilson, W.J. (1991) 'Public Policy Research and the Truly Disadvantaged', in C. Jencks and P.E. Peterson (eds) *The Urban Underclass*. Washington, DC: The Brookings Institution.

Wilson, W.J. (1987) *The Truly Disadvantaged*. Chicago: University of Chicago Press.

Windlesham, Lord (1993) *Responses to Crime (Vol 2): Penal Policy in the Making*. Oxford: Oxford University Press.

Witkin, H.A., Mednick, S.A. and Schulsinger, F. (1977) 'XYY and XXY Men: Criminality and Aggression', in S.A. Mednick and K.O. Christiansen (eds) *Biosocial Bases of Criminal Behaviour*. New York: Gardner Press.

Wolfgang, M.E. and Ferracuti, F. (1967) *The Sub-Culture of Violence: Towards an Integrated Theory in Criminology*. Beverly Hills: Sage.

Wolfgang, M.E., Figlio, R.M. and Sellin, T. (1972) *Delinquency in a Birth Cohort*. Chicago: University of Chicago Press.

Wonnacott, C. (1999) 'The Counterfeit Contract: Reform, Pretence and Muddled Principles in the New Referral Order', *Child and Family Law Quarterly*, 11(3), 271–87.

Wooland, K. (2003) *New Opportunities Fund Intensive Evaluation of Splash Extra 2002*. Cap Gemini: Ernst & Young UK.

Woolf, Lord Justice (1991) *Prison Disturbances April 1990: A Report of an Inquiry*, Cmnd 1456. London: Home Office.

Wootton, B. (1959) *Social Science and Social Pathology*. London: Allen & Unwin.

Wootton, B. (1962) 'A Social Scientist's Approach to Maternal Deprivation', in M.D. Ainsworth (ed.) *Deprivation of Maternal Care: A Reassessment of its Effects*. Geneva: World Health Organisation.

Wright, R.A. (1993) 'A Socially Sensitive Criminal Justice System', in J.W. Murphy and D.L. Peck (eds) *Open Institutions: The Hope for Democracy*. Westport, CT: Praeger.

Wynne, J. and Brown, I. (1998) 'Can Mediation Cut Re-offending?' *Probation Journal*, 46(1).

Young, J. (1971) *The Drug Takers: The Social Meaning of Drugtaking*. London: Paladin.

Young, J. (1986) 'Ten Points of Realism', in R. Matthews and J. Young (eds) *Issues in Realist Criminology*. London: Sage.

Young, J. (1994) '"Incessant Chatter": Recent Paradigms in Criminology', in M. Maguire, R. Morgan and R. Reiner (eds) *The Oxford Handbook of Criminology*. Oxford: Clarendon Press.

Young, J. (1999) *The Exclusive Society: Social Exclusion, Crime and Difference in Late Modernity*. London: Sage.

Young, R. and Goold, B. (1999) 'Restorative Police Cautioning in Aylesbury: From Degrading to Reintegrative Shaming Ceremonies?', *Criminal Law Review*, 126–38.

Youth Justice Board (2000) *National Standards for Youth Justice*. London: Youth Justice Board.

Youth Justice Board (2001a) *Risk and Protective Factors Associated with Youth Crime and Effective Interventions to Prevent it*. London: Youth Justice Board.

Youth Justice Board (2001b) *Good Practice Guidelines for Restorative Work With Victims and Young Offenders*. London: Youth Justice Board.

Youth Justice Board (2002) *Youth Justice Board Review 2000/2002: Delivering Change*. London: Youth Justice Board.

Youth Justice Board (2004) *Government Response to the Audit Commission Report – Youth Justice 2004: A Review of the Reformed Youth Justice System.* London: Youth Justice Board.

Zimring, F. and Hawkins, G. (1973) *Deterrence.* Chicago: University of Chicago.

Author Index

Subject Index